MW01244509

Profiles in Success

Profiles in Success

Inspiration from Executive Leaders

Volume 8

GORDON J. BERNHARDT, CPA, PFS, CFP*, AIF*

Copyright © 2014 Gordon J. Bernhardt, CPA, PFS, CFP®, AIF®

ISBN: 979-8-9861435-7-6

All rights reserved. No part of this publication may be reproduced, distributed, or transmitted in any form or by any means without the prior written permission of the copyright holder, except in the case of brief quotations embodied in critical reviews and certain noncommercial uses permitted by copyright law. For permission requests or information on bulk purchases, contact the copyright holder.

First edition

Gordon Bernhardt conducts interviews of business leaders primarily in the Washington D.C. area who come recommended by their peers. The profiles included in this volume are a result of these interviews. As a result of these additional insights Mr. Bernhardt has published these profiles. Gordon Bernhardt is the President and CEO of Bernhardt Wealth Management, a registered investment adviser with the Securities and Exchange Commission. Registration is mandatory for all persons meeting the definition of investment adviser and does not imply a certain level of skill or training. The business leaders may or may not be clients of Bernhardt Wealth Management. These interviews are independent of investment advisory services and do not imply any endorsement of Gordon Bernhardt or Bernhardt Wealth Management by the business leaders.

This book exists because of all the inspirational individuals who so graciously shared their stories with me. I am thankful for the opportunity to get to know each and every one of you. I feel like a better person thanks to what I learned from you and your story.

To my team at Bernhardt Wealth Management—Tim Koehl, Bonnie Armstrong, Trent White, Olivia Dewey, Kate Brodowski, and Emily Burns. I would never have been able to do this without your efforts and support throughout the process. Thank you for all you do for each other and for our clients.

I am deeply grateful to Brian Roberts, Founder and CEO of Croix Connect, and to Peter Schwartz, Master Chair of Vistage Worldwide, for your help and encouragement on this project. Thank you.

And lastly, this book would not have been possible without the guidance and creative support of Karen Embry.

Table of Contents

Foreword

G ordon Bernhardt has assembled a collection of profiles that reveal the human side of entrepreneurism. As you read these stories, you discover people who become business leaders by overcoming obstacles of all kinds; internally, personally, professionally, economically. You'll learn how they've pushed themselves over and through these barriers, showing a passion and determination that is inspiring.

For small business owners and CEOs, our businesses are intertwined with our lives and our employees are our family, making it difficult to separate emotion from our decision making. Therefore it is necessary that we create a 'work life integration' that blends what we do personally and professionally in order to make both work. Unlike the stories the press often tell about "Teflon-style" CEOs, the individuals showcased in these profiles are very human—striving to make the best possible decisions while serving their communities and leading the way in job creation.

After 15 years in the Air Force, I entered the business world in 1992 working for startups and small businesses before founding Croix Connect in 2001, a management and technology consulting company. I've been fortunate to have diverse experiences working with both government and commercial clients in large companies, small businesses, and even as the sole employee of my own firm. I've had clients from the Fortune 50 to those with less than 10 employees, and they've been a mix of B2B, B2G, and B2C. There have been many highs, including incredibly fast organic growth, IPOs, and M&As. There have been many lows—dot com and telecom industry meltdown in 2000, followed by 9-11 in 2001, the Great Recession, and in the early 2010s, the government sequestration and shutdown. As with all things in life, the real learning and growth comes from the tough times. I've learned that flexibility is the key. You've got to be a Gumby to survive.

Outside of my duties in the USAF at the White House Communications Agency during the Reagan years, serving as a Vistage International executive peer group leader has been my most rewarding professional experience. The entrepreneurial CEOs who participate in these groups are inspirational in their continued desire to learn and improve themselves personally and professionally, while also growing their businesses.

I'm a true believer in executive peer groups: helping each other to consider creative solutions to challenges, figuring out the best way to approach an opportunity, or serving as a supportive sounding board. I've found spending one day per month working ON our business in an executive peer group is so very powerful. You think you've seen and heard it all until you meet with a group like this where you can be humbled by what other executives are undertaking or how they are handling formidable situations. As we CEOs move towards our goals, obstacles and challenges inevitably pop up. The Vistage peer group becomes our "Executive GPS"—helping to recalculate and adjust our bearings as we journey forward. Here are a few lessons I've learned from this group:

Have a child-like approach to everything in life, including business. Be inquisitive. Don't act like you have all of the answers because the only thing you know is that you don't know it all.

Listen. Learn. Embrace and Act. Treat every employee the same, from C-suite executive to the lowest skilled employee. By living the Golden Rule your employees will be there when you need them to help take your company to great heights.

Stop avoiding a difficult situation or conversation. It isn't going away and could only get worse, so confront it. I tell my team to "bring me the good news fast and the bad news faster." Having a foundation of trust in your organization is the key to removing any fear of conflict, on your way to effective communication, accountability, and ultimately results.

Determine what activities boost your energy, and do more of those. For those activities that literally suck the life out of you, find a way to outsource or delegate them whenever possible. When it's not possible to delegate, compartmentalize by doing those activities all at a certain time of day.

If you aren't a CEO or owner but have been thinking about taking that leap of faith—DO IT and don't look back. In 1519, Captain Hernán Cortés landed in Veracruz to begin his great conquest. Upon arriving, he gave the order to his men to burn the ships. Here's the lesson: Retreat is easy when you have the option.

I hope the following stories will inspire you to turn it up a notch and to be better tomorrow than you are today.

– **Brian Roberts**
Founder & CEO, Croix Connect
Vistage Chair, Vistage International
broberts@croixconnect.com

 *Brian Roberts works with executives who have a desire to learn and grow personally and professionally, and grow their businesses. He provides executive advisory services through Croix Connect, Inc., and as a Vistage Chair, he provides that service as well as the facilitation of CEO and executive peer groups. In 2013, Brian received Vistage International's Chair Excellence Award for outstanding overall performance. He hosts a business oriented radio program called "Taking Care of Business with Brian Roberts," where he interviews top local business and government executives.*

Introduction

*"All highly competent people continually search for ways
to keep learning, growing, and improving."*
– BENJAMIN FRANKLIN

Competence

One of six core characteristics of a trusted financial advisor (**character, chemistry, caring, competence, cost-effective and consultative**), competence is certainly a non-negotiable requirement for any professional. But what exactly does it mean to be competent? And is it enough to just be competent?

At its core, competence is defined as having the necessary skill set, knowledge, resources and ability to do something successfully. "Successfully" being the operative word—not just satisfactorily or good enough—but rather possessing and demonstrating these abilities with proven success.

In my experience as a wealth manager, a competent advisor must provide the knowledge and insight necessary to chart an investment course customized to the unique situation of each client—as well as the discipline necessary to keep them invested when markets get choppy. I once heard an advisor's role compared to a pedestrian bridge over an eight-lane highway. Yes, it's possible to cross those lanes of traffic on your own, but getting to your destination will be a little more harrowing than if you cross safely over a pedestrian bridge. An advisor can point out the route best suited to your tolerance for risk and ultimate goals or destination.

In addition to providing investment expertise, getting clients safely over the bridge requires helping them to make good decisions. One based on the facts of a situation not the emotional reactions to that situation. Therefore, the competent advisor must ask questions, listen to clients' answers, develop thoughtful investment and wealth management strategies, carefully monitor their progress, and serve as a personal Chief Financial Officer. This process keeps investors from reacting out of fear or "irrational exuberance," and keeps them on the road to reach their goals.

Many professions require practitioners to hold specific degrees and pass comprehensive exams. For example, as a Certified Public Accountant (CPA), my credentials demonstrate a measurable standard of competency in accounting which is universally recognized by the profession, as well as consumers.

Unlike the legal, medical or even accounting professions, anyone can call themselves an investment advisor. That creates confusion, because consumers of financial advice often wrongly assume that 1) there are standards of expertise and care that all advisors share, and 2) anyone who provides investment advice must act in the client's best interests.

In reality, only professionals registered as investment advisors with the Federal Securities and Exchange Commission (SEC) or comparable state regulators who operate as fiduciaries are legally obligated to put their clients' interests first. Conversely, salespeople who work for brokerage firms place their loyalty primarily with their employers, not with their clients. That is, while fiduciaries always make recommendations that are in their clients' best interests, brokers must adhere only to a "suitability standard." This lesser standard requires only that the investment products they suggest and sell "suit" an investor's financial needs and risk profile. And that leaves portfolios wide open to more expensive, less effective products.

While there has been much discussion about identifying a single standard of competency for financial advisors, there is currently a wide variety of designations for financial advisors, which can be confusing or even meaningless without an understanding of their particular area of expertise. Perhaps the most recognizable designation is the CERTI-FIED FINANCIAL PLANNER™ (CFP®) credential which signifies demonstrated competency through education, experience and examination. It entails an increasingly broad and rigorous educational curriculum, including a comprehensive exam with questions that require applied knowledge. A minimum level of experience is also mandated. At this time, CFP is perhaps the closest to providing for a minimum level of competency as well as a requirement for fiduciary. The fiduciary component is absolutely critical to establishing a trusting relationship by ensuring the investor receives objective guidance from an advisor who is required by law to put their clients' interests first.

Certifications alone cannot guarantee successful outcomes. The capacity of a person to understand situations and to act reasonably and effectively over time will ultimately prove their competence.

Because a leader in any profession never stops learning, at Bernhardt Wealth Management we strive to expand our circle of competence through constant learning and a deep interest in all matters related to finance. As a team, we continue to develop our bench strength in order to best serve our clients and cultivate trusting relationships. We accomplish this by taking advantage of ongoing educational opportunities, taking our role as fiduciaries very seriously, and by spending the time necessary to thoroughly understand each of our clients' unique circumstances and goals.

I hope you enjoy reading about the executives featured in Volume 8 of the Profiles series. They have each demonstrated competencies in their professions that exceed expectations and achieve extraordinary triumphs.

– Gordon J. Bernhardt, CPA, PFS, CFP®, AIF®
Founder, President and CEO
Bernhardt Wealth Management, Inc.
www.BernhardtWealth.com

 *Since establishing his firm in 1994, Gordon Bernhardt has been focused on providing high-quality service and independent financial advice in order to help his clients make smart decisions about their money. He specializes in addressing the unique needs of successful professionals, entrepreneurs and retirees, as well as women in transition throughout the Washington, DC area. Over the years, Gordon has been sought out by numerous media outlets including MSN Money, CNN Money, Kiplinger and The New York Times for his insight into subjects related to personal finance.*

Profiles

———

BERNHARDT
WEALTH MANAGEMENT

David Anderson

No Room for Fear

David was already beginning to feel the familiar signs of unease before giving his presentation to forty pastors and laymen from around the world at a Risk Management Conference for the Seventh-Day Adventist Church. Shy by nature, he always felt anxious when asked to speak in front of a room full of people, but he had gotten in the habit of reminding himself he had done it hundreds of times, whether in running a board meeting, speaking at a town hall meeting, or reporting financials to his staff.

Just before he was to start speaking, however, he was informed that several other sessions that afternoon had been cancelled, so instead of speaking to forty people, he would be speaking to 500. "Twenty years ago, I would have been scared to death. I don't know if I could have done it," he says. "I'm more comfortable now, probably because I have to do it all the time, but that day was the hardest by far. I had a difficult time managing that stressful situation internally, but I didn't let my fear take over. Instead, I grew from it."

At that time, David had been the Director of Human Resources at Washington Adventist Church for just under two years, so he was still finding his stride within his new leadership role. Now the Chief Operating Officer of Lerch, Early, & Brewer, a commercial law firm based in Bethesda that represents entities of all sizes and practices around Washington D.C. and Montgomery County, he's not only hit that stride, but truly taken off.

Because he is essentially responsible for keeping the distinguished firm on a thriving trajectory, David's introverted nature has become more of an afterthought than a roadblock. "I think my shyness defines me in terms of how I approach my work, but it certainly does not limit me," he says. "I'm grateful my position forces me to be out of my comfort zone all the time. It's all about the bigger picture; running a business is really a lot like sports. You're working with a group of people towards a common goal, so everyone has a role and a pattern to run to get the ball to advance. If you let your own fears hold you back, you hold everyone else back."

In alignment with David's perspective, Lerch, Early, & Brewer was built on the same foundation of teamwork towards a common goal. When Henry Wallis and Harry Lerch founded the firm in 1950, they created a unique culture of ease and practicality, such that even today, everyone is on a first-name basis, and clients can reach their attorneys directly, rather than having to navigate a cumbersome switchboard. "We operate through team effort when solving problems, and in everything we do," David affirms. "It's better than one individual working alone, and it distinguishes us from our competition."

The firm's main focus today is servicing the needs of businesses and business owners in the areas of family law, estates, trust administration, and some executives. They have a large litigation practice, and most recently, they have a growing white-collar criminal practice that deals with Medicare fraud issues. While the firm has grown exponentially over the past decades, they have adopted a trend more commonly seen in larger firms, in which non-attorney professionals like David manage the practice like a business. "From this perspective, the lawyers can do what they do best and practice law, while the non-attorney professionals can keep the train running and the books balanced," David explains. "Attorneys are very skeptical people; they want to see the numbers and data before agreeing to anything, or they feel like they're having the wool pulled over their eyes. Fortunately, they really trust the CFO and me, so I find it to be a great system."

David's team mentality, which has led him to success so often in the business world, actually stems from a love of sports cultivated from an early age as a natural result of having two older brothers. "I was big for my age, so I would tag along with them to play football, baseball, or whatever was going on that day," he says. "I could only play if I could keep up, so I developed a competitive edge right away."

David was born in New Hampshire, where his father, a minister, ran three churches: two within the state, and one in Vermont. When he was five years old, the family moved to Northern Ohio, just outside of Canton. "Back in those days, ministers moved around quite frequently," he explains. "My father would get a calling to a new church every three to five years, and he would decide if he wanted to go." After seven years, they moved to Monroe, Ohio, a small town north of Cincinnati, where David spent his formative years becoming an avid Cincinnati Reds fan. "I would listen to the Reds games every day on the radio after school," he recalls. "My school had a program where A-students got free tickets to the games, so I went from being a B or C student to straight A's because I had suddenly had a reason."

His love for baseball continued even when the family moved to Mount Vernon in Central Ohio for his final three years of high school. "It was a nice place to live, but I realized the small town life wasn't for me," he says. Part of this realization came from observing the connection between labor-intensive jobs and the small-town environment. David attended a private boarding school, and while he was a day-student, the class schedule was set up so that students could work in the afternoons, so to make extra pocket change, he cut grass, drove laundry trucks, worked construction, and cleaned his father's church. "Those jobs really taught me the value of money," he says. "There was something enticing about the ability to go buy baseball cards with my earnings, so I took every opportunity I could to make extra money."

While he had no complaints working labor-intensive jobs as a teenager, David aspired to work a job that utilized his analytical skills, even though he wasn't quite sure what that might be. Neither of his older brothers went to college, and while his father had started school, his calling to the ministry pulled him away before he could finish. Many of his counterparts finished college, however, so David saw through their career paths that college would be the appropriate next step for him.

While he had little direction from his family about which college to attend, he was heavily recruited by Seventh-Day Adventist Colleges affiliated with his religious private school. He received invitations for visits and interviews from local schools in Ohio as well, but he ultimately decided to continue on with his religion and attend one of the three most popular Adventist schools reaching out to him: Andrews University in Michigan, Southern Adventist University in Tennessee, and Columbia Union College in the suburbs of D.C. "Most of my friends were going to Andrews or Southern, but I wanted to break away from the path I was on, so I needed something different," he says. "I was really intrigued by the D.C. area as well, so I picked Columbia Union."

He began college in 1981, taking mostly general courses initially with a slight lean toward accounting. After realizing that his childhood dreams of becoming a professional football or baseball player might not become a reality, he considered taking computer classes, since his brother had gone to trade school for computer programming and it seemed like a field rife with future opportunity. He also considered the financial track since he was a strong math student, and his introverted nature made him adverse to public speaking, so he was unsure of a career in management.

During his freshman year, David was hired in the school's bookstore, where he was formally introduced to the art and science of running a business. "I was involved in ordering books and book buyback at the end of the year, as well as displaying supplies and marketing strategies," he says. "They taught me about natural mark-ups for profitability, so I had a huge lesson in retail essentially laid in my lap." During his time at the bookstore, personal laptop computers started to escalate in popularity, so the store's manager decided to offer them for a significantly discounted price. "With that philosophy, we picked up tremendous clients, including businesses, since they would come to us for our cheap prices over anyone else," he says. "During that period, I was averaging $100 thousand in sales each month, and since we kept a part of what we sold, I was making more than some of my professors."

As soon as the administration learned of what was happening in the bookstore, they cut the program entirely. David took that as his cue to find a new job on campus, so be began working as a student accountant while also serving as the RA to his dorm. He was motivated to have his own spending money, but more so, he was paying for his tuition single-handedly, so between classes, baseball, and dating, he always made time to work, even if it meant selling microwavable burritos in his dorm's late-night snack shop.

David only had nine credits to fill during his senior year, so he spent the majority of that time at his accounting job. He enjoyed tax work, as well as the problem-solving strategies used in auditing, so he thought he might enjoy becoming a CPA. He graduated with a Bachelor's in Management and an Associate's in accounting, but by that time, he was ready for a change. "I can keep books, but it gets boring for me," he explains. "After one cycle, there are no more new challenges. I didn't want routine in my career, I need a lot of variety in my life and constant new challenges."

Shortly before graduation, while David was involved in a softball game with another school, Andy Seidel, the Director of Human Resources at Washington Adventist Hospital, approached him with an opportunity for an entry-level HR candidate. David accepted and worked in his entry-level position for four years, learning as much as he could about Human Resources, from recruitment to benefits and compensation.

When Andy left at the end of the four years, the hospital went through four massive reconstructions, which included many layoffs, so David began taking on new responsibilities at a rapid pace. "What I really liked about HR was that every day was different. Every person had a different problem that called for us to develop a unique set of solutions," he says. "I utilized my math skills when working with benefits and my sales skills for recruitment, and I developed my communication skills by leading an orientation every month for new employees."

The department went through a series of active directors over several years until David was promoted to the position. "I was suddenly the leader of a 1,500-employee facility, so my learning curve hugely escalated," he says. Fortunately, the Vice President at the time mentored him as he quickly took on more and more responsibility, so that in a short period, he went from Director to Chief Human Resources Officer and eventually to Vice President of Adventist HealthCare. "It was a lot to take on at first," he says. "I'm the type of person that wants to be liked, but when you're in a leadership position, you're not going to be liked by everyone all the time, so you need to have conviction that what you're doing is in the best interest of everyone, including the business."

During his fifteen years in Human Resources, David had to close down a hospital, place 450 employees, and oversee a merger between Washington Adventist Hospital and Shady Grove Hospital. "We merged all the benefits and policies between the two hospitals and remodeled the HR system under my tenure," he explains. "It was a wonderful experience for me because I was given a lot of latitude and support to do the things I thought we needed to do to accomplish the goals of the organization."

In the wake of the merger, David was selected to implement a cost reduction initiative, which would measure the activity of the hospitals to analyze how they could streamline their processes for efficiency. Although the program seemed very promising at its conception, it ended up failing when the CEO and CFO left and essentially deflated the project's momentum. The new leadership rewrote the project to focus on streamlining operational strategies between the two hospitals; however, it ended up attracting negative attention that questioned the quality of care being offered. "We were able to defend ourselves, but once you get a bad reputation, it just snowballs out of control," he explains. "So we had to return to having separate presidents at the two hospitals, as well as frequent joint commission reviews, which can be very stressful."

Over a three year period, David went through five reviews, all of which were extremely intense and caused him to begin feeling burned out in his role. He and his wife had two young daughters at home, which made it even more difficult for him to spend fourteen-hour days at the hospital for six days a week. "One day, I confided in a close friend that I really needed to try something else, because the hospital was taking its toll on me," he says.

That friend decided to reach out to Robbie Brewer, a Principal Attorney at Lerch, Early & Brewer. The hospital had worked closely with the law firm for years, so they were already familiar with David when his friend suggested they look into taking him on. "I'd worked closely with the firm since I was 26 years old, and Rick Vernon had been my attorney, so we already had a strong relationship when this conversation was put on the table," David says.

When the firm approached David, he jumped on the opportunity immediately. "It sounded like interesting work that would continue to challenge me," he says. "I also knew I enjoyed the people working there very much, so the rest was history." In May of 2001, David became the firm's first COO, which has since doubled in size. "The founders wanted the company to grow naturally by providing services to clients, and they recognized that to do so in an efficient and effective manner, they needed outside perspectives, which I was able to provide."

Shortly after starting with the firm, David's father-in-law died suddenly of a heart attack at the age of sixty. "He seemed to be in perfect health," David recalls. "He had played tennis all that morning and was working on an extension on their house when it happened, so I realized that if that sort of thing could happen to him, I should get a physical."

David went for a check-up shortly after his fortieth birthday, and to his shock, was diagnosed with a Mitral Valve Prolapse, a condition that would require open-heart surgery. "I was completely taken aback, especially since my family had a strong record of longevity," he says. "I had the surgery two years later at the Cleveland Clinic, and it was one of the scariest moments of my life. It was something I couldn't beat or run away from—I just had to accept it and hope everything turned out alright."

Fortunately, the surgery went well, and David made a full recovery, so that all that remains from his surgery is a mug from the Cleveland Clinic. "I keep it in my office to remind me that every day is precious; every day is a gift I've been given back," he remarks. "I truly want to cherish every moment."

While he is thankful for each day since his surgery, he is especially grateful for the time he can spend with his wife, Connie, and their two daughters. The couple met in college and was married before Connie, who is two years younger, received her Bachelor's. She is a nurse who has worked in various roles at Washington Adventist Hospital, as well is currently at the American College of Cardiology, where she works as a consultant administering a registry to track the results of certain procedures so that hospitals can improve the quality of their service. "She's a vivacious, outgoing, fun-loving person, and exactly the opposite of me in that she's extremely extroverted and always the center of attention," he laughs. "She drags me along to things I wouldn't ordinarily do, but I always love it, because I love meeting new people. She pushes me and really encourages me to challenge myself, which I'm very grateful for."

His two daughters are currently 20 and 22 years old, both working towards careers in pharmacy and physical therapy, respectively. As his own children enter their adulthood, and with it the business world, he offers them the same advice he would offer to all young people starting out. "You are going to be judged on your character and on your work ethic, and if you stand out in those two things, you will do well at whatever you do," he says. "I've found through my career that those in a position of power always noticed when I worked hard, and with that came greater responsibility and compensation. There's an attitude circulating these days that if you are paid well, you will work hard, but that's backwards. Don't focus on what you want, but what you're doing, and do it well."

David has found that he is the type of person that thrives from being involved in as much as he can, so when he's not at work, he sits on the Board of Directors of Leadership Montgomery, where he served as Assistant Treasurer in 2011 and Vice President and Treasurer in 2012. He also sits on the Board of Directors of Rebuilding Together Montgomery County in 2012 and has held high roles within his church's infrastructure, where he remains an active member. "I really feel that the greatest recognition I can receive is being elected to a leadership position," he says. "That indicates I have a skill that adds value to whatever it is I'm doing, which is important to me."

At the end of the day, David's story has coursed with such a strong pulse not in spite of his obstacles, but because of them. "I have a horrible fear of heights, but my brother and sister-in-law gave my wife and me a hot air balloon ride for my fiftieth birthday," he says. "It was one of the scariest activities I've ever done, but my wife loved it, and I didn't want to hold her, or myself, back because of fear. Life isn't about that—it's about pushing through that fear to go beyond yourself." Whether it is sports or business, family life or a personal journey, pushing through obstacles and leaving no room for fear is a sure route to lifelong evolution, and lifelong success.

Gino Antonelli

A Legacy of Family

"One of the many reason I decided to start my own business was because it allows me to pull my family together for Sunday dinners," says Gino Antonelli, President and COO of Spear, Inc. The company, founded by Gino and his business partner, Richard Pineda, is dedicated to delivering IT solutions and management consulting services to the federal government, as well as strategic business partners. The company has achieved remarkable success in its mission, yet what makes its professional endeavors so remarkable are the personal elements behind them. "Co-founding Spear allowed me to take my kids to Redskins games, or to host our loved ones on a trip back to Italy," Gino continues. "Family time is what I cherish most, and it's the reason I am constantly inspired to work harder every single day."

Indeed, in today's world, people often have to choose between work or family, but for Gino, one wouldn't be complete without the other.

He works to provide the absolute best for his family—an unparalleled source of passion that lends him incredible impact in the business world. His is purpose-driven work, and it shows.

Focused on providing cutting edge business solutions, Spear offers three core services. The first is cyber security, currently in high demand within the Federal space. Spear also offers data analytics solutions to help the government sort through and make sense of the massive amounts of information it accumulates on a daily basis. "From the Department of Defense to the IRS, the government harvests the largest amounts of data known to man," he explains. "But it's only useful if it can be organized and put into digestible terms; otherwise it's just noise. The computing tools we offer for these analytics provide solutions to business problems by maximizing the usefulness of the data collected." The final tier of Spear's business is providing classic IT and management consulting assistance to the government, from network management to capital management to human resources.

While the company is still in its infancy, having been founded in 2012, it has experienced significant success in a short time, which Gino insists is a direct reflection of their dedication to people—a dedication that starts with the firm's own employees. "We are a people-focused organization," he says. "It's very important to us that we build a solid team that has a spirit of kinship around it and the sense of working towards a common goal. Office politics and defacing others is not tolerated in any way." In addition to building a strong team internally, Gino places a heavy emphasis on understanding how the customer is being measured on a professional level. "We understand that our customers are individuals just trying to do their jobs correctly, and often times they depend on us to do just that. For that reason, we try to understand each customer and their objectives so we can accomplish exactly what needs to be done."

While helping individual customers is a source of deep satisfaction for Gino, he strives to select clients that help the greater good, particularly with a focus on patriotism or broad societal concerns. "We appreciate customers who work toward the service of the citizen, such as through national defense or cancer research," he says. "We feel that helping them reach their goals allows us to make a broader positive impact on our country."

The company is currently striving to balance investment with growth—a period that all startups experience at one point or another during their maturation. Together, Gino and his partner Richard decided to forgo external funds due to the complications they often engender, and instead opted to invest their own personal funds to move the company forward. And while this carries its own risks, it seems to have paid off. "We are very proud that we've achieved a top secret facility clearance to work in the intelligence space within the government in such a short period of time," he says.

Gino believes a key component of the success of his company is his natural tendency to treat people involved in the business like family—an inclination he credits to his loving father's influence throughout his childhood. His father immigrated to America with his family at the age of sixteen, leaving their mother country of Italy behind but bringing their strong Italian culture with them. After their farm in Eastern Italy had been destroyed during WWII, his grandfather's brother-in-law, who owned a brick laying business in Washington, D.C., sponsored them to enter the country. Settling in the same area, Gino's father joined his uncle as an apprentice in the brick-laying business, eventually moving to journeyman before deciding to start his own brick laying business.

As a young man in his late twenties, his brick laying business was successful; however, he grew tired of often being short-changed due to general contractors falling short of their financial obligations and pay-ment terms. His brother-in-law realized his problem and suggested the two enter the underground utilities business together, where they would lay water line pipes in the suburbs of Washington. "Fortunately, it turned out their new line of business was far more lucrative, since they were reimbursed based solely on their progress laying pipes down, as opposed to putting a price on the job before it was even started and receiving slow to no pay," Gino explains.

Gino's mother was also a second-generation Italian-American, and when they married, the couple moved to the suburbs of Maryland, where a large population of Italians had settled. Gino and his three younger siblings spent most of their childhood playing with their neighborhood friends, participating in bike rallies, roller skate clubs, go kart races, and soccer. He excelled in sports and academics, finding that the greatest reward he could receive was his parents' pride. "Every time my Dad introduced me to anyone, he made a point to be very boisterous about how proud he was of me; that I was a good son and did well in school," he says. "He was a very affectionate father to all of us. He was very successful and was able to set himself and his family up well financially, but he made it clear that his greatest asset was his children." However, while Gino played hard, his father made sure he worked hard as well. By the age of eleven, he and his younger brother spent every summer working for their father. "I was the boss's son, so the expectations were extremely high," Gino recalls. "But I reflect back on that experience, being down in a ditch all day working in the heat, and I know it did a great deal for my work ethic."

When Gino was eight or nine, he took a particular interest in trips to the bank. "I remember walking into those banks and thinking how cool they were," he said. "To me, they represented a big job, so I decided as a kid that I wanted to own a bank one day." After graduating high school, he attended the University of Maryland, where he studied finance to align himself with his goal, even though he considered taking over the family business when his father retired instead. "I brought up the idea to him, but he told me that he wanted me to use my head rather than my back to make my living, so I should work hard in college and pursue whatever really struck me," he recalls. "I took his advice and really dug into my finance studies, deciding I wanted to be a Vice President by the time I turned thirty-two. "

For his last semester of college, with the help of his brother-in-law, Gino landed an internship with Centel Federal Systems, a telecommunications company from the Midwest with an IT division on the East Coast. He had an immediate connection with the CFO, and before Gino graduated, he was offered a full-time job working in the finance and accounting department.

For four years, he generated all the operating plans and budgets for the company while also juggling responsibilities for miscellaneous projects. He evolved to a liaison role with the commercial division; however, when they created their own accounting staff, he realized he wanted to change his career track before falling too deep into finance. "I began realizing the guys around me were making in one month what I was making in a year, and I decided I wanted the opportunity to have that kind of financial growth," he recalls. "I decided to ask the CEO if I could have the opportunity to explore a role in business development. He had been in finance as well, so I think he was disappointed at first, but eventually he decided it would be a good idea to have a finance type sitting on the businesses development side, so he gave me a shot."

Gino worked with Centel for another two years in his new role before moving to Telos Corporation, where he joined as a Director of Business Development. The company had won a major contract, which Gino was given responsibility for. He brought together a team and built a sales organization that brought Telos a great deal of success and led to Gino's promotion to Vice President of Sales and Marketing, meeting his goal of achieving VP status by the age of thirty-two. "I was very proud of the team we put in place," he says. "I really feel I should credit my executive mentors, who had an immense impact on my professional growth. They taught me how to interact with people on the business front, and how to deal with ever-changing and evolving situations."

After eight years with Telos, Gino moved to a company called Intelligent Decisions as Vice President of Business Development. In his new role, he naturally gravitated toward the operational side of business, moving up the ranks to Executive Vice Present. During his nine and a half years with the organization, he helped the company grow from double digit million dollars to half a billion dollars in revenue.

For the last few years of his time with Intelligent Decisions, Gino began feeling his entrepreneurial instincts stir within him. "I felt I had done what I had come to do with that company, and if I was ever going to do my own thing, now was the time," he recalls. His wife, Danielle, who is a CPA, could sense his desire to take a chance on himself, and she was extremely supportive. "She's always been a rock for me, and was especially so when I decided to try my hand at Spear," he says.

Before he left Intellectual Decisions, Gino had met and worked with Richard Pineda. It quickly became apparent to both men that they shared similar business and leadership philosophies, and the two developed a close personal friendship. As fate would have it, they happened to leave their respective companies around the same time, prompting a lunch that changed both of their lives. "By that point, I was about to put my own company in motion," he recalls. "I had the financials worked out and was in the process of seeking out an executive team when Richard suggested we partner together. I thought it sounded like a great idea, not only because it was shared investment and shared risk, but also because it gave me another sharp mind to relay ideas with."

As it has turned out, the two made a perfect match and have been able to build their company around the core values that matter most to them. "Richard is a wonderful business partner. He's like my brother," Gino says. "A partnership can really be like a marriage. It's either going to be great or very tough, but we figured out how to make it work. We are both very capable and proven executives, and we work extremely well together. We feel it's very important to have candid conversations with each other, and we are able to do that effectively."

An essential facet that the two agree on is the importance placed on the people within the company. Just as Gino strives to understand and value his clients' objectives, he does the same for his team. "When it comes to leadership, I feel it's imperative to step back and let my employees do their job," he says. "I make an effort to lead by example, rather than by micromanaging. That gives them the autonomy to flex their own professional capabilities a bit, and makes whatever task I've delegated that much more important to them. Additionally, I feel as the leader of this company, it's my duty to open the doors to career growth for my team, just as it was done for me at other companies."

While Gino certainly believes opening doors for his employees is crucial, he knows that the fundamental component of any young person's success comes from within. "I think what sets certain young people apart from others is the ability to set aside the notion of entitlement and focus on doing the best job one can," he explains. "If I could offer advice to people entering the workforce today, it would be to lower your expectations initially, put your head down, and do the work. It's the only true way to prove what you do and do not deserve."

Looking back, Gino feels extremely proud of the company he's grown, as well as the choices he's made along the way. "There couldn't be anything more rewarding than hearing our folks at Spear talk about how much they love what they do and where they work," he says. "Richard and I are making financial sacrifices and hard decisions to move the company forward, so we celebrate hearing that we've created an environment and a company that our people truly appreciate."

Yet while his company is certainly a cornerstone of success in his life, Gino readily admits that all he has accomplished would be hollow without the love and support of his family. "I have a beautiful wife and wonderful children, and I'm lucky enough that my mother and three siblings all live close enough to each other that, when our schedules allow, we can descend on Mom's house on Sunday for dinner," he laughs. "I feel so much appreciation for what my father did, coming to this country and teaching himself English, reading, and writing. He personifies the American Dream, and it's my hope to carry on his legacy to the next generation. If I can be half the man my father was, I'll feel extremely satisfied about my life." Indeed, by carrying on his father's legacy in this way and bringing the spirit of family to the business environment, Gino has helped cultivate a company whose culture serves as a reminder to all of us of what really is most important in life.

Marc S. Berman

The Grand Tradition

While other twelve-year-old children slept in on Sundays or spent their mornings leisurely watching cartoons, Marc Berman followed a markedly different agenda. He would wake up early, hop on his bike, and ride across town to a deli in Silver Spring, Maryland. Inside, he would pull up a chair at a table where three old men—his grandfather and his grandfather's two brothers—discussed business. As they talked, Marc listened and listened, week after week.

Marc's grandfather never made it past the tenth grade, but was a brilliant businessman and dealmaker with a prominent hand in building our Nation's Capital city. Much of his savoir-faire came from his own father, who invented the wire coat hanger and the screen that turned hot water into steam for use in irons. He owned 28 dry cleaning stores throughout Washington, DC, paving the way for his three sons to start Diener's carpet, one of the city's largest carpet conglomerates.

Marc's grandfather went on to develop an expansive real estate portfolio that was augmented with the purchase of local and national radio stations, and he discussed these deals in detail at the Sunday morning breakfasts, with his eager grandson at his side.

"He was filled with this wisdom that permeated his whole demeanor, and I was completely in awe of him," Marc remembers. "He was like a fortune cookie, with general wisdom for everything. He'd talk to his brothers about a shopping center they were developing on Rockville Pike, and afterwards, I'd jump in his car and we'd drive up to look at the construction progress together. I've emulated and admired him my whole life." Now the President of Vector Technical Resources, Marc has wholly embraced this entrepreneurial spirit as his own, and continues in his family's grand tradition of shaping Washington, D.C. with its work and vision.

Marc was born at George Washington Hospital to one of the largest, most prominent families in town. "In those days, buildings were owned by people, not companies," he reflects. "In those days, it felt like royalty to be a Diener." Having grown up a Diener herself, his mother, Marlene, was raised with a silver spoon, but never let it go to her head, drawing the love and warmth of all she met.

Marc, the middle child of two sisters, grew into a young boy with a fierce love of sports. His father built a basketball court in their backyard, and all the neighbors would come over to play. Marc had an impressive 39-inch vertical jump and excelled at athletics, inspired in part by his father's priorities. "He pushed athletics, not school or business," Marc recalls. "But my grandfather didn't care as much about sports. He loved to discuss business and made it clear that it was his favorite topic of conversation."

As a fourth generation Washingtonian who hails from a richly entrepreneurial family history, Marc's identity as a business leader and innovator is innate, but circumstances in his early life made entrepreneurship a necessity rather than just a passion. His parents divorced when he was fourteen, and as his mother was a homemaker, it fell to Marc to provide for her and his two sisters. His character acquired new depth as he became the head of the household and launched his first business before he turned fifteen. "I was successful very early in life, and that came with a price. I made a lot of mistakes, but my grandfather had taught me that most successful businessmen fail at some point in their career," Marc says. "I was ready, and I wasn't going to let it discourage me."

With his expectations in check and his sights set on providing for his family, Marc launched a modest business at the age of fourteen, installing various kinds of stereos in cars. 8-Track players had just come out, so he learned how to remove radios and insert the new technology. Within a year, his grandfather stepped in to help support the small family in his father's absence and began gifting Marlene pieces of real estate and other investments, as well as providing a generous monthly stipend. She was restored from rags to riches overnight, but that didn't stop Marc's drive to succeed. Before long, his business took off, and he was making $25,000 a year—a sizeable sum for a boy of his age in the early 1970s.

As a high school student with three employees and a considerable salary of his own, Marc quickly garnered the excitement of his business teacher. The teacher assigned the class to design flyers for him and pass them out all over town. An article on his business was written for the school newspaper. "I came from a very tight-knit community in Silver Spring where everyone knew each other, so the word of this new concept got out," he says.

Meanwhile, at age fifteen, Marc was hired as a stock boy at Spring Electric Supply by the father of his best friend, Gary. Gary's father, whom Marc admired deeply, bought the company several years later. Gary went on to college at the University of Maryland to study electrical engineering, and while Marc started college as well, he ultimately decided he didn't need it. "I was trying to run my business, and my father and grandfather didn't seem to think furthering my education was important," he says. "My grandfather would say that, when we go to school, we learn our lesson and then we take our test, but in life, we take our test and then we learn our lesson. I was so successful at 17 that I thought I didn't need school, but now, I really regret that I didn't spend those years experiencing that time with my peers, playing basketball and learning in that kind of environment. I later attended The University of Maryland in the evenings because I realized how important college was, and now, as a father, I push education so much."

Instead of college, Marc focused on the radio business and was promoted to general manager of Spring Electric Supply, running the whole operation. At the age of 21, he married a young lady named Tammy and bought his first condo. They had a daughter named Lisa, and Marc went into business with Tammy's brother, Ronny, to start a property management and construction company. He had felt the pull of his grandfather's influence and decided to try his hand at buying real estate. As he built that portfolio, he helped a friend build a hair salon in Rockville and made $25,000, so he and Ronny decided to pursue similar opportunities in the construction business as well. They moved into an office in Wheaton and then in Silver Spring, excelling over a four-year period until several customers missed payments and the company tanked.

By that time, Marc and Tammy had divorced, and he decided to go into business with Carl Rowan to launch another construction company that focused on interiors. The venture was somewhat successful, but Marc didn't love it, so when Gary called to let him know about a new opportunity in D.C., he jumped on it. Pepco was paying $50 rebates to people to replace their incandescent fixtures with compact fluorescents, so the two started an electrical contracting company that grew into one of the largest energy management companies in the country. "We would go into buildings, retrofit the fixtures at no charge to our customers, and collect the rebates from Pepco," he recounts. "Over the next several years, we were unbelievably successful and morphed into a service company. We eventually sold the business to a small company in Gaithersburg in 1996, and Gary still runs that company today."

In the vacuum left from the sale of the business, Marc and his second wife, Margarita, decided to launch a staffing company. He had a strong relationship with several technology executives that he met through their mutual love of boating, which leant the venture an IT focus. Margarita had a strong background in staffing, and Marc learned from her round-the-clock wheeling-and-dealing. "She was a master recruiter," he remembers. "She rarely went on the various popular job boards, but instead did everything over the phone or in person. She'd be on the phone at all hours, calling up key candidates who could refer her to the best of the best to fill a given opening. It was incredibly impressive, and I learned the art of the industry from her."

Their staffing business flourished from 1996 until the bottom dropped out of the market in 2001, at which point Marc joined the leadership team of another IT staffing company, now known as ALTA IT Services. ALTA served companies like HP and Lockheed Martin, and its President, Howard Stein, was an incredible mentor and model. As Marc's success mounted, so did his reputation, coalescing to attract even better talent. He oversaw every transaction, making sure recruits were taken care of and the right thing was done. Cognizant that his name is his word and his word is his business, he committed each day to making "Marc Berman" the brand of choice in IT staffing. He developed an extensive network built on solid credibility, and those same people became his references later, when he set out on his own in search of an opportunity to build a company according to his own vision.

After ten successful years at ALTA serving as Executive VP and Partner, that opportunity came in the form of a small government contracting company called DOMA Vector, owned by Rob Williams. It was a Service-Disabled Veteran-Owned Small Business with a top-secret facilities clearance that had won some good opportunities since its launch in 2007, but Rob was ready to retire, and the company had little wind left in its sails. When Marc came across the opportunity in 2011, he was happy at ALTA, but the entrepreneurial Diener blood in his veins called for a true test. "I had often wondered if ALTA would be my last job," he reflects. "I had always felt as though I was missing something, and then the memory of my grandfather became very clear to me, and it dawned on me. I didn't want to be a partner; I wanted to be at the helm of something great. So one day, I decided to do it."

Thus, in July of 2012, Marc took over as President at Rob's company, immediately enacting a complete rebrand and reconstruction of the entity into Vector Technical Resources. And while it was a move that his trajectory had tended toward since those early days riding his bike to meet his grandfather on Sunday mornings, a marked igniting spark came with the unparalleled support of his wife, Patti. The couple married in 2009, after Marc's mother introduced them just before her death. "I have never met another person like her in my whole life," he avows. "She motivates me every single day and night. She's incredibly intuitive and brilliant, and she selflessly cares for others in ways I can't even imagine. She always helps me see the positive. She's my inspiration, and I couldn't have done it without her."

It took grit to jump from a lucrative position, to no income, to making a substantial investment in Vector's future success, but from the shell of a business, Marc built a staffing company that is now 25 employees strong. With a focus on government contracting and services, it has grown in part through the acquisition of smaller businesses making good profit but lacking the resources to grow. The company is also focused on high-level marketing, and Marc continues to evolve his identity and brand as a leader through organizations like SmartCEO and EO. "The work is hard, and I might prefer to go home to Patti at the end of a long day, but it's important that I'm out there, networking and making a name for the company and the tremendous work that we do. We're changing the way staffing companies do business, putting an emphasis on core values and on bringing in the A players."

Vector's company culture revolves around the key tenets of honesty, equality, and respect—values that pay off in spades even as they add substance and sincerity to client and employee relationships. They are the echoes of a memory in which Marc's grandfather was preparing to buy an office building on M street. He had a meeting in one of the top-floor offices with the corresponding echelon to close the deal, but when he entered the building, he instead took the elevator down to the basement to spend some time chatting with the maintenance staff. "Without fail, my grandfather treated everyone like gold," Marc explains. "It was how he thought all people should be treated, and he ended up saving a million dollars on the building because he was able to find out what was wrong with it. His example really hit home how important it is to treat people the right way, no matter what you're doing."

In advising young people entering the working world today, Marc emphasizes the importance of finding what you love, even if it's not readily apparent with your first job. "As you move laterally or vertically through various professional opportunities, pay attention to the things that really drive you, and through it all, focus on doing the right thing," he says. "Do unto others as you'd have them do unto you, always being fair and honest." Beyond that, Marc's example is one that underscores the true value of failure in building character and business acumen. After rising to incredible success at such a young age, owning a construction company by the time he was 18 and then amassing ten rental properties, he hit rock bottom at the age of 22 but emerged from those experiences with the knowledge and skills to build solid, sustainable success.

Just as it always has been, both the root and bloom of that success goes back to family. His oldest daughter, Lisa, shares his entrepreneurial spirit and owns a successful insurance company. His son studies law at the University of Baltimore, and his youngest daughter is a senior at Loyola. Patti has two children of her own—Samantha, who attends Florida State, and Sophie, their last child at home—and the entire family blends together with beauty and balance. Their family life has elements of older generations, as Patti cares diligently for her ailing parents. Lisa's son—Marc's grandson—also lends the joy of generations to come, and all are connected through the arc of vision and achievement that is the hallmark of their family's legacy. "It's something I live and breathe, just as I am living and breathing Vector right now," he says. "My entire life force is dedicated to being the best father, husband, mentor, entrepreneur, and business leader I can, because each of those roles is connected. It's the grand tradition of the Diener family, and it certainly won't stop with me."

Jake Bittner

The Difference

Today, when Jake Bittner laughs and talks with his daughter, he hears his own father's voice speaking through him. Though he grew up in Cleveland and St. Louis with his mother while his father lived in Detroit, the two spoke all the time and were more like friends than father and son. They took epic road trips together to New Jersey, where they attended reunions at his father's alma mater, Princeton University. "I remember being on campus and realizing that an Ivy League education was attainable," Jake remembers. "It wasn't out of reach."

Meanwhile, Jake's mother, an incredibly hard worker who emphasized the importance of education and follow-through, was a manager in the motorsports department at a large PR firm in St. Louis. She often brought her son along when she traveled across the country on weekends, and thanks to this exposure to different cities and ways of living, the young boy was encouraged to dream even bigger. With airline miles racked up from business travel, she was able to take him on trips to Mexico, Puerto Rico, St. Martin, Hawaii and Spain. "I had seen a lot of the world, and I wanted to see more of it," he recounts. "Most of the kids who graduated from my high school stayed in St. Louis, but I had other aspirations."

Because of these influences during his formidable years, Jake prioritized his studies and was admitted to Yale University, which changed the course of his life, catapulting him into a higher echelon through his college years and inspiring in him the confidence to play at any level. After spending four years working with some of the brightest students in the country, learning both from and with them, Jake had the feeling he could attain anything in life, and now, as the cofounder and CEO of Qlarion, that sense of potential has made all the difference.

Qlarion was launched in 2010 as a spinoff of Cadence Quest, a data analytics company that focused on the commercial space and retail analytics. It grew to fifty employees before its commercial piece was sold to Accenture in 2010. Jake, along with Adam Roy and Dendy Young, bought the government piece, which had been whittled down to four employees. They rebranded the business as Qlarion and grew it to a team of nearly forty employees, following a growth trajectory between 40 and 50 percent and finishing 2013 at around $5 million in revenue.

Today, Qlarion helps public sector organizations leverage their data to operate more effectively, applying analytics and data management capabilities to augment the way they seek to achieve their missions. Through the complex world of analytics, the company helps organizations extract intelligence from their data sources. "The intellectual property and solutions we invest in are all about simplification," Jake explains. "We believe that, through simplification, we can proliferate the use of analytics and encourage more people to use data to make better decisions. By changing the way organizations operate and showing them that they can be more data-driven, making decisions based on real-time, historical, and predictive analyses, we believe we can have a major impact on mission achievement."

While roughly two-thirds of projects in the analytics market fail, Qlarion boasts a success rate of a hundred percent—in part because its entire focus is dedicated to analytics, and in part because it approaches such projects from a business perspective. The company understands that, when a business decouples from its technology, these two elements become misaligned, and time and money are misspent. "We've designed an approach and methodology that allows a customer to maintain its focus on the business outcomes it needs from the data," Jake affirms. "The world of data is vast and full of red herrings, but by focusing on the mission at hand, we give our clients a chance at real success."

These clients include the Centers for Medicare & Medicaid Services, the Department of Energy, Fannie Mae, the U.S. Postal Service, the Department of Defense, the IRS, and the City of Boston. From asset management, to staffing strategies, to predicting future trends, Qlarion is leading the charge in showing organizations that, for many of the questions they face, the solution is in the data. "More and more people are beginning to realize that, to increase efficiency and make smarter operational decisions, one of the best things you can do is invest in technology and analytics," says Jake. "I'm passionate about this field because of the difference it makes. When I can help someone look at a problem in a different way—a way they've never been able to visualize before—and I see the lights go on in their head, that difference is palpable."

In a way, Jake has been preparing for his role at the helm of Qlarion all his life, beginning from the time he was a young boy observing his father's entrepreneurial ventures. He was born in Boston, but his family moved to Pittsburg and then Cleveland. His father was the head of marketing for the Cleveland Grand Prix, and when he vacated that position to move to Detroit and put on the Detroit Grand Prix, his mother took on the job. Their marriage dissolved when Jake was six, and when the company in charge of the Cleveland Grand Prix went under shortly thereafter, Jake's mother found the job in St. Louis, where she was very successful.

Young Jake would travel alone frequently to see his father, and he gained an incredibly comfortable sense of independence. On these trips, he watched as his father launched a community recycling company to address the massive piles of tires that cluttered the city. "Dad had some good ideas, but he was more about shooting for the moon than about building steadily and solidly," he recalls. "He didn't make the right financial decisions, building out a big facility without having any customers to use it. In retrospect, I asked myself, what could I learn from his mistakes? Financial soundness became important to me, so I decided I wasn't going to just run off, start a company, and see what happened. I would prepare myself financially, skill-wise, and knowledge-wise."

Aside from some babysitting and yard work for neighbors, Jake earned his first paycheck working at a miniature golf course in town. He also worked as a camp counselor, but spent most of his time playing soccer, baseball, and basketball. His best sport, however, was football, and he worked incredibly hard through high school in the hopes of playing in college. As a freshman, he played tight end and was named the most valuable player of the year. As a sophomore, the varsity team needed an offensive guard, so that became his spot.

Jake was a junior in high school when he tore his ACL playing basketball, putting his entire athletic future in jeopardy. "When an orthopedic surgeon told me I would never play football again, I hit the lowest of the low," he recounts. "I couldn't go to the next basketball game because I was in surgery, and I couldn't walk. People were telling me I didn't have a future. I worked my ass off for so long to play football in college, and it looked as if it was all taken away in a heartbeat."

Thankfully, Jake sought out a team doctor who took a look at the injury and saw a different future for him—one that involved a full recovery. From that moment on, he hit the gym three times a day for six months of rehabilitation. At one point, his determination even broke a workout machine. "The whole experience taught me to never give up," he says.

Thanks to his tenacity, he did indeed go on to play football at Yale, where the sport served as a character-building force that still influences his life on a routine basis today in the business world. Though he was a straight-A student in high school, he often had to make value judgments as a college student that taught him how to quickly assess critical items on the table and make a decision. "The truth is, I learned how to prioritize what needs to get done in a certain amount of time, rather than aiming for perfection and taking forever to finish," he says. "When resources are scarce, you have to be able to allocate them appropriately to get the maximum benefit. If studying for five hours meant I might get injured or let my team down, it often made more sense for me to get a B on a test instead of an A." The experience of meeting his obligation to his teammates while balancing his personal obligations evolved in him unparalleled discipline, as well as an internal sense of time with which he can pinpoint exactly how long to spend on a given task.

Jake majored in mechanical engineering and had already secured a post-graduation job at MicroStrategy, when tragedy struck during his senior year of college. His fun-loving, upbeat, optimistic father passed away suddenly from a heart attack, leaving Jake devastated. He focused on getting through graduation and then moved to D.C. in August to start his new job in a new city, with new people and a new life. The fresh start did him good, and as he found himself enjoying the world of technology, he settled into analytics. When he was 24, he moved into a sales position as part of a broad plan to achieve future success. Though he had always hated selling things when he was younger, he had his sights set on one day running his own company, and he knew that mastering sales would be a vital component of that achievement.

The sales job at MicroStrategy was a bit of a stretch for a recent college graduate, but the company decided to take a chance on him. This decision was in part due to the success he had already garnered, underscored by the fact that he had attended Yale, and by his boldness in stepping up and asked for the opportunity. Jake did well in this capacity, and after four years at MicroStrategy, he transitioned over to Informatica, where he worked in sales for another four years.

Though he was making good money, he eventually realized he had learned all he needed to learn in that capacity. It was now time for him to leave the larger corporate climate to experience a smaller company, so he found a position at a startup called Intensity. "It had incredible technology but was poorly run," Jake remembers. "I learned that small companies can drown in opportunity when the market loves what they do. At a small company, you have to be selective with your time and resources in terms of the opportunities you pursue."

From there, Jake went on to a startup group within a company called Business Objects. In that capacity, he was charged with selling a new product to their existing customer base, giving him a taste of entrepreneurship but with a safety net. He learned the value of a disciplined and formalized sales process, which helps to align an entire sales team, and which has been key in Qlarion's success. When Business Objects was acquired by Oracle, Jake felt he had built up enough knowledge and expertise to launch a business successfully, so he brought the idea to the one person whose opinion could make or break the dream: his wife, Chandra.

Through their marriage, Chandra knew Jake was considering starting his own business, but neither of them had known for sure if he actually would. Jake had watched his father's poorly planned entrepreneurial ventures lead to two divorces, and he was resolved never to put his own family at risk. Chandra, in turn, knew her husband wouldn't take the leap if he wasn't sure he could do it, so when he said he was ready, she gave him her blessing. "Her confidence in me was a big source of support," he remembers. "When you've got a good thing going with a stable paycheck coming in each month, it's hard to pull away to take a risk and a step down in income, but we were ready."

Thus, after mastering sales and working with software companies of all sizes to observe what worked and what didn't, Jake joined forces with two former colleagues to acquire Cadence Quest and create Qlarion. Jake focused on new customer acquisition, seeing the big picture, and guiding the direction of the company. Adam Roy took responsibility for delivering to those customers, and all the company's consultants now report to him. Dendy Young, on the other hand, has a private equity investor company of his own that advises businesses like Qlarion, so his input has proven invaluable through its inception. "We're all about pushing and growing, but he reminds us that we have to be doing certain things today to get us where we want to be tomorrow," Jake explains. "We're all a great team of complementary strengths, and Qlarion in thriving because of it."

In advising young people entering the working world today, like his own half-brothers, Jake emphasizes the value of trying new things. For him, what began as an experiment in analytics just out of college evolved into a successful entrepreneurial venture that is changing the way businesses operate and problem-solve. "College can be like a cocoon, so put yourself in positions that expose you to the world, because you never know what you might find," he says. "It's also important to be able to adapt—a skill that becomes increasingly important in leadership positions." As a leader, Jake assesses the behavior that will be most effective depending on the people involved and the situation at hand. He maintains a set of core principles and then adapts, depending on what each scenario calls for.

His life mission extends beyond the bounds of the company, as well. A member of MindShare, a forum for CEOs of emerging technology companies, Jake is also passionate about bringing the advantages of data analytics to charitable organizations, hoping to create a consortium of resources to help such organizations operate more effectively. He and Chandra are passionate about local issues, particularly those pertaining to children and hunger. "In life, I employ the same tenet we embrace at Qlarion," he says. "If it makes sense, do it. Chandra and I try to do the right thing for the community, just as the company strives to do the right thing for our customers. It's what the concept of analytics is all about. If we can be a more data-driven society, many problems of scarcity and discord naturally evaporate, and there's a sense of unity in rationale and purpose. That's the difference, and that's what we're about."

R. Bruce Buchanan

The Mathematics of Life

Bruce Buchanan gazed up at the equation written on the chalk-board high above his head. After recognizing a strong interest in math in the second grade student, his teacher had walked him upstairs to the third grade classroom to see if he could solve the problems taught to the older children. The third grade teacher had scrawled a long equation on the board, and the moment of truth was upon them.

The only help Bruce needed to solve the problem was a boost so he could reach the top of the board—a defining moment for him that showed the young boy there was something special about his aptitude for numbers. But what was even more special about him, and what has served him just as vitally throughout his professional career, was the deep empathy that has always allowed him to connect with others. Now the Managing Partner of Berlin, Ramos & Company, P.A., a CPA firm serving the D.C. metropolitan area, Bruce's work is about more than numbers—it's about the mathematics of life. "The accounting profession is not cold and clinical for me," he affirms. "I enjoy really getting to know people, connecting with them and seeing what's important to them."

Berlin Ramos can be traced back to Paul Berlin's first CPA firm, which was launched in 1947. He joined forces with Rene Ramos in 1970, and Bruce joined the firm shortly thereafter as an entry-level accountant. Having just graduated from college, he was the youngest employee for a period of two years. Now among the firm's second generation of partners, he's currently working on cultivating the third generation. The Berlin Ramos team now has 50 professionals and support staff, including six active partners and a dozen managers. About a third of its employees are 35 years or younger.

Berlin Ramos excels at building strong client relationships that span generations and is still serving clients it took on sixty years ago. It owes much of its longevity and success to its commitment to focus on key service areas. It has a long history of doing tax work for successful family real estate businesses in the D.C. area, with that segment of the firm's business comprising over a third of its total volume. Twelve percent of their billing comes from audit, and about ten percent from third party administrator work for qualified retirement plans. The firm excels at helping clients evaluate what kind of qualified retirement plan would work best for them, based on their unique goals. The firm has a diverse mix of business clients, including a number of professionals. Berlin Ramos also prepares about a thousand individual income tax returns, mostly for business owners and exceptionally complex cases. It stays away from SEC work and the risk that comes with accounting for publicly traded companies, and does not work with financial institutions.

"Having watched me for all these years, my wife will often emphasize the 'public' in public accounting because, especially at the leadership level within the firm, we're not just sitting in the back room grinding through numbers," Bruce affirms. "Our main focus is striving to make the financial lives of our clients better, and in order to do that, we have to get to know them. We focus on listening so we can learn the aspects of their financial situation that cause them anxiety, and then we work to relieve that and help them achieve financial security. We try to ask good questions to find out what's really important to them, so we can pursue solutions that are sensitive to their goals. When I have the opportunity to see an improvement in someone's situation—not so much their net worth, but their frame of mind with respect to their lives, it's extremely rewarding."

Bruce grew up in the small town of Hollidaysburg, Pennsylvania, as the oldest of four children. In the winter of 1957, the family moved into the home that his mother still lives in today. "We had such a stable home life," he says. "My parents were married for 56 years before my father passed away in 2006. My mom's parents lived in the same town, and we'd go over to their house on weekends so I could spend time with my grandparents, who loved us so much. I grew up in that community, and I graduated from high school with many of the same kids I started elementary school with. My roots are there."

Bruce's father ran Buchanan Lumber Company, a group of building supply centers in Central Pennsylvania that his grandfather had started. At one point, the family owned lumber companies in Cumberland, Maryland; Kaiser, West Virginia; and Altoona, Pennsylvania. After the businesses were acquired, his father took an early retirement at age 58 and opened a travel agency. "He loved traveling, as well as the people side of that business," Bruce remembers. "I think a lot of my attributes, both professionally and personally, come from him."

Bruce's mother was a homemaker and would take the children to baseball games and piano lessons, radiating warmth, kindness, and patience as a parent and as a member of the community. "She was always determined that we sit down and have family dinner," he says. "It's more important than a lot of people realize, and I think our culture would be stronger if we had more families sitting around the dinner table together."

Beyond strengthening the fabric of American society, family dinners might also be the perfect setting for children to practice their passions in life, as Bruce did. At the table, his father would challenge the children to do math problems in their heads. "I think it was more a cause of indigestion than encouragement for my siblings, but I always enjoyed it," Bruce laughs. "Five times five times four divided by 10 plus two. Those were the kinds of run-on problems we'd solve as he strung them out in the air." Bruce earned good grades in school, and his paternal grandfather would pay him small sums of money for A's on his report card.

While he was somewhat shy and sensitive as a small child, thanks to the encouragement of his parents and teachers, Bruce's confidence blossomed, and in each year's school picture, his smile grew a little broader. He took up baseball, basketball, and golf through his childhood. At age 15, his friends convinced him to play the Hammond organ for their rock and roll band, which thrust him in the spotlight and brought out his extroverted nature even more. The four-member band was paid $57 per gig, and with $5 of expenses, that meant Bruce was pocketing $13 for three hours of work—more than he was making in his minimum-wage job at his father's lumber company. "Those were my concurrent first jobs," he says. "My dad would get frustrated when I'd play a gig in the middle of the week and get home late, so he said I had to choose between my job with him and the band. I picked the band!"

Bruce also vividly recalls the summer of 1967, when a friend invited him to attend a week-long Young Life camp in Colorado. A sophomore in high school at the time, he had had no prior experience with the organization, and though he attended church on a regular basis, he hadn't really connected with the Christian faith. "That camp was full of fun and adventure, but there was a serious element to it as well, and it was the first time I really understood what it meant to trust in

Christ," Bruce remembers. "It resonated with me immediately." When he started college at Bucknell University several years later, he connected with the Christian community there, beginning with attending a prayer meeting on campus in the wake of the Kent State shooting of 1970, and his faith grew deeper.

Bruce was one of the best students at his high school, but found himself an average student at Bucknell. It was hard to adjust at first, but looking back, he's thankful that he was academically challenged in a small-school environment. He started his college career as a Math major, but experienced a sudden change of heart during his sophomore year when he enrolled in Principles of Abstract Algebra, taught by the dreaded Dr. Kim. By the end of the first class, the severity of the professor had converted five of its approximately 30 enrollees from math majors to accounting majors, including Bruce. "I wanted to do something more concrete and less abstract," he says. "That class was the turning point, leading me to realize I wanted to pursue applied mathematics as opposed to theoretical math."

In anticipation of his upcoming graduation, Bruce interviewed with several large accounting firms in the spring of his senior year. "The idea of being on the 34th floor of an office building in Philadelphia with one of the Big 8 firms was a bit daunting to me," he remembers. "A professor of mine encouraged me to interview at Berlin Ramos, so I drove from Lewisburg down to Silver Spring, Maryland, and borrowed a red tie from a friend's father, at her insistence, to look professional. The firm seemed warmer, with a company culture that was more closely knit. Having grown up in a small town, the smaller firm environment seemed more appealing to me, and since accepting their offer, the firm and I have both evolved tremendously over the decades."

The success of that evolution is chronicled on a small framed 5 x 7 piece of paper that now sits on Bruce's desk—a Christmas gift he received several years ago from the Berlin Ramos staff. In the center, in green typeface, is his name, surrounded by words and phrases written by staff members about him. *Leader. Enterprising. Analytical. Charismatic.* The ones that mean most to him, however, are those that speak to his character. *Encouraging. Patient educator. Principled. Giver. Understanding. Kind. Boss but not bossy.* "I'm thankful to God for his grace in helping me to show some degree of good character," he says. "I really appreciated the thought that went into that gift. The kinds of comments I got from the staff encouraged me that I'm doing at least some of the right things. I believe in servant leadership, and we have a lot of really wonderful people and strong relationships at the firm. They're an essential part of why people enjoy coming to work here."

This positive company culture has been formally recognized by a national survey of employees conducted by *Accounting Today*, naming Berlin Ramos among the top ten accounting firms in America to work for through six consecutive years. "This has been important for the firm's morale and great for recruiting, as well as being meaningful to our clients," he says. "We have a low turnover rate and a lot of satisfied employees who are doing great work for them." Bruce himself was recognized as a SmartCPA by SmartCEO Magazine, but far more meaningful to him are the small, direct acknowledgments from the people he serves. "Recently, a client said I was the most accommodating person she knows," he recalls. "Another time, I got an email that said, 'Thank you for your excellent, conscientious service.' Those are the kinds of words that I treasure."

None of this could have been possible, however, without the love and support of his wife, Carla. When they met through Young Life, Bruce was an extrovert in full bloom, while she was quiet and pensive, with a beautiful inner life that captivated him immediately. As Young Life leaders, the two would see each other on a weekly basis, and they married in 1977. Active in the Presbyterian Church of America together for almost thirty years, Bruce is now an elder, and Carla dedicates her time to hospitality efforts, mentoring young women, food pantry work, and other vital services. They're also very supportive of the Cystic Fibrosis Foundation and Camp Friendship, a camp for kids with cancer. "It would be impossible to overstate Carla's role in my success," Bruce avows. "I have no idea what I would have done without her and the incredible love, support, and encouragement we share."

In advising young people entering the working world today, Bruce highlights the lessons that are often forgotten for their simplicity. "The small things make a big difference," he notes. "Persistence, daily diligence, and dedication pay off. Do the good work God's given you the gifts to do." This focus on using your gifts stands at the heart of Bruce's work, helping his clients to make sense of the mathematics of life and to improve their lives because of it. "For many people, the numbers side of life feels like a mysterious black box they don't understand," he says. "When we don't really understand something, we tend to be anxious about it. To feel that I have some gifts I can use to help alleviate those fears is really what I've wanted all along. When I was a kid, I thought about my future and hoped I'd be able to make a living using my gift for math in a way that was fun, and I'm so grateful for the opportunity to do that every day."

BERNHARDT
WEALTH MANAGEMENT

Cari Guthrie Cho

The Natural Healer

Successful adults often name childhood role models, mentors, teachers, and parents as the influences that set them on their professional paths early in life. Cari Guthrie Cho, however, can't name any particularly intuitive therapists or inspiring teachers, and wasn't steered toward counseling and the field of mental health by any particular adult hand. Rather, her career choice was inspired solely by her own experiences, particularly those spurred by her parents' divorce and the role she played in its aftermath.

Cari was ten when her parents separated, and while the divorce wasn't acrimonious, it nonetheless represented a major upheaval for a family with young children. Though much too young to fully understand the scope of adult problems, it fell to Cari to console her mother and comfort her confused younger sister—responsibilities she took on with innate grace. Her family found her to be a natural talker and listener, with a presence that soothed the ache of the situation and allowed them to see it as an opportunity to rebuild. "My mother was very open with me about what she was going through," Cari acknowledges. "I remember sitting on her bed late at night, talking about her fears and hopes." Though the situation wasn't ideal, Cari and her mother developed an incredibly close relationship that persists to this day. Over the next few years, Cari talked extensively with her family and began to dream of a career spent helping others face their problems and defeat their demons.

As a child, Cari dreamed of helping other families deal with the trauma of divorce, but as she entered the world of mental health, she began to encounter people experiencing truly severe psychological issues. These people desperately needed the attention of someone dedicated, and she knew she had found her calling. Today, Cari is President & CEO of Cornerstone Montgomery, an organization that provides a vast array of services for the mentally ill in Montgomery County. Because people suffering from mental illness tend to fall through the cracks of an imperfect social safety net, they often lack access to proper psychiatric care, and homelessness, drug addiction, and unemployment plague their ranks. Even beginning to tackle these problems, entangled and complex as they are, requires a tremendous commitment of time and energy that most people balk at. Ever the optimist, however, Cari has spent her career helping people fight for their lives, even if they gave up all hope of a normal, happy existence long ago.

In 2012, two organizations—Threshold Services and St. Luke's House—merged to form Cornerstone Montgomery. Both were well established in the area; St. Luke's had been providing services to the area's mentally ill for four decades, while Threshold had been doing the same for three. Both had begun as grassroots organizations founded by community members—St. Luke's by members of a local Episcopalian Church, and Threshold by members of the National Alliance of Mental Illness (NAMI). The NAMI members sought to provide housing for their family members in need, while St. Luke's hoped to bring a range of services to the area's homeless. Over the years, both groups grew and evolved, and both came to provide residential services, day programs, and clinics staffed with psychiatrist and therapists.

Although similar in these many respects, each organization had a unique focus and range of programming to bring to the table. "St. Luke's had a tremendous employment support program and were the best in the area at helping people with mental illness find, secure, and keep jobs," Cari explains. "On the Threshold side, we brought the co-occurring disorder program, working with people that have both mental health and substance abuse disorders. Our missions were similar and had overlap, despite their distinct specialty programs. We felt that joining forces as one entity that had a broader range of services would be a good thing, so the two boards met and agreed to merge."

Today, Cornerstone Montgomery employs a staff of 300 and operates on a budget of $18 million. Until she actually stepped into the role, Cari had no idea she'd be running an organization so large, serving as its CEO, President, and default COO. Although her dreams of becoming a therapist date back to her early childhood, she never imagined taking on an executive role. But the position required unique competence, dedication, loyalty, and passion for the mission, all of which were manifest in Cari's own philosophy and approach to service.

Cari was born in Des Moines, Iowa—the town both of her parents called home. A mere two weeks later, the family moved to Clemson, South Carolina, where Cari's father enrolled in an animal physiology graduate program. Four years after that, they moved to London for two years while he completed his post-doctorate work. Finally, the young family settled in Maryland, where Cari's father had found work as a research scientist for the U.S. Department of Agriculture.

Growing up in Laurel, Maryland, Cari did well in school and, with some encouragement, discovered a lifelong passion for choral singing and music. "My mother made me join the choir at church," she remembers. "I was vehemently opposed and didn't want to go, but of course it turned out to be a lifelong passion for me. She would laugh at me and say, 'You never want to do anything new. Just try it, you'll like it!' And I did. I've had wonderful choral directors all my life and have been lucky enough to sing in places like Westminster Abby and Notre Dame Cathedral, and with the Baltimore Symphony Orchestra."

Divorce notwithstanding, Cari loved middle school and high school, flourished socially and academically, and felt the constant support of both parents. "They never doubted I could do anything I wanted to do," she says. "They were at every concert and every piano recital." After high school, Cari headed to The College of William & Mary, where, she immediately began studying for her Bachelor's of Psychology. "William & Mary was sort of a last-minute decision, but I visited the campus and really loved it," she recalls. Even through her formative years and the personal evolution from childhood to adulthood, her interest in studying psychology and becoming a therapist never wavered, and although she liked some of her professors at school, she got her most memorable education back home, employed at Montgomery General in the psychiatric unit. Cari's mother was working for a law firm at the time, and the hospital was one of the firm's clients. She got Cari an interview, and Cari began to work as a psychiatric technician, where she was quickly trained as a nurse's assistant and thrown into the deep end. "My mother remembers me coming home with these stories about clients and the issues they had, and she just couldn't even fathom it," Cari remembers. "But none of it shocked me. It fascinated me." She grew close with her supervisor, Rosemary Walters, a wonderful teacher and mentor who immediately recognized the young woman's unusual dedication to the work. Indeed, Cari worked not only every summer, but anytime she could get home at all. "I'd call them and say, 'I'm coming home for Christmas. Can I work?'" The answer was always a resounding yes.

Although she loved her work at Montgomery General, Cari wanted to explore all of her options before taking on her first full-time job after graduation. She interviewed for a position at Threshold Services, and the organization appealed to her. "It struck a chord with me because it worked with people in the communities where they lived," she explains. "I realized I liked that better because I liked seeing the clients when they were doing well. In the hospital, you're only seeing them if they're in crisis." At Threshold, Cari could watch as her work helped turn lives around. She could be there as clients improved, began to engage in life productively, and rediscovered hope. She was hired as a counselor and quickly promoted to site administrator, which added administrative and managerial duties to her counseling work.

After three years with Threshold, Cari headed back to school to earn her Master's in Social Work from the University of Maryland at Baltimore and soon found a job in the area with John's Hopkins Bayview Medical Center, where she'd interned as a student. She planned to stay in Baltimore, but she never forgot her life-changing experience at Threshold, where her younger sister now worked. A few years into her time with John's Hopkins, Cari's sister called with news. There was an opening at Threshold for a Program Director. "I never would have come back to Montgomery County if my sister hadn't called me," she says. "I was happy up in Baltimore and wasn't looking to leave. But I went in and interviewed, and that's what led me to where I am now."

Cari came back to work as a Program Director in 1997, supervising one of the residential programs and quickly establishing herself as a rising star. "We joke that, over my years at Threshold, I worked at every site," she recounts. "I was a counselor and a supervisor, and I did on-call." By 2001, she had been promoted to Rehabilitation Director, where she oversaw all the program directors. She began to develop a close relationship with Craig Knoll, the Executive Director, who became a mentor, role model, and friend. "We really started working closely together, and we had a really great partnership," she says. "Our strengths definitely supported each other, and we could build on that." In 2005, Craig asked her to step up to the COO position, and often mentioned his expectation that she would fill the CEO role upon his retirement. Cari, however, was reluctant to commit to the idea. "The job definitely entailed more glad-handing, more fundraising, and more political juggling," she explains. "I thought, 'Do I really want to do that?' I wasn't sure." Although Cari had always been more dedicated to her clients than professional glory, Craig knew no one else would be able to bring as much dedication to the mission and as much knowledge of the organization. In July of 2012, as the merger went through, Cari promised Craig she would seriously consider taking over upon his retirement in five years.

Those five years turned out to be more like five months. Craig was diagnosed with cancer and took a leave of absence while he recovered from surgery. Then, in January, he announced that he wouldn't be coming back. It wasn't the smooth transition anyone had envisioned, but Cari stepped up to the challenge. "I felt I owed it to the organization," she says. "I have a lot of loyalty to this mission, and I knew I had it in me." In July of 2013, Cari was officially named CEO, and she took over a fledgling organization without the guiding light she'd looked to for so many years. But today, she is happy to report that Craig is recovering well, and business, too, has begun to thrive after a dramatic restructuring and adjustment process.

As the newly anointed leader of a young organization, Cari has undergone a fair amount of adjustment herself. She is never a micromanager and always a coach—one who models her "open door" leadership policy after the management style she observed as a Threshold employee. Now, at Cornerstone, she's learning how to effectively communicate, touching base with each employee as frequently as possible. "I want to feel connected and be available for feedback, but I don't want to tell people what to do," she says, of her leadership style. "I try to be hands-off and flexible, but I also try to hold people accountable."

As a trained counselor, Cari is better equipped than most to maintain a healthy, productive work environment, and to young people entering the working world today, she emphasizes good communication skills as an absolute necessity. "The biggest challenge for people is dealing with conflict at work," she says. "I see it all the time. Don't be afraid to respectfully deal with conflict. People struggle with respectful conflict management at all levels, but it's extremely important." She also urges young graduates to take advantage of all the opportunities that come their way, never dismissing or ignoring experiences that could turn out to be life-changing. "Look at all your options and don't just say no to things that come along. Be willing to give them a try," she says, echoing the encouragement of her mother years ago. "I've been very lucky to have a lot of great opportunities come my way." Indeed, it may have been luck that brought Cari her opportunities, but it was dedication and compassion that turned them into something much more.

David Cohen

Doing Something About It

Change is an amorphous concept. Everyone wants it in some form; few know how to bring it about. It's a word that represents untold millions of ideas, proposals, and possibilities. It's a word so encompassing and so daunting, that almost no one takes the time or energy to define exactly what "change" would look like, and even fewer push the limits of their ability to implement it. Instead we tend to fall into complacency and passive complaint, angry because change is too big, too scary, and too impossible to take on.

David Cohen, on the other hand, has spent every day of his career taking on the world's most ambiguous and ambitious task: improving the state of humanity. Since his teen years, he's been identifying problems, defining goals, and building practical solutions, all in the face of a widespread defeatism that so often cripples ability. As a teenager, David was no stranger to such defeatism. The adults in his community, including his parents, often railed against politicians and policies, but these opinions were accompanied by a decided lack of action. "I noticed that a lot of people were very opinionated about politics and complained a lot, but never really did anything about it," David remembers. "I got the feeling that, if you're going to complain, you should learn about what you're complaining about and do something about it." This realization would shape the course of his career, and indeed, his entire life.

As a senior in high school, David was elected President of the student body. Right away, he began challenging the notion that change was out of reach for the little guy. Car washes and bake sales didn't hold much appeal; instead he looked into Florida State education laws and took up a cause. It was well into the 1970s, and the Red Scare still loomed across textbooks and classrooms. In fact, the political education in Florida at the time was pure propaganda. "The law said that schools had to teach Americanism versus Communism," David recalls. "It said that Communism had to be taught as everything evil, while our capitalist free enterprise system had to be taught as everything wonderful. But I thought we're smarter than that."

Certain that the young people of Florida were capable of drawing their own conclusions, David worked with the student council to draft a revised version of the law. They sent their proposal to the State Legislature in Tallahassee, where it was received by Bob Graham and Bill Nelson, two then little-known members who both went on to become United States Senators. The following April, during the legislative session, David got a call. He was invited to Tallahassee to testify in support of his initiative.

David was a high school kid with no experience and few connections, but that didn't stop him from trying to impact his community. His success taught him a lesson he lives by to this day: to get something done, all you need is a good idea, a little ingenuity, and a lot of passion. Today he runs David Cohen Consulting, where he provides a wide range of services to NGOs, governments, businesses, and other groups related to food security and agricultural development. The company's services, abilities, and accomplishments are so vast and varied that they cannot be reduced to a sound bite. They write and edit proposals, provide strategies for business development, facilitate public-private partnerships, work with governments, and handle communications for an array of clients. David Cohen Consulting is present in every aspect of project development, implementation, and analysis, on both the private and public sides, and its clients have included USAID and the Department of Agriculture, as well as the Alliance to End Hunger, Shelter for Life International, Counterpart International, ICF International, and Relief International.

With over thirty years of experience in agricultural policy and international development, David is well-positioned to help these groups achieve their various goals. Currently, he's working with Cooperative Resources International in Wisconsin to manage USAID grants in South Africa and Nicaragua. He's also in talks with the Philippines Ambassador to the U.S. to introduce more sustainable methodologies in the region's marine aquarium export trade. In Minneapolis, he worked with an NGO on an initiative to take "crop residue" in Uganda—everything left on the field after it's been farmed—and use it to produce construction materials. The UN estimates the total value of discarded crop residue to be around $2 billion—just one example of the waste and inefficiency of current structures. He's travelled to more than fifty countries with as many distinct needs, but across the spectrum, he's noticed a commonality in the human spirit. "The thing I've learned is that no matter where you go in the world, human beings are a lot more connected than apart," he remarks now. "We speak different languages, have different color skin, and worship differently, but at the end of the day, we share a spirit of innovation and ingenuity, and we want the same things, like protection for our families. We share stories and have fun together. And we want change together. Humanity is connected."

In a world increasingly beset by environmental problems, agricultural practices all across the globe are ripe for reform. "Everything in international development starts with agriculture," David explains. "People have to eat, so communities have to grow food." Over the last few years, he's focused on creating economic engines through market-oriented solutions to development, which translates to business-led, sustainable development. Where older, charity-based models fall apart in the long-term, the newer models provide mutual gain and are able to sustain themselves. David has been at the forefront of this movement, constantly seeking out innovative and improved solutions for the world's seemingly intractable problems.

David was always ambitious, but he could hardly have imagined the extent of his future success while growing up in rural Easton, Maryland. His parents were both first-generation Americans, each born of immigrants fleeing Eastern Europe and Czarist Russia. His father's father left Ukraine at age twelve with nothing more than fifty rubles and his own two feet. He began walking west, bribed his way across the Prussian border with cigarettes, spent a year working on a dairy farm in Holland, and made his way to London. From there, he saved enough money to book passage on a ship to Canada, where he stayed with a relative in Toronto. For a few more years, he wandered, working the docks in Chicago, meeting up with his brother in Philadelphia, and finally ending up on the Eastern Shore of Maryland, where the family settled. There, David's grandfather founded a scrap metal business, which his father reluctantly but dutifully took over. "He hated it, but that's how it was," David explains. "My father was born in 1912, so he was in his twenties—his prime years—during the Great Depression." Although he disliked the business, David's father worked hard to provide for David and his two older sisters. His mother, too, worked to keep the family business afloat, and David attributes his work ethic to the strong example set by both parents.

Just before he entered his junior year of high school, David's parents moved the family down to Florida, marking one of the hardest experiences of his young life. In Maryland, he had a life and friends, and had already been elected Junior Class President. True to form, he had persuaded the school to hold elections early, because he wanted to get a jumpstart on his term by organizing and planning over the summer. "After moving to Florida, I remember thinking I might hop on a bus and find my way back to Maryland," he says. "I was devastated for a while."

But inevitabilities never kept David down for long. Soon after settling in his new community, he set to work rebuilding. He proposed a reading program that encouraged independent learning by allotting 30 minutes a day for private reading. The administrators and students embraced the idea, and, buoyed by his initial success, he again petitioned to move the student council elections from fall to the proceeding spring. A mere nine months after arriving in Florida, David was elected Student Body President. During his term that year, his experience with the state legislature vividly illustrated the power of a single voice. "Why did that happen?" he reflects. "Because nobody told me I couldn't do it. I took that experience, and when I went on to college I became a lobbyist for the student body."

The University of Florida sent David to Tallahassee three years in a row to represent the 120,000 students attending all of Florida's public universities. His work there installed a new student member on the State Board of Regents and gave the student population a voice on a range of issues, including tuition costs. His achievements were hardly the norm; he was a college student, surrounded by a lot of young people searching for meaningful experiences—some in all the wrong places. "I started getting into these leadership positions and thought, 'This is kind of fun!' Now, I wasn't a total nerd," he laughs, "but not everyone was as driven as I was, and I liked accomplishing things where I could see a positive impact. At a young age, I learned that self-esteem comes from overcoming adversity to achieve success." David's productive time in Gainesville only reinforced what he'd already begun to recognize back in high school: that the only real limitations in life are those we imagine for ourselves.

Fresh off of earning his Bachelor's Degree in Political Science, David headed to Washington, D.C. to pursue his Master's of Public Administration at American University. The degree comprised an internship, and David, as usual, went above and beyond what was expected. For a year, he interned as a Congressional Affairs Specialist for the Farm Credit Administration while at AU, where he helped found the Center for Congressional and Presidential Studies and helped design and implement government relations seminars for IBM and USPS executives. His accomplishments stood out, and in 1980, the year he graduated, David interviewed to work for Ed Jaenke, a former governor of the FCA. Jaenke was a prominent public official who'd been shortlisted to serve as the Secretary of Agriculture under President Carter. When Nixon came into office, he moved over to the private sector and founded E. A. Jaenke & Associates, a consulting firm that worked with governments, agricultural trade associations, commodity groups, cooperatives, and virtually every other player in the field.

For fourteen years, David worked closely with Jaenke, who became a close friend, mentor, and father figure. Together, they successfully lobbied to save the National Cooperative Bank and the Farm Credit System from legislative assaults. They advised the Japan International Agricultural Council on policy, helped launch the Citizen's Network NGO, and undertook countless other projects in the name of sound agricultural policy. And in that time, David learned firsthand how to build a business on the back of one's values. "That job defined my career," he says. "We got to do the most interesting things. We picked what we wanted to participate in and didn't do what we didn't want to do. Jaenke was a rainmaker type who knew lots of people. And I got the echo of that, which created everything for me. He believed in me, and I believed in him. He was loyal, and I was loyal. I knew the only way I could pay him back was to pay it forward. A former young staffer and I have almost the same kind of relationship today." The people David met and the relationships he built while working with Jaenke continue to serve him well to this day.

All good things, however, must come to an end, and in 1994, Jaenke announced his imminent retirement. Although he had hoped David would take over the business, the offer was declined. "I knew what I couldn't do," David explains. "I could run it day-to-day, but I wasn't the guy to bring in new business. I didn't have the stature." Jaenke sold E.A. Jaenke & Associates to what was then the largest agriculture consulting firm in the country, Sparks Companies. David went with it as the key executive and was given the title of Vice President of Policy Monitoring and Analysis. He could easily have stayed in the position for life, but two years later, he found himself unhappy with the vastly different culture of the firm. True to form, he decided to do something about it—even though that "something" meant taking a huge risk. His wife, Michele, was pregnant, and he had no new job waiting, but he believed deeply in himself, his ideas, and his abilities. That year, in 1996, he founded his first consulting business, David Cohen and Associates.

David began consulting for a range of clients, including many he'd worked with before on the agricultural side, as well as groups like the Foundation for Democracy in Africa and Women for Women International. During his first year of independent consulting, he began hearing more and more about the then-nascent concept of using business, rather than charity, to create development. One group doing such work was the Citizens' Network for Foreign Affairs, and David wasted no time hitching his wagon to their train. As usual, his methods were simple and direct. "I knew the CEO from years earlier, so I walked in and basically said, 'Hey, I like what you're doing here.' A week later, I started working there."

The organization created a position for him, and David began working with agri-business firms, drumming up enterprise-led development partnerships in countries in Eastern Europe and Russia. He held a full-time job at the Citizen's Network for Foreign Affairs for the next three years, all the while also consulting through David Cohen & Associates. Then, in 2000, one of his major clients, Counterpart International, asked him to come onboard as Director of their Program Development unit. He accepted, and for five years, he improved proposal writing and win rates, and was promoted to Vice President in 2005.

By 2007, David's work with Counterpart was more than a full-time job. He had been promoted to Vice President of Food Security and Nutrition, choosing to give up his private consulting for the time being. Under David's stewardship, Counterpart's handful of projects in Senegal grew to an array of projects across the region. Business overall grew by 130 percent, and the proposal win-rate climbed to an unprecedented 77 percent. The projects themselves were hardly typical; the group was already working on impact investment, getting capital into impoverished economies, and consistently anticipating international needs. "In Niger, we partnered with the U.S. Geological Survey to work on climate change issues with the Minister of Environment," he says. "Even though the way things are run can be focused and narrow, we were looking for innovation."

David spent four more years with Counterpart before deciding it was time to move on. Work, to him, had always been about the pursuit and achievement of progress, and he had come to feel he could best accomplish this vision by re-starting David Cohen Consulting to regain flexibility and agility. Since 2011, he has remained steadfast in his self-guided pursuit of meaningful projects. "I've been very fortunate that I've gotten to do the things I believe are important and that truly make a contribution," he says today. "I want to leave the world a better place than when I got here." Of course, it's more than good fortune that got him here—he can also thank his hard work, talent, and continual innovation.

As a leader, David believes that success is built not only through one's hard work, knowledge, and creativity, but also through the team that surrounds you. "I think the most important position in a company is HR," he asserts. "People are everything. You have to find people who are compatible, and you have to treat them with dignity and respect." To young people hoping to someday achieve success, he advises boldness.

"Don't ever say no to an opportunity," he says. "Don't play it safe. Be passionate, because if you follow that passion, you'll be successful at whatever you do. You'll have fun, you'll love doing it, and you'll make a difference. And never give up. Be tenacious about everything."

Beyond this, he echoes the refrain of his favorite story, *Fiddler on the Roof*, which, at its heart, is an anthem of change and survival that underpins all enduring success. In a world that remains in a constant state of flux, rigidity guarantees failure. "You can stay true to your principles, but you have to be willing to adapt," he says. "Change is constant. It's the story of life. Success takes many paths, so don't stay stuck in one place. You have to be willing to change and evolve, and you have to be willing to do something about it, whatever 'it' may be."

BERNHARDT
WEALTH MANAGEMENT

Gaby DeLeon

Working Today with Tomorrow in Mind

When Gaby DeLeon realized he had the opportunity to start his own business, he did what any rational man would do: he consulted his wife, Selma.

Selma and their four sons had followed Gaby's career growth in project management throughout the Middle East and Europe. But now, she knew she had to put on the brakes, reminding him that his work was robbing him of the best years of his sons' childhoods. Through the years, she had supported his career growth and helped steer him in the right direction, so now, after a few years of overseas work, he needed her advice more than ever.

On the family's return to the Washington, D.C. area after his work abroad, Gaby was hired by a construction management company, but was quickly disillusioned by the goals and objectives of his employer and decided to resign after completing the first phase of a multi-phased project. The client offered Gaby the opportunity to complete the rest of the phased project as an independent consultant—an opportunity that came with incredible promise but tremendous risk. "When we returned from Saudi Arabia, we had to face the challenge of four college tuitions," he remembers. "With the ages of our sons, we had to pay all four tuitions in the same year. Whatever money was earned overseas was quickly used up, and the prospect of starting my own business presented risks of continuity after a project is completed, so we needed to do a serious evaluation. Selma was cautious but urged me to do it, as long as I kept in mind the next step. By nature, I am more focused on the present, while she is more focused on tomorrow, so together we embody the principle of shaping our work today to guarantee our work tomorrow."

Their approach paid off, so that today, Gaby is a founder and Principal of GRD Construction Consultants Inc. (GRD), a company dedicated to serving the private sector with construction consulting for real estate developers, commercial developers, and property managers. In 1998, GRD became certified by SBA as an 8(a) enterprise through the participation of Gaby's second eldest son, allowing the company to offer service contracts to the federal government. "We have a whole spectrum of real estate transactions now," Gaby explains. "Within a few years of receiving our SBA certification, we now have people working as contractors, budget analysts, financial analysts, project managers, and building managers that are full-time and on yearly contracts."

The company was started in 1985, shortly after Gaby was hired for the role performed by his previous employer. He ran the company by himself initially with no immediate plans to grow, but when his sons joining him, they established a new business line to include contracts for services with the federal government. The business partnership with his sons became so successful over the years that the firm has since grown to twenty employees. Gaby and his youngest son, also an engineer, run the private clients side of the business, while the two older sons, an engineer and a business major, run the government contracts.

"In general, our private clients invest in development projects, like office buildings," Gaby explains. "Typically, the building developer surrounds himself with a number of consultants who are experts in their lines of work, from real estate attorneys, brokers, architects, engineers, general contractors, and facilities managers, among others. I take on the construction aspects by coordinating the roles of the architect, engineers, regulatory agencies, and the general contractor. My focus is on understand what the client wants and making sure it gets delivered, familiarizing myself with their standards. My goal was to meet my clients' vision of a product that delivers their financial objectives. This assures me of repeat business, thanks to the record I've established by working with them before. This working relationship is done through clear and uncompromising communications. "-

Gaby grew up in the Philippines when the country was a young democracy undergoing big transitions. "The country was trying to find its identity, and its infrastructure was not yet in place," he explains. "My parents were tremendously impacted by all the changes and lost a lot, but we developed the understanding that, while any material object could be taken from us, our most valuable possessions—things that could never be taken—were in our minds." With that, education became the first priority for Gaby and his siblings, and their parents made it their mission to fund as much of their children's academics as possible so that expenses would never inhibit their progress.

Gaby was the ninth to be born of ten children, which instilled in him a nature that was at once independent and cooperative. He never met his three oldest siblings, who died young due to inadequate health care. As a result, the DeLeon family learned to treasure every moment together and took nothing for granted. During summer breaks, the siblings went to the logging camps in the family's concession areas and entertained themselves by hitching rides on logging trucks, learning how to do inventory on timber being hauled, and exploring neighboring villages. Their father was a hunting enthusiast, and when the children were old enough, they would pile into the family Jeep to go in search of deer and boar. As Gaby grew older, his father assigned him work bundling scrap timber and depositing proceeds of sales at the bank.

Gaby knew he wanted to work in the construction industry for as long as he could remember, having been inspired by his entrepreneurial parents. Shortly after the parents' marriage, his mother, a schoolteacher, started a grocery store and restaurant, while his father, a salesman, started a lumberyard, where he worked for most of his life. As a child, Gaby frequently tagged along and was able to see first-hand the pride his father took in the projects he was building. "He was a huge role model for me," he recalls. "He impressed upon me a sense of discipline, honesty, and integrity, and I realized I wanted to do the same work he did."

Gaby attended college at Mapua Institute of Technology in Manila, where he majored in Civil Engineering. While he was dedicated to starting a career in the construction industry, he felt engineering would give him a broader background to draw from. "I dabbled in architecture, but I was always more interested in the how and the why behind the construction of a building," he recalls. "I was very curious."

After graduating college, he got married to his first wife, with whom he had four sons. He and his family spent a few years together in the Philippines while he worked for his father's company until 1969, when he came to New York to attend Columbia University to earn a Masters in Operations Research. His time at Columbia was fragmented, however, by his obligations to his employer, first with a design engineering company, then a small general contractor. Gaby's search for his ideal employment led him to Bechtel International, where he was assigned various hotel projects around the world and could take frequent trips back to the Philippines.

Gaby worked for Bechtel International in New York for five years, focusing on construction project controls management. He fully developed his skills and expertise in that niche, which shaped the career that followed. After his wife passed away, he met and married Selma, and he spent the majority of the early 1970's traveling around the Middle East and Africa.

While Gaby enjoyed the work, he rarely got to see or communicate with his wife and sons. "I remember Selma telling me that it was wonderful how I was building my career, but I was missing crucial moments in life I could never get back," he recalls. "I wasn't very high up in the company yet, but I decided to go to my supervisors and tell them that they needed to either find me a job locally or send a posting for my family to come to me." Unfortunately, neither option was possible, so he began to look for opportunities elsewhere.

Gaby's ideal job with Bechtel had to come to a decision between career growth and family. The frequent international trips meant less time for Selma and four growing boys, so Gaby sought and eventually found employment with The Arabian American Oil Company (Aramco), prompting the entire family to move to Dhahran, Saudi Arabia.

Gaby's employment with Aramco presented numerous advantages in career and family. During their time overseas, Selma was able to practice her nursing education from Hunter College in New York as a public health nurse. At Aramco, she was able to work with the company's health system, doing research on communicable diseases in Saudi Arabia, and when the family was temporarily relocated to London for Gaby's work for two years, Selma earned a second Masters degree in medical demography at the London School of Tropical Medicine.

Gaby enjoyed his position at The Arabian American Oil Company for several years until his children reached high school. At that point, the company insisted on sending his children back to the United States so that they would not lose touch with their roots, but Gaby and his wife worried they were losing them too early. They decided their best option was to leave, but Gaby quickly realized how difficult it would be to find a new role in project management.

In 1984, the DeLeon family returned to Washington, D.C. in the hope that Gaby would find a role of equal stature that would allow the family to stay together. Shortly after arriving, he received a call from a former colleague, telling him to pack his bags for Paris. "He wanted me to join him in building five hotels for Disney in France," he says. "I thought it sounded very exciting, but my wife told me I was being tempted by the same things that made us return from overseas in the first place. As much as one part of me wanted to go over there, the idea of having my family split apart or uprooted again was just too much. In the tried-and-true tradition Selma and I had developed, I needed to choose my next move with the future in mind."

With that, Gaby turned his former colleague down and instead joined the local construction management company that ultimately led to disappointment. He and his boss did not see eye-to-eye on the nature of construction management, and the company acted more as a general contractor. "In true construction management, a client's wishes always come first," Gaby explains. "It's the construction manager's responsibility to make sure that the client's interests are served. If the construction manager does general contracting at the same time, everything becomes blurred. Thanks to this mindset, I had grown very close to my first client, so as soon as their first building was done, they offered to let me manage the rest of their projects."

With the help of that first client, Gaby started GRD Construction Consultants, and while he had no intention of starting a business empire, the company quickly started growing at a rate so fast that he needed to hire representatives for each project. By 1997, he was receiving offers from other companies to buy GRD, but he turned them all down, finding he was happy with the growth of his company and foreseeing a successful future. "Running your own company brings a great sense of accomplishment, and I really love the independence that comes with it as well," he explains.

Throughout his experience with GRD, Gaby has realized that the best way to lead is by setting a good example. "If you don't see your leader practice what they preach, their word doesn't mean anything," he says. "With this in mind, I try to model the pursuit of clear, intentional solutions. When I'm meeting with my employees, our first objective is to fully understand what the problems are. Once we hit on that, the underlying sources of issues come out and are addressed completely, paving a clearer pathway forward that leads to greater success."

Today, Selma has retired after starting a travel agency in Bethesda. After 20 years, she finally decided to cut bait and sell, and the couple works to carry on Gaby's parents' legacy of pushing education for their children and grandchildren through an educational foundation. "Selma and I have put the financial structures in place so that our kids will always be able to have the education they need," he says. "It was important to us to do this so that they have the freedom to do what I would advise any young person entering the working world to do: arm themselves with knowledge. I also encourage them to live by the same principle I have built my life around, working today with tomorrow in mind. There is always the challenge of what happens after a job is finished, and the way I guarantee the next job is by doing a good job now. It's the fundamental principle that's kept clients coming back to us for decades, just as it kept our family together when my sons were young, preserving the things that are most important in whatever context it's applied."

BERNHARDT
WEALTH MANAGEMENT

Barth X. deRosa

The Inner Voice

Sitting in the quiet solitude of the garden and reflecting on the twenty years of life he had lived so far, Bart deRosa heard something. It wasn't coming from the world around him, however; it was coming from within him. And it wasn't a transient, temporary sound; it had a timeless, certain kind of resonance—something not only greater than the earth, but beyond it, that had always been with him and would always remain.

Bart had always been a spiritual person, and St. Francis College, complete with its rural Pennsylvania landscape and natural wonder, was an idyllic place for the periods of personal reflection he was so drawn to. As such, he had been led by his inner voice before, but in that moment, it sounded different. Its scope echoed not within the confines of his own mind, but extended out through time, defining a horizon Bart didn't even know he had. "When it comes to conceptualizing of one's life,

I think people have horizons of different lengths," he remarks today. "Some see a month into the future, while others see years—three, five, ten. In that moment, I realized I was blessed with a thirty-year horizon. I suddenly saw myself going into law, practicing in Washington, D.C. and becoming a partner someday. Thanks to that voice, it was all very clear."

Bart had just spent the summer working in a laboratory where he met a young woman who struck him in a profound way, and though they weren't meant to be lifelong partners, she inspired him to think beyond the immediate and into the future, imagining the kind of life he'd like to live. And upon hearing that voice in the garden that day, he was inspired beyond imagination to action. Now a member of Dickinson Wright, PLLC, a prominent national law firm specializing in over 40 practice areas, Bart's life course has unfolded according to that divine cadence with its omniscient timber, and its subtle elegance shows in the details. "I've learned to trust my inner voice, and to rely on it," he affirms today. "It's never let me down, and I have tremendous faith in it."

Dickinson Wright is a Detroit-based firm with around 400 lawyers spread between its twelve U.S. offices and one office in Toronto, Canada. Founded in 1876, it has since developed a deep tradition of excellence in law and prudence in business. Paired with its close-knit company culture, complete with special Christmas dinners that bring its partners together every holiday season, Dickinson Wright attracts competent, high caliber lawyers who have gone on to become governors and state Supreme Court justices.

Bart came to the firm in February of 2008, where he specializes in intellectual property law with an emphasis on trademark and copyright law, including enforcement litigation and practice before the U.S. Trademark Trial and Appeal Board of the United States Patent and Trademark Office. He also provides general counseling on most aspects of business law, with an expertise in brand development, licensing, and the intellectual property due diligence aspects of corporate mergers and acquisitions. Yet even though he grew up in D.C. as the son of a prominent trademark lawyer who was one of the original twelve lawyers hired to administer the Lanham Act of 1946, he never planned on following in his father's footsteps and actually walked his own route to the profession.

Bart did, however, inherit his father's sense of humor and his mother's intuitive nature, which would become critical coping mechanisms through a childhood that found him transferring schools too often to establish a sense of stability and comfort. After kindergarten and first grade, he was sent to a private school that required him to repeat first grade. His family then moved further north, landing him in a school that had him skip second grade to enter third. Then, because of population growth, he was sent to a new school district for fifth and sixth grades. He was then sent to a Catholic parochial school in Silver Spring before he ultimately settled at St. Johns Military College High School, D.C.'s junior ROTC Catholic military school. "As soon as I'd get my footing in one school, I was sent to another," Bart remembers. "This left me extremely disengaged academically, and I did the bare minimum to get by."

Despite his academic challenges, Bart made close—albeit mischievous—friends in high school and really began to come into his own. "I remember hitchhiking down Rockville Pike with my friend Mike, looking for a job. We walked into Shakey's Pizza and asked for an application," Bart recounts. "The manager asked if we were tall enough to reach the ovens, which unfortunately, we weren't. On those grounds, he said he couldn't hire us." Together, Bart and Mike caddied at the local country club and worked in restaurants as busboys, dishwashers, shorthand cooks, and waiters. "My lifelong friend was instrumental in showing me how to break down barriers and do what's necessary to get a job," says Bart.

Next to his older brother and sister, who were national scholars, Bart's academic performance did not inspire the confidence of his parents. His mother suggested he consider trade school as a viable option, but despite his lack of interest in his studies, that inner voice was resolute that he not give up yet. With that, he graduated and enrolled at St. Francis College, now St. Francis University. Then, after seeing his thirty-year horizon at the outset of his third year, he transferred to George Washington University and fully immersed himself in his studies for the first time in his life. He got a part time research job at the National Legal Center for Public Interest, where his boss took a special interest in him and became his first mentor. "Leonard J. Theberge was a former assistant U.S. attorney for New York City and a Rhodes scholar," Bart explains. "He was charismatic and brilliant. I worked with him until I enrolled in the University of Georgia Law School in 1979. It was a tremendous opportunity to work with Mr. Theberge. I met key business leaders, Supreme Court nominees, members of Congress, and a number of Nobel laureates."

When he earned his law degree in 1982, Bart hoped to go into environmental and energy law, but as the Reagan administration was cutting EPA funding, jobs in that field were scant. He had an offer from the National Oceanic and Atmospheric Administration to oversee fishing quotas off the coast of Massachusetts but didn't foresee much of a future on that track. That's when his father suggested he try working at the firm where he'd built his own career, Watson Cole Grindle and Watson. It was 1982, and his father was in the process of helping the firm facilitate the signing of a licensing agreement that gave their client the rights to produce and market Trivial Pursuit. "That was my introduction to law in the real world, and it was a lot of fun," Bart remembers.

During that time, a beautiful woman with two small children moved in several houses down from Bart. Mary was half Italian and half Sicilian, just like him, and one Friday night, he found himself armed with a cannoli and knocking on her door. She invited him in for dinner, and the two hit it off immediately. "I knew by the second date that we were meant for each other," he laughs. "She understands me in a way nobody else does, and she has this incredibly calming effect about her.

If she were a newscaster and an atomic war were about to start, she'd be the one who could calm everyone down."

The two married and were blessed with two additional children. While Bart found his family life blossoming, unfortunately the professional atmosphere around him was less promising. Despite the firm's success since 1864, the concept of investing in the firm had not been embraced by the time Bart's father retired in 1988. It lacked the technological advancement and innovative drive of its competitors, which frustrated a young and forward-thinking attorney like Bart. That's why, in 1995, he helped the firm merge with another practice, Stevens Davis Miller and Mosher, LLP. The two firms complemented each other well for the next two years, until the Stevens Davis partners decided to pull out and invited Bart to join them. With that, the firm was reconstituted with four equity partners and grew to 25 lawyers. "We were a great firm with a strong culture, history, and partners, but as time went by we began to have different ideas of where we wanted to go," Bart reflects. "When our lease was about ready to expire, we decided to merge with a general practice firm. We met with ten major firms, from which we chose Dickinson Wright."

Bart's experience at Dickinson Wright has been rewarding and successful, earning him nominations as a D.C. Super Lawyer for 2012, 2013, and 2014, as well as a *Washington Post* rating as a top attorney in the D.C. area for each of those three years. Yet despite his love of law, Bart came to find himself disillusioned with the shifts of modernity that have deemphasized direct communication between lawyer and client. "I love engaging with clients, talking with them and getting to know their businesses, families, successes, and failures," he remarks. "But everything is done now through email, which is a great tool but has become the brick wall in developing those relationships that really drive me."

If a lack of human connection formed the bricks of Bart's obstacle, a lack of creative opportunity formed its mortar. "I'm a builder," he asserts.

"I have this drive to create—this sense that there's always something to build that's greater than myself." When his firm merged back in 1995, he had the opportunity to have his hand in multiple pots, building the company website and establishing its culture as he practiced law. Then, as an equity partner in a four-person firm, he was constantly involved in major decision-making that took him beyond the day-to-day. "I enjoyed those things so much that I've always wanted to start a side business to see what I could do with my creative energies," he says. "Mary was very supportive of the idea, but something would always intervene and I never seemed to have the time to actually pursue it."

All that changed, however, when Bart found himself at a legal conference in November of 2010. Exploring the art galleries of Phoenix's Scottsdale neighborhood, he stumbled across an olive oil and vinegar store, and the inner voice in his head said, "This is it."

True to form, Bart had been dedicating time to contemplating life and asking himself the kinds of questions that his inner voice is so good at answering. What did he and Mary enjoy? What was new; novel; up-and-coming? With that, and together with his continued 32-year dedication to law, Bart enlisted Mary's help and began pursuing his entrepreneurial dreams.

At first glance, an olive oil and vinegar store was a perfect venue to bring together the deRosas' love of art, antiques, and fine Mediterranean cuisine, but they were committed to exploring the idea much deeper. They researched extensively and took a trip to California to meet producers face-to-face. They found a location in Bethesda and developed a logo and decorating scheme, diving head first into the minutia of entrepreneurial creativity that Bart finds so rewarding.

Now the proud cofounders of SECOLARI, which means "age-old," the deRosas opened the first store of its kind in the D.C. metropolitan area and won a Best of Bethesda award for 2013. It features 30 different varieties of olive oils, vinegars, balsamic, and special oils, and has garnered enough success to warrant the launch of a second store, which opened its doors in December 2013 at the mall in Columbia, Maryland. "Growing businesses and selling olive oil is my passion," Bart says, speaking expertly on everything from the health benefits of his product to the climate, transportation, and labeling standards he adheres to which ensure such high quality. "It gets me out and meeting people, which I love." So much so, that Bart was elected to the Board of Directors for the California Olive Oil Council—the industry's trade, marketing, and certifying organization located in Berkley, California. He is the first non-California resident to sit on the Board in its twenty-year history.

This love is at the root of Bart's professional journey, and of the advice he extends to young people entering the working world today. "Do what you're passionate about, wherever that leads you," he says. And if one is to find out what that is, one must be able to tune out the din of the world—a task of mounting difficulty, considering the perpetual noise of advertising, social media, and our culture of perpetual connectivity. In a society where we're always plugged in to the world around us, it's important to take the time to plug into the voice within us, allowing it to speak to the path that's right for us. "I know there's something greater out there that stays with all of us," Bart affirms. "It's like a guiding light and a feeling of well-being. Listen to it, trust it, and have faith in it, and it will guide you to where it wants you to go."

BERNHARDT

WEALTH MANAGEMENT

Taylor Devine

The Power of Possibility

For all he's accomplished in life and all he's seen of the world, Taylor Devine is still profoundly moved by the simple notion of a blank piece of paper, or a clean white board, or words that have not yet been spoken. For all that's been written, he is impassioned by the possibility that lives in all that is yet to be explored. It takes particular strength of mind and openness of spirit to approach each encounter and experience with this attitude, but it's the best way to learn life in its truest form.

"I might have a loose agenda going into a given situation, but I force myself to have an open mind," he explains. "I bring a blank piece of paper and concentrate on listening and learning. Those moments are about creating opportunities and ideas that are new and meaningful, instead of imposing a pre-existing perspective." Now the founder and managing partner of The CDI Group, a financial and consulting services firm for business owners, corporate leaders, and other strategic partners throughout the Washington D.C. Metropolitan area, Taylor has used this philosophy to investigate success from all angles, and now brings a lifetime of expertise to enrich the prospects and value propositions of others.

Taylor launched CDI in 2001 as Corporate Development International in an effort to commercialize technology, but soon found himself wanting to shift its focus. He knew how to buy and sell companies, so the business transformed into an M&A house. "We looked at the market as strategists and saw an opportunity to bring our professional tools and approach to companies between $5 and $75 million in revenue," he recalls. "We had some competitors in D.C. and Northern Virginia with very strong pedigrees, but they were focusing on larger or smaller companies. So we decided to pursue success by changing the rules, targeting the particular audience that didn't have access to these services and filling that gap."

Through this work, Taylor began to notice that liquidity events were often missed because businesses weren't priced right, packaged right, or marketed right. He saw an opportunity for CDI to take on valuation services, so the company became an expert in the Uniform Standards of Professional Appraisal Practices (USPAP). This opened even more doors for the company, as valuations lead to opportunities for improvement. "In doing valuations, we came to understand the value drivers and detractors that particular companies faced and were in a unique position to address them. This paved the way for our second practice area, value enhancement, wherein we work with a consulting assignment for what ever time it takes to help the organization increase its value and provide quarterly progress reports."

As Taylor saw that value propositions could be dramatically increased with several years of foresight, CDI found a natural segue into exit and succession planning, which in turn provided a natural segue into a fourth practice area, Corporate Development and Strategic Business Plans. "Companies often need capital to fund the organic and acquisitive growth they envision, which involved planning over the life cycle of the business," he explains. "We used to farm this process out to FINRA-licensed investment bankers, but I saw the opportunity to deepen our client relationships by getting FINRA-licensed myself."

Now, CDI's services span the life cycle of a business owner, division president, or corporate executive, offering comprehensive and nuanced service that few other firms dare to master with such precision. With a lean and powerful team of eight, it serves the IT community, government contractors, and select segments of the healthcare market, averaging between twelve and fifteen transactions each year. "At CDI, it's no longer an M&A beauty contest with a liquidity event prize," Taylor affirms. "We build multi-year relationships over the entire life cycle, and if we can't bring the needed value to a relationship ourselves, we make sure our clients can get those skills and expertise elsewhere. We do five things very well, and if we need more horsepower or pedigree to really deliver for a client, we turn to other people in the market to maximize client success. It's about putting each client at the center of our professional world, where they can fully benefit from our extensive resources."

In a way, this strategy mirrors Taylor's own upbringing in Jamaica, a neighborhood in the New York City borough of Queens. His father was a factory worker at Sperry Gyroscope in New Hyde Park, while his mother was an accountant at a hospital down the street from the factory. She worked normal hours, while his father worked the night shift, but they made time each day to sit down for a cup of tea together before his father left for work. "Some of my fondest memories are of my mom working hard to be a good Cub Scout Den Mother for me, and of the horseback riding lessons my parents signed me up for," Taylor remembers. "Each lesson cost $2.50, so I'd get in the car each Saturday morning with my father, and he'd give me a two-dollar bill and a fifty-cent piece." There were no earth-shattering conversations during these car rides; rather, father and son spoke about school, riding, and Cub Scouts, quietly forging in the young boy an optimistic, inquisitive, and good-willed character.

As a boy, Taylor had no grand plan for the future and no dream job—rather, he focused on enjoying life. A testament to his work ethic, this meant earning his first paycheck at age twelve, before he could even get legal work papers. He spent several Christmas breaks packaging gift packets at a local liquor store, and then the next several Christmas breaks filling in on postal routes, enjoying the opportunity to be outside and on the move. He wasn't a perfect student, but he enjoyed learning, and was only rarely slapped on the hand by nuns with rulers at his Episcopal day school. When he was younger, he played stickball in the street with a broom handle and a rubber ball, and when he grew older, he ran track and cross country.

The young boy's cheerful and laid-back approach to life would meet a brand new environment of structure and possibility when his parents, along with help from their Episcopal Church, decided they could afford to send him to Manlius Military Academy, just outside of Syracuse. There, Taylor spent his high school years not only earning a tremendous education, but also benefitting from the school's ROTC-inspired discipline and character-building principles. "I learned an expression there—Manners Maketh the Man," Taylor reflects. "Over a lifetime, that has translated into being nice to people, regardless of how they might be treating you."

At Manlius, freshmen begin as privates and later become corporals, or squad leaders. Juniors can advance to lieutenant status, and are responsible for their own platoons. Four students advance to become captains as seniors, and Taylor was one of them. In this position of leadership as a company commander, parents of new students would approach him with their hopes and goals for their sons, and at seventeen years old, Taylor found that leadership resonated with him at a deep level.

Taylor envisioned continuing his education at a small, Midwestern, co-ed college, so his guidance counselor introduced him to Hillsdale College in Michigan. A week after he started classes, his father passed away. As he had spent the past four academic years at Manlius and the accompanying summers working at a concessions stand at a national park near West Point, he had only gone home for holidays. The loss was a blank page that had lost its potential—never to be written on, and experiences with his father never to be lived.

Other experiences would take their place, however. Now that Taylor had to find a way to pay for his own education, he took a job in the college's dining hall, which was run by Saga Corporation. Launched by three veterans in the aftermath of World War II, Saga had a public restaurants division, as well as a division of contract food services in colleges, universities, hospitals, and white-collar business and industry. At Hillsdale, it had an eight-semester in-school management training program that prepared students for unit management jobs upon graduation. As Taylor worked through that program, he also won an American Freedom Foundation scholarship. Financed by the *Wall Street Journal*, the opportunity meant he would give short, semi-weekly speeches to Rotary clubs, chambers of commerce, and other civic groups, covering political and economic thought at the time. His college professors helped him delve into the subject matter, building his confidence and his network.

His academic pursuits centered on parallel themes. The school had a Business Leadership track, where students could major in business or accounting and minor in psychology or sociology, augmenting their studies with an honors program in leadership. Having settled on this avenue, Taylor was a representative of the school and gave tours to parents and prospective students. He became president of the Student Union and of his fraternity.

As Taylor prepared to graduate, a professional goal surfaced clearly in his mind for the first time. "I wanted to learn how to run a business with somebody else's capital," he remembers. With that, he interviewed with IBM and Proctor & Gamble, but it was ultimately Saga that would give him the best opportunity to develop his skills in pursuit of his dream. The company was ahead of its time in recognizing the value of investing in its people to generate top-notch business results, paying for Taylor to attend strategic marketing graduate courses at Columbia University and learn about the product life cycle stages of embryonic, growth, maturation, and aging. Its founders had adopted the thinking of Bill Crockett, the father of organizational development, and Abraham Maslow, whose hierarchy of needs could be applied to employees within an organization. "I apply these theories to my work today when I look at a person, management team, organization, or athletic team," Taylor explains. As a young district manager with Saga, Taylor was sent to a Xerox class that marked his first foray from operations into sales. "It was like Consultative Selling 101, and I still use those skills everyday," he says. "It's about finding out the needs and wants of the person you're talking to, and whether you can help them directly, or through a referral."

Taylor thought he'd never leave Saga, but after seventeen years with the company, he found himself stalled at the Division President level, three rungs away from the presidency. Rather than advancing internal candidates, the founders kept bringing in Harvard and Wharton MBA graduates, who spoke a language he didn't understand. He sought out the advice of a mentor, a board member who also happened to be chairman of the Graduate Marketing Department at Stanford University. Taylor realized that, to reach the helm of a public or private company, he needed to focus on his weaknesses, like quantitative analysis. His advisor told him to apply to the toughest quantitative school he could find, so even though Taylor had two children at the time and was going through a divorce, he landed a spot at the University of Chicago Booth School of Business.

The program exposed Taylor to a higher echelon of academia, lending him a new confidence that landed him a position at Arthur D. Little (ADL) upon graduation at age 39. Having worked as Sage's first strategist alongside Robert H. Waterman, who would go on to co-author the blockbuster business book, *In Search of Excellence,* Taylor continued to study the recipe of business success or failure at ADL. The company had just invented a practice in its Belgium office called the Strategic Management of Technology, and it needed a U.S. practice manager. "How does a contract food service and restaurant guy with strategy, marketing, and operations experience but no technology background wind up in that position?" he queries. "By sticking my hand up when nobody else wanted the opportunity. Back in the U.S., our first assignment was a problem with an R&D lab. Thanks to the product life cycle training from Saga and the financial perspective garnered from University of Chicago, I was able to go up to the white board and map out the ROI associated with the company's situation, explaining to the chairman which technologies should be invested in at which points in time. It was the culmination of everything I had learned up to that point."

Amidst his success at ADL, Taylor received a call from a headhunter about Mrs. Fields Cookies, a small family business in San Francisco looking for someone to help grow it. Debbie and Randy Fields were looking to relocate, and they charged Taylor with growing the company's 35 stores into 241 stores within a three-year period. Being a private company with no franchisees, the business's greatest challenge was convincing its typically teen-aged employees to adhere to its quality standards. Debbie, the heart and soul of the venture, decided to use a relatively new technology at the time: voicemail. They hooked up voicemail systems to units in each store so they could speak more personably and directly to employees hundreds or thousands of miles away about the Mrs. Fields way. "Rule books don't work for a 17 year old who doesn't have an emotional link to the company and wants to take a shortcut," Taylor points out. "It was brilliant."

At the same time, Randy Fields learned how to transmit data into and out of an IBM 36 and 38 using a touchtone phone. He had a good run with the company, and when they decided to part ways, he felt that the technology they had explored could be put to other uses. With that, he launched the nation's first voicemail service bureau company out of Park City, Utah, where he was living at the time. The company, called Inform, started with a server room of ROLM switches owned by IBM, and sold voicemail systems to companies on a subscription basis so they wouldn't have to make the capital investment themselves. The business excelled until the day IBM ROLM decided to give voicemail away for free, leaving Taylor and his partner no choice but to pivot and try to salvage what they could of their failed venture. He was able to sell it to a competitor but had lost copious amounts of money, so when he received a call from the same recruiter who had summoned him West in the first place, he was happy to listen.

As fate would have it, Wayne Huizenga had just purchased Blockbuster Entertainment Corporation, the parent of Blockbuster Video, and wanted the top national and international business builders. Taylor was asked to join a powerhouse team as a Regional Manager and was shortly promoted to Zone Manager, responsible for three quarters of the nation. Within a year, Wayne called him up and asked him to move to London as Vice President of International Operations, using it as a launching pad to make Blockbuster a household name around the globe.

Four years later, Taylor returned to the U.S. and began investing in startup companies. Among them was Takeout Taxi, a restaurant marketing delivery company that brought him to the Northern Virginia area for the first time. He then moved out to Portland, Oregon, as the CEO of a company called Coffee People, providing leadership as it sought to close private place memorandums and navigate an IPO. The company bought several other businesses and started a national expansion, finally marking the realization of the dream Taylor had set as a new college graduate just entering the world of business. When the company was sold, he returned to the D.C. area to help his daughter, Amee and her business partner pursue some entrepreneurial dreams of their own, where he has since built a life with his loving and supportive wife, Georga. "You know you're with the right person when you get back from a jog in the cold and realize how lucky you are to be coming home to them," Taylor affirms.

In advising young people entering the working world today, Taylor highlights the importance of knowing what one wants to accomplish, and why. "That kind of direction is invaluable, even if it changes several times throughout your life," he remarks. "For me, life isn't a spectator sport, so I believe in getting out there, competing, and playing. Lead by example and remember that input from others is valuable and meaningful as you make your decisions in life, so be open to everything you don't know." By being open to the unknown and meeting life on its own terms, Taylor's journey is the kind of tour de force that can only come from looking past one's own experiences and expectations to see the power of potential in all things and people.

BERNHARDT
WEALTH MANAGEMENT

Scott DiGiammarino

Everybody Can Be A Star

In 2010, after 25 years as an award winning senior executive at American Express, Scott DiGiammarino started his dream business, Reel Potential. At the root of this entrepreneurial venture is an unyielding belief in the human spirit, and in the idea that everyone has inner potential waiting to be engaged. With this proven philosophy, Reel Potential partners with some of the major Hollywood studios, using their iconic movie clips to help inspire and engage people in the workplace. The company also helps teach college students the soft skills they need to land a great job upon graduation, and motivates consumers worldwide to maximize their true potential. "I've always believed in people," Scott says. "Sometimes all it takes is a different way of communicating for a message to really be heard, and for inspiration to really be felt."

During his last few years at American Express, Scott himself began to lose sight of the motivation that had first inspired him. Ever since he was a child, he had been fascinated by people who had achieved success, both personally and professionally. "Through watching people succeed, I learned quickly that if you help others get what they want, you'll ultimately get what you want," he explains. "So I spent the better part of my life working toward a career that engaged others to believe in what could be, which, in turn, provided financial freedom for my family and me."

But because lifestyles of affluence don't often come easily, Scott had mastered the art of putting his head down to get the job done. "I call it Hustle 101, which basically means trying to outwork the rest of the field," he explains. This approach led him to he achieve tremendous success for over two and a half decades, but toward the end, he got the feeling that something just wasn't right. Internally, he wasn't as fulfilled as he'd been in the past.

Scott thought he was keeping that emotion to himself, but nothing could be further from the truth. One day, his two daughters, Amanda and Emma, approached him at one of their soccer games. "Dad, are you okay?" they asked. "You seem to be a little distant these days. You're quieter than normal. We want our fun-loving, passionate dad back."

Despite the numb exterior he had developed, his daughters had found just the right buttons to push to wake him up to what he really wanted his life to be about. "They were so right," Scott says. "I wasn't having fun at my job anymore. I felt stagnated, bored and unchallenged. My goal had always been to make a global difference in the lives of others, and I just didn't feel like I was doing that anymore." Thus began the quest to search for the next chapter in his life—one which would help him make that global impact he dreamed of. He wanted to help motivate, inspire and engage the masses, and above all else, he wanted to bring the old dad back for his daughters.

At the outset of that quest, his thought process reverted back to his childhood days in Marblehead, Massachusetts. Scott always felt a pull to help others—an emulation of his parents, who provided best-in-class love and support to Scott and his brothers. His father was an Assistant Principal at a local high school, and despite his success in the school system, there were some years when he had to work multiple jobs to provide for the family of five. He'd supplement his day job by teaching driver's education, working at a fish pier, painting houses—whatever it took to provide the lifestyle he envisioned for the family.

Scott's mother had a similar work ethic. She had three sons by the age of 22 and then secured a position working in the health care space as an administrative assistant for various practitioners. Both of Scott's parents were the shining example of Hustle 101, doing whatever they had to do, without hesitation, for their children. "I learned the value and importance of putting family first," says Scott. "I saw how important it was to have a strong work ethic and to genuinely love and care for your family."

Scott was the oldest of three boys, and the brothers loved sports from the time they could walk. While Scott played basketball, track, and tennis, and was the captain and All Star quarterback of his football team during his senior year, his true love was baseball and the Boston Red Sox. "Sports were everything to me," he remembers. "Whether it was bouncing a ball against the front stairs, buying baseball cards from the ice cream truck for a dime, or playing street hockey in the parking lot, I simply just can't ever remember a time when I wasn't playing something."

Scott's parents were always extremely supportive of him, never missing a single game. "Maybe it was an Italian thing, but I'll always remember my dad, sitting in the corner of the field during my practices," says Scott. "He'd be smoking his pipe, watching every play, every move, and every success and failure. During the car rides home, he would only focus on the positives. And as I think about it now, I am who I am because of my parents."

Scott actually planned on playing both baseball and football in college, but he was only 5'7" and a whopping 165 pounds, so he knew he'd eventually have to pick a different route. When he graduated high school, he attended Babson College, a small business school just west of downtown Boston. "I had a classmate who's father was an alumnus there, and he told me that Babson didn't have a football team," Scott explains. "He said I should go there and stretch my skills by starting one myself. He actually wrote a letter of recommendation for me saying that I would be an excellent entrepreneur. What's funny is that I didn't know what that word meant at the time. I had to look it up in the dictionary. When I found the definition, I thought it summed me up perfectly. It was everything I wanted to be."

When he finally started at Babson, Scott had already drafted up a business plan to start the team. He met with the administration several times to argue in support of the plan and his strategies to raise money for it, and even though it was ultimately rejected, his lifelong career as an entrepreneur had begun. "Babson has been the top school for entrepreneurial skills in America over twenty years," he reflects. "I learned so much about how to start and run a business, as well as the critical elements that you need to have in place to win. Conversely, they also taught us the importance of failing successfully and bouncing back when you're hit the hardest."

Scott graduated from Babson in 1984 with a degree in Marketing and Finance and set off on his career path with his focus on the advertising world. He applied to every advertising firm up and down the east coast, but was rejected across the board. "The only upside of that episode in my life was that you could get a free beer at the Babson Pub for every rejection letter you got," he laughs. Eventually, he was hired by Design Options, a startup computer consulting firm in downtown Boston. "What I didn't know was that they were going to teach me how to program in Cobol and Fortran... Right up my ally!" he jokes.

After several months, Scott was working with a client at the Bank of Boston who was developing a new financial product that would revolutionize investments, taxes, and people's retirement. It was called an IRA. Scott was so intrigued by the concept that he started researching financial services firms and was finally introduced to IDS Financial Services, which was then an eighty-year-old company based in Minneapolis. Scott was invited to an orientation meeting, and out of sixty candidates, he was one of only two hires.

Shortly after Scott started at IDS, the company was purchased by American Express and ultimately became American Express Financial Advisors. There was no office space, so Scott started off working from his basement, and with limited leadership and support, the first few years were a struggle. "I would wake up every morning, brush my teeth, and hit the phones," he recalls. "I had to build my own client base by cold calling, conducting seminars, buying and dialing direct mail leads, and asking for referrals. I had a $500-per-month draw, and I had to cover my own expenses, including gas, leads, and my state-of-the-art IBM PC XT for $6,000. As you can imagine, my parents weren't too happy with me. They thought I was nuts! My dad couldn't believe I was working a commission-based job after they paid so much for me to go to school, and after I had taken out student loans of my own."

After a couple years of working 15- to 18-hour days and achieving considerable success, Scott was ready to quit. He had been offered a salary position with a competitor and he was prepared to take it, but then Amex hired a new VP for the Boston region. "Larry Post came on board with an incredible background," Scott recalls. "We met, and he told me I wasn't going anywhere. I'll never forget the way he said to me, "You need to be smart enough to be dumb enough to do what I tell you to do for the next three years. If you do that, then I guarantee that you will have an incredible amount of success, both personally and professionally.' I thought to myself, "Wow! So that's what great leadership is all about—painting this compelling vision, sharing expectations, and letting me know what's in it for me.' I decided to stay."

Larry created a formal invitation-only leadership development program and asked Scott to join. It was an incredible opportunity for a 25-year-old who was starving for leadership and direction. Within six months, he was promoted to a District Manager position, and within a year, he was ranked the top manager out of 836 in the country—a spot he held for three consecutive years.

Scott was then promoted to Field Vice President in 1992. He was asked to take over the Washington, D.C. region, which was ranked 173 out of 176 at the time. "I had my choice of ten different regions to run, but the D.C. opportunity seemed special to me," he explains. When he finally arrived, he learned that he had his work cut out for him. With rampant compliance issues and employees blatantly not showing up to work, morale in the office was incredibly low. Scott took the office by storm, and within one year, he took the region to Number One in the country. "I took the system I learned in Boston and applied it to D.C.," he says. "We put in a common vision, principles, values, systems, goals, roles, rewards, and accountability. We put the right people in the right jobs, and if we couldn't change the people, we knew we had no choice but to change the people. And the key to our change was that we were extremely transparent in everything we did. Everybody knew what we were trying to do and the 'why' behind it."

Over a six-year period, Scott went from 32 employees to 1,600. They grew from one office to over 200, and the three leaders underneath him multiplied to over a hundred. He was trying to build a dynasty—one that would set record-breaking results each and every year. Soon, however, it became clear they were growing too rapidly—something his boss termed "uncontrollable growth"—and Scott started seeing his leading indicators shake. He knew that if he didn't do something creative, he could lose all of the success and goodwill he had built. But before he made any rash decisions, he and his team decided to take a step back and evaluate what was really happening—not only to their own environment, but also to the world at large. They wanted to understand how the new generation wanted to learn and what made them tick. Then, and only then, would they develop their long-term strategy.

Scott's research lent him remarkable insights. He learned that attention spans were shrinking, so the days of the three-hour meeting were over.

He learned that his employees wanted to learn by being entertained, especially by video. He also learned that, as people grew, so did the gap between the top performers and everyone else. "There's something called the 80/20 rule, which states that, in a given work environment, 80 percent of the work is done by 20 percent of the workforce," Scott explains. "I saw that that was absolutely true, and that the other 80 percent of the workforce felt very much like a number. As Pink Floyd would say, these people felt like just another brick in the wall."

With a strong belief in a collaborative approach to problem solving, Scott brought a cross section of employees into his office to find out what they thought the region should stand for. He wanted to find out what would make them proud to come to work each day, and what would motivate them to give their best efforts on a day-to-day, moment-to-moment basis. "If you had a magic wand, what would you want leadership to do to help you maximize your true potential?" he said, posing his signature question. "What could they do to help each and every employee get what they wanted, both personally and professionally?"

Over the course of the multi-day meetings, the focus group came up with over 200 themes that they wanted their work to be associated with. Among those were courage, teamwork, ethics, principle-based decision-making, fairness, and transparency. "I then asked them to prioritize the themes down to the top five or ten, and they pushed back," says Scott. "They said that they wanted to be known for all of them. I asked, how can we drive home over 200 themes in over 200 offices? 'That's what they pay you the big bucks to figure out,' they told me."

That weekend, Scott went to the movies and saw *Braveheart* and was struck by the sheer volume of scenes that inspired and motivated him. He found himself thinking how great it would be if he could share those emotions with his team. "That's when it hit me," he avows. "I decided I would figure out how to use movie clips to help drive the theme-based culture my employees wanted."

With that, Scott began sending out weekly theme-based emails to all 1,600 employees. For example, one week's theme might be courage. He would start with a brief explanation of why the theme is important and would then say, "It kind of reminds me of the movie *Top Gun,* starring Tom Cruise. And for those of you who've never seen the movie, it's about X, Y and Z." Scott would include a clip, and would then invite employees to share with him the most courageous decision they had ever made in their lives. "I'd receive back between 200 and 300 stories a week, and what was amazing was that most of them had nothing to do with business," he describes. "They were all about something that happened personally—maybe a story from when they were nine years old. I read each and every one of them, and with the author's permission, I'd share the most compelling and emotional stories with everyone else on a weekly basis."

Thanks to this story sharing strategy, the environment began to change dramatically. People started to feel more connected and team-oriented, which in turn prompted the employees to look out for one another. "I felt as though I went from 100 leaders to 1,600," Scott says. "If you were having a bad day or a bad moment, there was someone to support you. If you needed help, someone was always there to pick you up because they genuinely cared about you and your success. The team was more energized than ever before, and as a result, we maintained one of the top rankings amongst American Express divisions for over two decades. They had Best in Class metrics and, most importantly, Employee Engagement scores, and ours were through the roof." Scott won countless awards for his efforts, including the Leader of the Decade Award and the prestigious Diamond Ring—although neither could compare to the Coach of the Year Award he won when he led his daughters' soccer and basketball teams.

The Amex team's success soon drew the eyes of the corporate office, who sent in a number of internal and external consulting firms. "They wanted to see if what I was doing was legal, and to find out if it could be replicated across the entire global organization," he laughs. The observing firms published their findings in a study, a large section of which focused on the environment, the culture, and the galvanization of principles and values that came from the storytelling and movie clips, which strengthened the overall motivation, inspiration, drive of everyone involved.

The next thing he knew, Scott was giving keynote speeches at national conferences and mentoring countless leaders throughout the country. He was even asked to host an internal television show. Through all of this, he used the magic of film to help his messages come alive—something that especially hit home at a speech he gave in Las Vegas entitled, "Leaving a Legacy." Afterward, a woman came up to him. She had laughed and cried through the presentation, and she was so moved by the experience that asked if Scott had considered doing it full time. "My goal in life was to be a great dad and husband, so I didn't want to be a motivational speaker," Scott explains. "But she gave me the courage to start calling the Hollywood studios to see if there was potential. I knew we were onto something special, and I asked the studios to partner with me to try and change the world."

It took over nine years of negotiations, but Universal Studios finally stepped up and agreed to partner with Scott. That's when he left American Express after 25 years to start launch Reel Potential, the first and only company in the history of Hollywood to gain legal access to movie clips for B2B and Higher Educational purposes.

Today, Reel Potential uses these movie clips to help business leaders inspire, motivate, engage, communicate, and teach soft skills to employees and students. The experience is short, compelling, entertaining, and memorable, and therein lies its power and efficacy. The company has also expanded its impact by allowing people to share their experiences and stories on its new social community portal. "The ROI has exceeded all of the expectations we had for engagement scores, activity, and email open rates," Scott reports. "Everyone wants to see what the movie is."

Today, Reel Potential has over 3,000 expertly curated and meta-tagged movie clips. They work with medium- to large-sized companies, especially those that are decentralized. They also work with colleges and universities to teach students the soft skills that have become a necessity in today's inundated job market. They also use their movie clip library to help supplement e-learning and corporate strategy. A highly sought keynote speaker, Scott also delivered a talk at TEDxRockCreekPark, entitled "Why Movies Move Us," in which he discussed the impact movies have on humans and the neuroscience behind it. After a brief hiatus, he's back to living his dream of trying to inspire and engage the world, and at full velocity.

Throughout his extensive career, Scott has learned firsthand how to be an empowering leader. Some of the lessons came from his parents, while others came from his daughters, Amanda and Emma. But the most influential person in his life has been his wife, Shelley. The two met at Babson, and she went on to become a CPA in the audit division of Arthur Anderson. "She's brilliant," he beams. "She's my wife, my best friend, my business partner, and my confidant. Every decision I make, I ask myself if I'd make the same decision if Shelley, Amanda, and Emma were sitting on the couch watching me. Would they understand and support why I made the decision? Having them by my side through the years has been immense!"

Just like that pivotal day on the soccer field, Scott's daughters keep him centered and are a constant reminder of why he's doing what he's doing. In return, he tries to teach them life lessons, often showing them movie clips that he hopes will shape and change their lives. The exchange of film and inspiration has become so pervasive that now, the girls have started picking out footage of their own to augment their father's library of clips.

Now that the 80/20 Rule has been explored more thoroughly, we no longer have to wonder if underachieving employees lack some crucial element unique to top performers. Rather, they have just as much drive, determination, discipline, desire, and decision-making capacity as anyone. They're just as good, if not better, than the best of the best— they just don't know it yet. "I believe that there's so much opportunity out there for everyone," Scott affirms. "I have this deep belief that greatness is inside all of us—it's just a matter of finding it somehow, someway. Just imagine a world where we can truly tap into that greatness. Our success would be so incredible that we'd all be able to write our own Oscar winning, Hollywood story. I believe everyone has that potential, and Reel Potential is all about finding it."

BERNHARDT
WEALTH MANAGEMENT

Bob Dinkel

Connecting the Dots

I f you happened to be driving along the winding country roads up near Buffalo, New York, back in the 1950s, there's a chance you passed by a small picnic table in a ditch where two little boys were selling produce. Maybe you stopped to buy vegetables and had the chance to chat about the weather with Bob Dinkel, the older brother. You would have certainly noticed his easy charm and natural way with people—character traits he cultivated at the small roadside business that would later carry him all over the world. Now a Managing Director of Pierce Capital Partners (PCP), a boutique M&A firm launched in 1993 that helps package and sell small businesses to mid-market companies, Bob has traveled hundreds of thousands of miles since his days of selling vegetables, but his work has always been about bringing people together and connecting the dots.

"From 10,000 feet, our firm is about bringing buyers and sellers together," Bob remarks. "It doesn't sound very complicated, but when you start drilling down, there are a myriad of considerations and realities that must line up for our work to be effective." On the seller side, Bob works primarily with small business owners in the IT government contracting space for a period of time to get the business ready, ultimately packaging it into a document that effectively communicates its value to a prospective buyer and indicates how it might complement the buyer's growth and strategic plans. On the buyer side, he takes care to note restricted contracts. "A seller might have contracts that can only go to small, veteran-owned, or women-owned businesses, for example, so you can't just connect any two dots in making a sale," he explains. "You have to mix and match to make sure the buyer can continue to grow the asset."

In this line of work, social events and networking play a big role in Bob's success, and in a sense, he's never truly off the job. "I'm a big believer in the idea that everybody's always selling," he remarks. "Whenever you talk to someone, you get a sense of a particular topic or interest they have, and in the back of your mind, there may be a way to connect them to someone else who can help with that. That's what connecting the dots is about, and I really enjoy bringing that kind of value to people. To me, that's a home run."

Having been born and raised in a rural farming environment where hard work permeated everyday life and value structures were strong, Bob believes that life isn't defined as much by specific moments as it is by the context and tone set by one's upbringing and culture. His father worked at the local Ford plant, while his mother had an accounting position at a car dealership. They modeled an excellent work ethic for their two sons, and Bob began operating the family's tractor at age seven with his dad. Because he was expected to help out with farming operations year-round, there wasn't much time left over for sports and other leisure activities.

Bob and his younger brother were allowed to sell vegetables on the side of the road, instilling in them the idea that if you worked hard, you could earn a few extra dollars for new school clothes or other luxuries. They did well, to the point that his father built a structure so they could expand the modest business into a small farm market. While he was in high school, Bob was also invited to work as a dishwasher at a restaurant nearby, which he eagerly accepted.

"Going through high school, I was far from a scholar and never really found something that resonated with me," he remembers. All that changed, however, after he enrolled at the local community college and began to embrace school. He had the opportunity to take a course in the new field of data processing, where he mastered COBOL and other data processing languages. He worked for a while on the weekends as the desk clerk for a hotel, but ultimately gave that up for a job running a computer for a local Board of Education, cultivating a love of technology that would come to define his career. Meanwhile, his family sold their land, bought a lakefront home, and built a new farm market to develop the produce business further. But Bob, having had a taste of a different kind of business early on in school, knew he wanted to pursue something else.

After getting his associates degree, he transferred to Miami University in Ohio with plans to finish his college career. But when he was offered a job back in Buffalo by the Board of Education a year and a half later, he decided to pursue that instead. For the next two years, he learned systems programming and was responsible for keeping computers current with the latest software available. "When I landed this job that paid twice as much as my father was making at the Ford plant, we all knew it was a home run for the family," he remembers.

Bob's ascent up the economic ladder had only just begun. Before long, a former colleague urged him to come join a small consulting firm in Buffalo, which didn't offer the humdrum stability of the Board of Education job but instead involved more entrepreneurial adventure and risk taking. He spent eight years at the firm, called DataWare, honing his skills in programming, marketing, and sales, which called on both his technical ability and the people skills he had first started developing back at the family produce stand. It was while he was working at DataWare that he went out to a local restaurant with friends and was introduced to Kathleen, the woman he would marry and spend his life with.

The company grew to about 40 people during Bob's tenure there, expanding and putting in place international distributors to sell tools and programs for people looking to convert from one computer environment to another. One evening, he got to talking with the distributor responsible for selling their products in France and Spain. One of the distributor's other clients was a company in Washington, Johnson Systems, who needed someone with Bob's software and sales expertise.

The next day, Bob received a call from the company, inviting him for a cup of coffee to explore the possibilities. In no time, the company offered him a relocation package and the opportunity to run the federal group they wanted to launch. "I didn't know much about that line of work, but they had spoken with a lot of local people about managing and driving a federal program, and everyone kept giving them reasons why they couldn't do it," Bob says. "The owners decided to bring someone in from the outside who had a fresh perspective on federal sales. The way I see it, sales is sales. You've got a product and a buyer with a need, so you connect the dots and make it work."

With that, Bob and Kathleen did the unthinkable and left the comfort of the Buffalo area for Washington in the summer of 1981. "No one in either family had ever thought of that kind of treason," he laughs. "We had been married for a little over two years, and the idea of taking my bride and moving south was unheard of." But the couple was committed, and Bob immediately set about establishing himself in D.C.'s sales and software arena.

Having come from a services background in Buffalo, he enjoyed learning the products side of business. Then, in summer of 1984, Johnson

Systems was acquired by Computer Associates International, Inc (CA), who wanted Bob to run a federal group for them. While the rest of the Johnson Systems staff was merging into the CA structure, Bob was given the leeway to take a piece of CA and run it as a federal group. He was on his own, and it was up to him to show his value and worth, but he wasted no time in showing the new company what he was made of. With a platform that he could truly grow with, Bob took the opportunity and ran with it, setting himself apart as someone who could deftly aid in the smooth integration of companies after they were acquired.

From then on, he was involved in virtually every one of CA's acquisitions in one way or another, which tallied up to well over 50 transactions involving a number of competitive firms. This entailed working on integration, as well as turning his expert eye on the various parts of a company to see which components would fit with CA and which wouldn't. "CA gained a reputation for being somewhat harsh at acquisition time, which was sometimes hard," Bob reflects. "But we made a point to let people know where they stood from day one (in, out or temporary), versus falsely expressing a career that would never materialize. As the process matured, we provided outplacement for former employees if they ever needed anything from us later on."

Bob spent a total of 23 years at CA, where he had an exceptional stable of mentors from which to learn and grow. He saw firsthand how large organizations implement sales teams and support and manage products on a global scale, and he had the opportunity to develop close relationships with CA team members and their families all over the world. Bob and his family moved to Chicago in 1986 to run the company's Midwest region, and was then asked to move to Long Island in 1988 to work at their corporate headquarters. In that capacity, Bob was responsible for Canada, Latin America, the federal practice, and the company's corporate events. "I had no idea what I was getting into at the time," he laughs. "Our Latin American operations, for instance, were run out of Sao Paulo, and included everything south of the U.S."

Several years later, Bob was sent back to Washington to run CA's government unit. By that time, he and Kathleen had two daughters, and when he was called back to corporate several years later, the family decided to stay put and continue fostering its D.C. roots while Bob commuted back and forth to Long Island. "Kathleen has always been a phenomenal partner and soul mate, and she really took care of the home front through all of that," he reflects. For the next four years, they made it work, and Bob still made the time to serve as a trustee at the Connelly School of the Holy Child, where his daughters attended.

In the late 1990s, after establishing itself as a multi-billion dollar global product licensing company, CA decided that it would only be able to further evolve toward its vision if it expanded into services. This transition finally brought Bob back to D.C., where he ran all of the firm's government work and also became the new Senior VP. He was later assigned to a small subsidiary, Computer Associates Services Inc (CASI), which he grew to $80 million and a staff of 400. CA's commercial sectors began to use his model as an example for their own work, and CA continued to acquire services companies through the early 2000s, until it realized that 85 percent of those service efforts were going toward supporting non-CA products. With that, Bob was asked to divest and reorganize the global services organization, responsible for its North American, European, and Latin American regions, and traveling weekly to new opportunities. He also spent three years developing alliances with some of the companies CA had divested to, until, at long last, it was time to retire and move on to something else.

Upon leaving CA in 2007, Bob was approached by a small D.C. consulting firm that wanted to partner with him and see what they could do. He then identified another firm to partner with, connecting the dots and pulling the companies together into something they could build upon. This yielded FedResults, a company geared at helping outside organizations enter the government sector via business development, GSA schedule support, and product resale. "We were essentially a local sales team for outside organizations," Bob explains. They built that company for three years until the economic crisis of 2008, at which point they decided to package and sell it with the help of Pierce Capital. "We sold it locally to a firm in Herndon, and upon that sale, the managing partner at Pierce asked me to join them," he remembers.

Having established himself at Pierce and acquired a familiarity with the different mid-market buyers, systems integrators, and small businesses within the community, Bob now especially enjoys the seller side of his work. "I really enjoy working with owners, talking about their challenges and where they hope to go," he remarks. "I also like that you have to really learn a company's history, customer base, and inner dynamics in order to match it with the right buyer. Typical buyers are interested in revenue and profitability, the agencies a seller works with, and the contract vehicles it has, and I love holding a refined lens up to those considerations to achieve successful transactions."

As a leader, Bob makes a point to be fully engaged, providing feedback to those who invest real time and effort into their work. He also leads by example, never asking someone to do something he wouldn't do himself. He replicates these tenets in the leadership roles he plays in organizations like the Northern Virginia Technology Council (NVTC) and the Small and Emerging Contractors Advisory Forum (SECAF), and as a father when his two daughters call him up to ask for advice. In these phone calls, and in advising any young person entering the working world today, Bob says it's not enough to just get your feet wet. "You've got to just jump into the deep end of the pool and see how it goes," he says. "You'll learn from mistakes. And pay attention to the little things, like arriving a little early, staying a little late, and keeping things organized, as that can go a long way too."

Beyond that, he emphasizes the importance of taking a step back and really looking at where you are and where you want to go. When he takes this advice himself, pausing the process of connecting the dots to take a look at what his efforts have created over time, he sees a balance of family trips around the world, transformative work experiences, and quiet afternoons buzzing around the hills of Great Falls, Virginia in the 75 TR6 he's had since his days in Buffalo. He spends his free time enjoying his volunteer efforts for child advocacy groups, the panels and local business clubs that now ask him to come share his expertise, and the business colleagues he feels honored to know. His example shows that taking the time to connect the dots yields the complete picture of a full life, sacred in its breadth and rich in its detail.

Babs Doherty

The Fixer

For many children experiencing the dissolution of their parents' marriage, the trauma of so many shifting realities can push them to a breaking point. Even those mothers and fathers who have inspired in their children a strong work ethic, a spirit of adventure, and firm values can nevertheless be consumed by the difficulties of separation, and their children can be left without the attention they need.

But for Babs Doherty, founder and CEO of Eagle Ray, Inc., breaking was not an option. As a young teen in an environment of crisis, Babs didn't just survive. Left to her own devices in the margins of her parents' attention as they struggled with each other, she flipped the breaking point on its head and emerged with the resourcefulness, determination and drive that would one day lead her to great success.

"I was almost completely on my own to solve my own problems," Babs says today. "My parents were focused on the divorce, and that became the epicenter of our home life. It was because of this that I became such an independent person." The youngest of three children, Babs watched her older brothers attempt to move on with their own lives, as she found herself very much alone. "I had to be resourceful," she continues. "I had to make sure I could get things accomplished and handle my own problems."

Babs did indeed master these skills, but perhaps the greatest trait that evolved through the experience is one that focuses outwardly, to external problems. It's an ability that has defined her personal and professional success, and that has become her core attribute: the power to take the skills she used to survive her own life, and translate them into skills that can identify and fix the problems in any system. "The things I enjoy doing are the things I can fix," Babs explains. "Classically, you see in male-female relationships that the guy is usually a fixer, and the girl just wants to talk about it. In my case the roles are reversed. I'm the fixer. In all aspects of my life—at home, at work, and with my children—I fix stuff. And that is integral to my ability to manage programs. It's a natural fit. It's easy for me because I do it without thought. And I believe that's the recipe for success when it comes to entrepreneurship. If you find something you are inclined to do naturally and without thought, success tends to follow."

Success followed for Babs in many ways through an aggressive and adventurous career, and culminated in her decision to found Eagle Ray in 2002. "I saw a need in the government space to make management skills and methodologies teachable, thereby allowing more people to be successful in managing projects and programs. I felt like these skills would be particularly vital with projects where you're building and deploying software in high-risk environments, such as for our intelligence agencies and in homeland security."

Throughout her career as a process and project manager, Babs saw individuals who were exceptionally talented in their field promoted to management roles, only to falter. She became convinced that if those individuals were equipped with the right tools, they would excel. "Individuals with mastery of a certain skill can become excellent managers if they have the right methodology," Babs says. "So we develop standardized methodologies for IT organizations to define, build, test, and deploy. In essence, we build a framework for building projects and moving them forward."

For Eagle Ray's customers, the program has proved to be an addictive service. "We may handle just one part of process engineering or leadership and mentoring to start," Babs says. "Then our clients want more and more, until we're handling the entire lifecycle of project management—from the initial conception of a requirement, to defining that requirement, to actually supporting it once it's built in."

After eleven years, Eagle Ray has built a team of over one hundred employees and sees its annual revenues at almost $30 million. This year the company was recognized by the Virginia Chamber of Commerce as one of 2013's 50 Fastest Growing Companies in the Commonwealth. Babs, herself, is a 2013 SmartCEO Brava! Award winner, and Eagle Ray has also been recognized by Washington Technology's Fast 50 list.

As a fixer, Babs has naturally developed a spirited character that eagerly meets any challenge, which is evident in the contracts her company takes on. Its main customers are found in the intelligence community, including the Office of Naval Intelligence and the Department of Homeland Security. "Our passion is the customers that provide mission critical products and services," Babs says, "because we understand the importance of getting things done rapidly. We like being in the line of fire because that's an environment we really thrive in."

While her parents' divorce made her stronger instead of weaker, Babs's character and ability were also influenced by the unique strengths of each of her parents. Indeed, her tenacity and drive to fix problems and processes would not have been nearly as formidable without the vital lessons and values that both her parents instilled in her. "I saw in my father that work always comes first," Babs says. "You have to get it done. You do your best, and that's your responsibility." Babs's father, an Air Force pilot, also set an example of patriotism that shines through his daughter's work today.

"On the other hand," she continues, "my mom taught me the vital lesson of attention to detail, which has been essential to my success. She also taught me so much about socialization and how to be a human being in the world—that it's important to get to know people and to understand agendas. In the professional world, just as in the personal world, you have to empathize and understand what is important to others. If you can foster genuine, mutually-beneficial relationships and help others get to where they want to go, you will ultimately succeed and get where you want to be as well. When those skill sets came together in my repertoire, they gave me a great balance between networking capabilities and the capability to follow through and get things done."

Armed with these mutually-affirming strengths, Babs seized her independence by necessity and ran with it. Although there was no money for college, she achieved opportunities that few mere high school graduates could hope for. Living in Northern Virginia, she got an administrative job at the Naval Research Lab and cut her teeth on the Wang word processor, a primitive computer system that required her to learn basic programming skills to operate. Between her early computer skills, her problem solving ability, and her gradual introduction to the classified intelligence world, doors began to open. By her early twenties, Babs was traveling abroad through her work, and by the time she reached her mid-twenties, she began pursuing her bachelor's degree through night classes. She learned the programming languages COBOL and FORTRAN and ultimately left the government to join private industry, where she followed role models and mentors to several small companies before landing at the last place she would ever work for someone other than herself: BTG, Incorporated.

"I joined BTG as a task leader for a software job," Babs says. "And before long, I met the owner, a gentleman named Ed Bersoff. It was the first time I had met the owner of a company of that size, about one hundred employees. This guy was different."

At 6'5", Ed's physical presence was already intimidating to Babs. But as she had more direct contact with him through special projects, his influence on her professional development grew. "He would know the answer to our questions before we even asked," she recounts. "Numbers would stream out of his head on demand. It was a validation of what I was learning in my classes about how a business should be run, and it left a mark on me. He would command the respect of those who worked for him, inspiring the team to bring their best skills and best selves to the table."

Babs was working at BTG when she completed her bachelor's degree. When she graduated, she was given two copies of her diploma—one to keep, and one to dedicate—and naturally, the honor of the latter went to Ed. "By then the company was over 300 people," Babs says, "and he still didn't know me very well at the time. But I set up a one-on-one meeting with him and presented him with my diploma. I said that whether he knew it or not, he was my inspiration to finish my degree and continue on my path of growth."

Fifteen years after starting with BTG, Babs was finally ready to launch her own company. Before she committed, however, she called Ed and asked for guidance. "He said it wasn't the right time," she recalls. "The economy wasn't good, and there was a lot of uncertainty in the world. He suggested I come work with him at this other company. I thanked him, hung up the phone, logged onto my computer, and incorporated my company right then and there. When I let him know, he invited me to dinner. We've met once a month since then, over the last eleven years, and today he's Chairman of the Board at Eagle Ray."

Since transitioning into a leadership role herself when her entre-preneurial dreams were realized, Babs has continued learning from her role models and mentors and has cultivated within herself her own leadership style. "Through little failures along the road, I have learned that my way is really just one way, and not the only way," she remarks. "I've learned to find the right people for my team who have value systems similar to mine, but who may have different approaches to the same problem. The important thing is to end up at the same place, but if I allow someone to take their own way there, then we may pick up something extra along the way that makes our company even better. With this in mind, as a leader, I am finger-on, not hands-on. I want to know what's happening and to be a part of what's going on, but I'm not going to tell my employees the exact way to do their jobs. My role is to provide the end vision and empower those under me to achieve that goal. People get stifled when they're not allowed creativity and space. That's what I've learned the most."

For her own space to be creative and entrepreneurial, Babs has her husband, Dan, to thank. Married for seventeen years, his support has been fundamental to her professional success. "He was extremely encouraging when I set out to found Eagle Ray, and to this day he picks up all the slack at home," Babs affirms. "He is definitely the rock that is holding down the house and the home so I can move forward with Eagle Ray and do the things we need to do, and I'm so thankful for that." Through their teamwork, the Dohertys are able to contribute to society in other vital ways, giving generously to the Breast Cancer Society and the Lung Cancer Society. In the past, Babs was also President of the Board for Volunteer Fairfax. The daughter of a military man, she donates to and volunteers for the Military Order of the Purple Heart, and every year around Christmas, Babs, Dan, and Eagle Ray adopt four to five families through Our Daily Bread.

Today, Babs and her company continue to thrive in high-risk, mission critical environments that demand results and capitalize on her trademark instinct as a fixer. The company's name, however, alludes to the something that runs as deeply in her character as it does in the world: the ocean. Since being taught to SCUBA dive by her father when she was a young girl, the experience of diving has been something she cherishes not only as an adventurous activity, but also as a powerful metaphor.

"I have a real affinity for the ocean," she avows. "It goes beyond the sport of SCUBA diving. My dad and I used to dive together, and I certainly hold those memories dear, but it seems as though diving permeates every aspect of my life in a deeper sense. My husband and my daughter are both certified divers because of me. My vacations are planned around whether I can SCUBA dive while I'm there. My longing is to be in water. Salt water is in my blood. And the very steel and smell of the tank—there's something about it that's relaxing and inspirational to me. When you think about it, oceans are a huge part of life. We spend all our lives above them, but I like to be a little bit below, just to see what's underneath."

In a sense, the solitude, clarity, and peace achieved when Babs dons a diving suit and disappears underneath the surface is a state of mind she brings to her clients each day. Reminiscent of the tremendous inner fortitude she cultivated amidst uncertain external forces as a young lady, she now dives with life-affirming enthusiasm into the unknown, confident in her silent skill as she confronts new terrain and submarine wonders. Like diving, her work through Eagle Ray—and her life itself—is an exercise in the expert handling of pressure that, to others, could be dangerous and disconcerting. But Babs, able to address such situations with a unique grace cultivated through years of rising to challenges of all kinds, wouldn't have it any other way.

BERNHARDT
WEALTH MANAGEMENT

Candace Duncan

Making Your Point

Raised on a farm just outside Wichita, Kansas, Candace Duncan learned at a very young age that there wasn't anything she couldn't do. Raising livestock, wheat, maize, alfalfa, and corn, she and her younger brother and sister were expected to help with anything and everything. Her mother taught school, while her father worked for a Mobil oil refinery in nearby Augusta, so Candy was responsible for making dinner for the family. There were always animals to be tended to and homework to finish, and her father had her driving a tractor before she knew how to drive a car.

Beyond teaching her the tremendous, incrementally escalating value of a hard day's work, this upbringing instilled in Candy a strong sense of self and an unwavering belief in her own ability, which would prove invaluable down the road when she found herself the only woman in the male-dominated field of accounting. "When I got into the business world, there were very few females, but I always had the confidence that I could do anything I wanted or needed to do," she affirms today. "The way I was raised, I just knew I had it in me."

This didn't mean Candy didn't notice the lack of equality in the workplace around her—only that she never took it personally, and never allowed it to hold her back. In 1978, she was hired in the Norfolk office of KPMG LLP, one of the largest accounting firms. She was one of two women on the professional staff, and while the other quit a month later, Candy rose through the leadership ranks to senior associate and then to manager.

"Sometimes it was hard to be different," she concedes, remembering being invited by clients to lunch at clubs that didn't allow women. "But a friend and mentor of mine, Dr. William Harvey, was one of the only black gentlemen at Harvard in the early 1970s, and he told me that if you're different, people will remember you. So if you're different, make your point, and people will remember it. That has been true my whole life." Candy has spent her professional career not discouraged about being different, but empowered by it, using it to amplify the points she believes are worth making.

Today, KPMG International is among the largest professional services companies in the world, employing 155,000 people and specializing in audit, tax, and advisory services. "It's a firm that really lives its core values of integrity and ethics, firmly committed to doing the right thing in the right way, and that attracts phenomenal people," Candy affirms. "Many public accountants end up moving on to other things, and there were several times in my career that I considered doing that, but it always came back to the people. This job has given me the opportunity to advise a wide array of companies and industries, and I've been able to facilitate a lot of good things with a lot of good colleagues for these people and organizations. I've really enjoyed that."

The other key consideration that has made her tenure at KPMG so lengthy and prosperous has been the opportunity for continuous learning and growth. "As soon as I would get settled into a position and feel like I had gotten good at it, they'd give me another job," she reflects. When Candy was admitted to the firm's partnership in 1987, she was the first female partner in Virginia. Later, she was asked to lead KPMG's Virginia audit practice, and then the Mid-Atlantic area, which included Virginia, Pennsylvania, Maryland and Washington, D.C.

Through that time, several partners asked that she run for the board, but Candy wanted to focus on mastering her responsibilities and ensuring everything was running seamlessly, so she declined. After five years of leading the Mid-Atlantic area, Candy felt that the numbers were good enough and that running for the board was the right thing to do—and her instincts were solid. "Looking back with what I know today, I'm still a little shocked that I got elected to the board," she remarks. "Of the firm's nearly 2,000 U.S. partners, there are only 15 board members. But I agree with the leadership of KPMG that diversity in gender, background, upbringing, function, and geography makes for the best boards, and I am thrilled to be a part of that."

Candy was elected to the board in 2009, and to her surprise, within 30 days, she was asked to move to Washington, D.C. to become the first female managing partner of the firm's Washington Metro Area practice. "My husband and I had been in Williamsburg for 25 years, so it was hard to give that up, but this has been a great and welcoming community," she says. "And in terms of helping people grow and furthering the strength of the firm, I feel like I've made a difference, which has always been my number one goal."

As she prepares to retire from KPMG following 35 years of service to the firm, Candy recalls how much the accounting profession has changed. She can still remember several jobs she had hoped to lead, only to be told that women were not put on such jobs. Several decades later, she finds herself a top-tier executive, serving as the lead on those same accounts. The time in between these two extremes was spent evolving both personally and professionally in a firm that has been as committed to change as she is—one of the reasons Candy felt KPMG was the right place for her. "I've been doing this for over 35 years, and I learn something new every single day," she avows. "Whether it's about people, leadership, growing a business, or taking something from concept to a tangible product, the constant learning has made for an incredibly rewarding career."

Candy's love of learning and finding better ways to do things extends back to the earliest days of her childhood, when her family's farm in Andover, Kansas grew popcorn that she had to shell by hand. The stalks would grow five feet high, and the shelling was hard work for a little girl, but she and her siblings were allowed to sell the produce at the family's vegetable stand in the summers for pocket money. The daily grind of shelling changed, however, when her parents gave her a popcorn sheller for Christmas. It was a symbol of the kind of solutions-oriented approach that would fascinate and compel her throughout her life.

Candy's siblings and grandparents also played a big influence in her life. Her brother was often sick as a child, so she and her sister would sometimes stay up the road at their grandparents' house. For the first four years of school, they attended a one-room schoolhouse, and the grade-levels in her high school had less than 80 students. Team sports were a favorite pastime, and Candy loved softball, basketball, and volleyball. As their property was on the main road between Augusta and Wichita, there was a small country club near their house, where Candy would lifeguard and teach swimming lessons to earn money. She also cleaned houses to supplement her modest income.

While hard work and help with the chores was expected, Candy's parents only asked that their children do the best they could do, and Candy internalized this as her dream for the future. "I never had any one thing in mind that I wanted to do with my life, but I knew I wanted to be the best I could be," she remembers. "My parents taught me to do a good job every day, and this lesson was as powerful as it was simple." By taking life one day at a time and always doing her best, Candy excelled in sports and was valedictorian of her class, in addition to earning academic honors and serving as student body president. "I always liked leadership, which began with the vegetable stand I ran as a young girl," she remarks. "My sister would sack up the produce and my brother would carry it for the customers, while I kept a ledger of everything we sold each day. I really enjoyed that sense of responsibility and ownership of the business' performance."

This love of leadership stayed with her at Kansas State University, where she served as a resident assistant in exchange for free room and board. During her sophomore year, she was responsible for one dormitory wing with 60 girls. The next two years, she was responsible for a co-ed floor of 200 people—an exercise in dealing with people and interpersonal issues that honed her leadership skills even further.

In her junior year, Candy chose to major in accounting not only because she found the classes enjoyable and a good match for her skill set, but also for its high marketability. "I noticed that everyone coming out of the major got a job fairly quickly, and a job was what I needed," she says pragmatically. "I did an accounting internship and liked that as well, so I decided to get my CPA."

After graduating *magna cum laude*, Candy took an accounting job in Kansas City, where her boyfriend, Mike, a fellow Kansas State University graduate, was in medical school. The two had met in high school in Andover and married just before he earned his medical degree. Mike was then summoned to the East Coast to practice at the Portsmouth Naval Hospital. Around that time, Candy passed her CPA exam and, with two years of experience under her belt, was hired on at KPMG in Norfolk, Virginia.

Prior to her retirement, Candy served as the face of KPMG in the Washington Metro Area. As managing partner, she focused on community outreach and attended important meetings and events, but she still enjoyed the more client-centered activities. "I love pursuing new work, interacting with existing clients, and working with audit committees and boards," she remarks. "That's my upbringing and my roots. There's a lot of pressure to grow the business, which is all about cracking the code of our clients' problems to find solutions." To do that, Candy focuses on bringing the best and brightest people on board through recruitment, competitive hiring practices, and spending time with the firm's interns. "Making sure we have the right people in the right seats on the bus is crucial, and I know that if we help our people find their way and be successful, our clients will be happy, too," she affirms.

This attitude speaks to the leadership style Candy has cultivated since those early days on the farm, which has nothing to do with titles and everything to do with enabling others to find a path to success. "I try to show, teach, encourage, follow up, check in, and make sure our team members can see where they're going," she says. "I begin with the end in mind and set a clear vision of the future, knowing that it just takes time and lots of small steps to get there."

This brand of leadership takes equal parts conservative implementer and risk-taking dreamer. By nature, Candy is the former, which is why her husband's influence was so important. Ever the dreamer himself, Mike left his successful medical practice to work at NASA, where he was responsible for international space physicians from Germany, Russia, Japan, Canada and the U.S., and was required to spend considerable amounts of time at the cosmonaut training facility in Russia. "Likewise, I spent time in Russia as well, and often in less than optimal conditions, but it made my world broader," Candy says. Mike was one of the four NASA personnel who played a key leadership role in the rescue of 33 Chilean miners from an underground chamber in 2010—a testament to his remarkable ability to broaden the world not only for his wife, but for others. Mike passed away in 2012, but his legacy of leadership through unrelenting vision continues to touch the world in profound ways.

Influenced in part by her late husband but bringing to the table a flare that is all her own, Candy has been on *Washingtonian Magazine*'s list of the 100 most powerful women since 2009, and is distinguished as one of the Kansas State Business School's outstanding alumni. She sits on the executive committees of the Board of Trade, the World Affairs Council, and the Cultural Alliance.

As co-chair of the Leukemia & Lymphoma Society's annual ball, Candy is leading efforts to raise more than $3 million dollars in support of the non-profit's mission. She also raised nearly $1.5 million as chair of the 2012 Heart Ball for the American Heart Association of the Greater Washington Region. "I'm very proud of helping to raise that money because I know it will make a big difference in the lives of people," she says. "I'm also very proud of the operating results of KPMG's Washington office, which is a leader in the firm from a growth perspective, and of my KPMG family tree—those people I've touched and had the opportunity to work with, mentor, and grow. Dollar Tree Stores is one of those clients who had 20 stores when I first began working with them. I was with them every step of the way as we took the company public and helped them buy companies, and they're now an almost $8 billion business."

Focusing on excellence every step of the way is the technique Candy employs each day to bring success to clients like Dollar Tree Stores, and serves as the advice she would give to any young person entering the working world today. "It might be tempting to come in a little late some days, or leave early, or cut a corner here or there, but if you can do a great job every single day, it really adds up," she affirms. "When you look back at the end of a year, or five, or 35, you'll realize you've really built something incredible." And in being our best each day, we not only build incrementally a lifetime masterpiece, but also make sure that we are prepared in any given moment to put our best foot forward, make our point, and show the world what makes us different and worth remembering.

BERNHARDT
WEALTH MANAGEMENT

Jan Fox

When Opportunity Knocks

Jan Fox couldn't tear her eyes from the screen. At six years old, she was watching her first Miss America pageant at her Aunt Lottie's house, finding herself completely lost in awe over the elegance and grace she saw in the women. "I didn't realize it at the time, but my mother was chronically depressed and didn't know how to raise kids," she explains. "Our house was always filthy and disorganized, and while watching that pageant, I really noticed for the first time how matted my hair was and how ratty my clothes were compared to theirs. I went home, wrapped my old bed sheet around me like a gown, and looked at my reflection in the mirror. I distinctly remember thinking to myself, 'I'm out of here.' I knew I was capable of more than this filth and neglect. I wanted whatever that Miss America pageant had represented for me."

Decades later, Jan Fox is not a Miss America, but a four-time Emmy Award winner. She's now five years into her newest adventure, Fox Talks, a consulting business focused on delivering speaking and leadership coaching to individuals from all walks of life. "My goal as a speaking coach is to help you SPEAK! For FULL-BLOWN IMPACT!" she says with enthusiasm. "I strongly believe in the power of tweaks. I can teach you to speak better in order to sell more, or help you gain media attention, and it's all done through exercises and tiny adjustments." She's also a sought-after speaker.

Jan started the business shortly after retiring from D.C.'s Channel 9 News, her final assignment as a reporter for a total of nearly 30 years in the field. Clients began asking for coaching, but she wasn't quite sure how to charge them. She decided her best option was to go to a brander, where she was able to corral her stories. She wanted to know what would have the most impact on those who sought her services. "Looking back on my journey toward Fox Talks, I realized my pattern was just jumping in and doing it," she says. "If I saw something out there I was interested in, I would follow the path and ask questions. When a little crack in the door appeared, I would stick my toe in and see what happened. My dad always said, 'Opportunity knocks; in walks Janet Fox,' and I guess he was right."

Jan and her younger brother grew up in Shelbyville, Indiana, not far from most of her 32 cousins. Her father was a watchmaker for the early years of her childhood, running a little town shop and hunting raccoons on the weekend. His deepest love was serving as a lay preacher for his storefront church. Because Jan's mother had been divorced long before marrying her father, his denomination forbade him from holding the position of Reverend, but he constantly volunteered to help the church. "He was asked to speak everywhere: nursing homes, jails, even substituting for preachers at other churches," she recalls. "When he died, more than 350 people crammed into the funeral home. He really touched people's lives. He had a fierce commitment to his family and his work. It gave deep meaning to his life and ours."

At the onset of the Cold War, her father was summoned to work in the naval ordinance at Fort Benjamin Harrison, using his fine instrument techniques to aid in the construction of bombs. The job came with a pay raise, but the family seemed to always struggle for money, most likely due to her mother's inability to manage a household. As Jan would find out in her adulthood, her mother battled depression and anxiety. She was physically and verbally abuse to Jan and her brother. "Dad would belt us sometimes, but at least we knew what we'd done and how many licks we were getting," she recalls. "Mom was outrageous. It was horrible. I often wondered why he never protected us from her, and my only guess is that he believed in 'honoring thy father and mother.' She was our mother, so we had to do as she said."

Despite her troubles at home, Jan managed to stay a positive, upbeat child, frequently playing baseball at the field by the factory across the street and working in the town dime store or Broadway Café. She served as Secretary/Treasurer of her class, and would sneak off to twirl batons when her father preferred she play the saxophone in the band. She earned good grades and aspired to become a teacher, after lots of playing teacher as a kid. She once taught a boy with special needs to write his name.

"I was always on the fringes of the cool group since I was from the other side of town," she recalls. "I wore my friends' hand-me-down clothes. Even though I sang in the Singing Stars group in high school, I couldn't help but feel less than, so on the inside, I was always pushing for something bigger and better. I could see it and feel it, so I went to work to find whatever it might be."

When she graduated from high school, Jan's father borrowed $500 from the bank to send her to a small church college where she could study to become a teacher. "My mother was against it, but I was determined," she says. "I worked every job I could find to pay my way. Growing up the way I did, working came easily."

In college, she became a cheerleader and finally made it to the in-crowd, making countless friends and falling in love during her freshman year. "He was the smartest guy in the college, and I was very attracted to his linear thinking," she recalls. "He told me he liked that I was a bubbly cheerleader, and that when he took me home, I would do all the small talking with his family so he wouldn't have to interact with anyone." In the middle of her sophomore year, he proposed and they married during her winter break, despite her parents' dismay. "I was only 19, so my mother was livid," Jan recalls. "My father was only okay with it because he came from a good family and had plans to join the Peace Corps after graduating." Her husband's Peace Corps dreams were interrupted, however, when he enlisted in the military to avoid the draft that came with Vietnam. He was assigned to Germany, and Jan finished college a semester early to join him and teach at the Army base nursery school in Munich. Kristin, her daughter, was born there.

After a couple of years back in the states, they divorced. Never one to be down for long, Jan enrolled at Lesley University and earned her Masters degree in education. She went on to teach kindergarten through second grade, and eventually ran workshops for the Greater Boston Regional Education Center. She also worked as a consultant for the Follow-Through Project, a program dedicated to continuing the Head Start Program in grades 1 through 4. She then returned to Lesley to teach graduate education courses and direct the outreach program.

During these years, she frequently traveled for her various positions and worked closely with parents, teachers, and community members. A therapist and instructor from her Master's program was invited to be a guest on a talk show in Boston, and he needed two people to argue as husband and wife, so Jan agreed and spent four Sundays appearing on the show. Eventually, the host position opened, and a photographer encouraged her to apply. She did, but she did not get the job.

A year later, she met a show producer at a little church in Harvard Square who asked to see a sample tape of her TV work. With nothing to lose, Jan hired a cameraman to film her reporting on fake stories to show that she could do the work, if it were offered. A few days later, the producer called, asking her to fill in for a talk show host who had called in sick. "They wanted me to interview the new choreographer of the Boston Ballet, and I said sure," she remembers. "I had no idea what I was doing, and it was on live TV! Somehow I did it, and they continued to call me to report for the show. After a few months, the host left. They offered me a thirteen-week contract that ended up turning into a permanent position."

Jan stayed with the program for several years until the TV station was sold to another network, which cut all local programming and left Jan without a job. With a daughter in high school and no leads, she heard about an opening for a reporter in Portland, Maine, so she flew up for the interview. The meeting went so well that the News Director asked her to sit on set with the anchorman and read the anchorwoman's part. Jan had no experience as an anchor, but she made it through the scripts and landed the job. "It was a huge honor, but also terrifying," she confesses. "It was a big job, and a lot of the responsibility for the ratings would ride, in part, on my performance. I decided to go to every parade, every festival, kiss every baby, and make every appearance possible so that, even if I flunked myself out of the job, I would be embedded in the community."

Jan stayed with Channel 6 for four years, and during that time, she met her current husband, Michael O'Sullivan. After several years of dating, he was offered a job in D.C. that would allow him to put his three sons through college, so Jan began looking for jobs in the area. With the help of her Portland news director, she was invited to meet with Channel 9. "After my interview, they asked me to join them in the conference room so I could meet the rest of the team," she says. "I met one gentleman who was excited to talk with me about Portland and his love of Maine Lobsters. Another gentleman asked me if I would crave the anchor position, since I had been an anchor. I told him that I was at an age where being an anchor wasn't as important as longevity in the business." By the end of the meeting, the general manager told her they were very interested, and that they would be in touch.

Their phone call never came. Jan waited weeks for Channel 9 to follow up, and even despite her calls to the secretary and hand written notes, she waited in vain. She was about to give up hope, when one day, walking down the streets of Portland, she saw an advertisement that read, 'We ship lobsters anywhere in 24 hours.' She went into the store, bought two lobsters, and shipped them to Channel 9 in D.C. with a note that said, 'It would be hard to leave these bad boys behind, but for you, I would.' Sure enough, the station called her soon after to formally offer her the position of General Assignment Reporter.

Jan served many roles while at Channel 9, filling in for the weekend anchors when Glenn Brenner was rushed to the hospital after running in the Marine Corps Marathon. She covered heart-wrenching stories of murders and fallen soldiers, fires and bad car accidents, snowstorms and floods. Eventually, her boss asked her to serve as the consumer reporter on *9 Wants to Know.* "I'm very grateful for every day of that job," she reminisces. "The producer and I worked together with the Fairfax County Police and the Safe Kids' Coalition to start car seat checks, and it made a real difference in people's lives."

After five or six years as the consumer reporter, a new news director disbanded the unit, and several people over the age of 50 were relieved of their duties. Jan was spared, but was later transferred to the Morning Show, which she saw as the metaphorical end of her career. "I wasn't happy about it, but I took the job, went to the ladies room to cry for a minute, and then put my smile back on and went on with it," she says. "The hours were terrible—I should have gone to bed at 7 pm every night, but I wanted to have a life with my hubby. Eventually I realized I was living my life in a stupor from lack of sleep."

After five years of maintaining an unfathomable schedule, Jan finally felt she had had enough. "My husband had just brought home an HD TV, and when I saw myself on the screen, I thought, 'Oh no, I look just like my great aunt Marian!'" she laughs. She decided that, at 62, she was ready to approach the news director and declare her retirement. "I'd interviewed presidents and many celebrities, gotten people their money back, sent thieves to jail, and made a business pay a million dollars in fines to the State of Maryland," she recounts. "I had the opportunity to do some amazing things, but even at my age, I knew there were lots of other things out there that I could get passionate about, and I wanted to do something else. I asked for a severance package for my years of being a loyal and faithful servant, a farewell cake from a nice bakery, and most importantly, a chance to say goodbye on my shows, because so often people just disappear with no explanation. I was very grateful to be given that opportunity."

After Jan retired from Channel 9, she worked for Billy Casper Golf. "I hoped taking that job would mean I was playing more golf but I ended *up talking* about playing golf and working a lot on excel spreadsheets, which really was way too hard for me," she laughs. "After a couple years, the management realized I could help them work on their speaking and presenting skills. I also produced videos for the annual meeting. I kept getting asked to speak and coach on the outside, so I realized I could actually build a business around it. I see the gaps in my clients' communication and have the ability to make those gaps seem smaller. Over time, I learned the art of taking a few steps backward, changing their point of view, helping them through their fear, and helping them move forward."

Although Jan had never held a professional position of authority, she now frequently coaches leadership skills by drawing on her experience at Channel 9. During her fourteen years with the station, she saw at least, nineteen different News Directors and General Managers come and go, creating a culture that was always ready for change. "Because I was able to see such a fast turnover of leaders, I feel I have the authority to speak on what leadership feels like from the inside out," she says. "When I work with CEOs, I tell them that they are the lions and lionesses of the jungle, while I have spent my career as lion food. Because I have fourteen years of experience from the lion food point of view, I can see how the way you speak and present affects those you lead. It's a rare person who can lead fairly, honestly, and from the heart, but I believe the way you speak about yourself and your business determines whether or not people will follow you. Leadership is all in your mouth. It better be driven by heart."

When Jan is not busy with Fox Talks, she devotes her time to her blended family of kids and grandkids, and her husband, Michael, to whom she has been married for ten years. After several years together, Michael showed up on the morning show and proposed. "I can honestly say I love him more today than I ever did before, and I'm so grateful because we are modeling a good marriage for our kids," Jan affirms. "He and my daughter have a wonderful relationship. She was 16 when they met, so he often says she embedded his buttons rather than pushed them." Michael has always been incredibly supportive of Jan's career, so much so that he even came up with her business's name. "I was struggling so much over the branding decisions, and no names were sounding right to me," she recalls. "My husband eventually just said, 'Why don't you call it Fox Talks, because you certainly do!'"

Since starting the business, Jan has written *Get Yourself on TV* and a Minibuk of her speaking practice plans to hand out to clients like brochures, which have been extremely successful. Additionally, she continues to speak all over the country. Her clients are so varied that it's hard to describe her niche. She's spoken at events as vast and varied as International Car Week in New Orleans, a Fantastic 50 IT company in Chantilly, Virginia, and a number of women's conferences. She's spoken at CEO coaching groups like Vistage International, at the D.C. Bar, and at meetings of the International Association of Pet Cemetery and Crematory Owners. "And I only have gold fish!" Jan laughs.

"I have no plans of slowing down any time soon," she affirms. "My husband always says that if I hear a 'no,' I will try a hundred ways to get a 'yes.' It can drive him nuts, but I know that's how I operate, and it's how I succeed. I also do believe somebody bigger than I am laid the path for me and I just walked it. I didn't have *What Color is Your Parachute* back then. That path, coupled with plain, old-fashioned work, helped me go from such meager upbringings to the accomplishments I've experienced over my life, and I wouldn't change a thing. When opportunity knocks, I know what to do."

BERNHARDT
WEALTH MANAGEMENT

Richard Greene

Taking Notes

Through his entire life, Richard Greene has been taking notes. Very early each day, he starts with a fresh piece of paper and writes down the things he plans to do during the day, framing the immediate future with purpose and intention. Then, as the hours unfold, he adds to his daily notes and writes down important matters from his conversations and meetings for later follow through. Keeping up with technology, Richard now scans these notes for safekeeping and later reference, in his computer files.

"I believe the mind absorbs more when you write things down," he remarks today. "And beyond the internal benefits lent from living a thoughtful, reflective life, I also believe strongly in the power of communication within a professional setting. In meetings, my best practice advice is to write down the most salient one-liners and then distribute these "Key Points" to attendees to see if anything needs to be modified or expanded, and to remind them of who is to do what, by when. It's the most literal way to make sure we're all on the same page, and it does wonders for promoting progress, streamlining strategy, and creating a harmonious company culture."

Now the founder of RGA Business Advisory & Venture Funding, Richard has synthesized the salient points from a lifetime of professional experiences and now uses them to help companies and nonprofits achieve success of their own. "As a business advisor and coach, my greatest passion is helping people," he says simply. "I have more years of experience than I'd like to admit, and so many one-pagers of Key Points that my computer memory is packed to the brim. I think there's something in all of that which can help make the road easier for others, and that's what RGA is all about."

Richard launched RGA in the late 1980s. "On the business advisory side of the coin, my goal is to help companies and nonprofits increase their income," he says. "Oftentimes, these organizations concentrate on volume and sales, which are important, but net income at the bottom line is at least as important as revenues. One of my objectives as an advisor and coach is finding specific ways to help clients increase their bottom line by reducing their expenses without reducing the quality of the products and services they acquire, taking advantage of the often little-known tax incentives and credits available to them, such as research and development tax credits, which apply to a broad range of innovations."

Richard also helps with business plans and strategy, often interviewing a company's employees to get their opinions on how it's run and what can be improved, and then reporting back to executives to help implement positive changes. On the venture funding services side, he serves as President of the D.C. Metro chapter of Keiretsu Forum, the largest group of accredited investors in the world. In that capacity, he's part of the Mid-Atlantic region, consisting of New York, Philadelphia, Pittsburgh, and the D.C. metropolitan area. "The overall operation of the Forum started in 2001 on the West Coast, and just like weather, it swept east," explains Richard, who was asked to help form the D.C. chapter. "We blend together early stage companies looking for funding with accredited investors who have the money, and over its 14 years, the members of Keiretsu Forum have invested more than $450 million in early stage companies. Thanks to our extensive vetting process, our cooperative mentality, and our dedication to informing our investors, we're much more than just another angel investing group. By performing comprehensive due diligence on selected companies, reports are issued, so that investors become informed investors before they make their investment decisions. We're a connector between entrepreneurs and investors, and in one capacity or another, we stay with those companies that get funded all the way through their exit."

At its essence, Richard says he is in the "know business." The phrase is derived from one of his heroes, Socrates, who said, "The smart person is the one who knows what he (she) knows, and knows what he (she) doesn't know," to which Richard adds, "but knows where to get it." With an extensive knowledge bank of his own and a keen sense of where to go to get the information he doesn't know, he has an army of experts with which to tackle most business problems and an intuitive understanding of when, and who, to connect. "I'm a true networker at heart, to the point that I've collected more business cards than most people can imagine," he laughs. "I revel in the challenge of connecting the right people to accomplish great things."

Even as a young boy, Richard aspired to pursue a profession where he would be involved with people. He was born in Norwalk, Connecticut, and moved to D.C. with his family at age five. His father had done well as a salesman for Metropolitan Life Insurance in New England, but after the relocation, he got involved in the jewelry business and ultimately ended up with a store of his own on 14th Street in D.C. "I used to spend a lot of time there, and I was his runner," Richard recalls. "I would take the trolley to the jewelry repair shops on F Street for him. Other times I was a young salesman in my father's store, and after waiting for him to finish tinkering late Saturday nights, he'd take me to the Hot Shoppe for a hot fudge cake as my reward." Richard's mother, who had worked in the FBI in Herbert Hoover's offices before Richard and his older brother were born, helped out at the family jewelry store as well.

As a boy, Richard enjoyed playing basketball, baseball, and checkers at the playground just down the street from his house, and he made his first buck collecting for a newspaper route from subscribers. He also took up clarinet and participated in a number of orchestras and bands, including the Police Boys Club band, in which he marched in an inaugural parade. Later on, while attending Roosevelt High School, he joined a fraternity and was given an award for being its best member. He also found the time to organize events for charity, foreshadowing the leadership roles he would play down the road. "My parents taught us to care about people and help others, and my grandmother reinforced that message," Richard remembers. "She was religious, and a lovely lady. She once met a young couple who needed some help as they got on their feet, and even though we lived in a small row house, she invited them to stay with us."

Richard also looked up to his uncle, a prominent local attorney in town who inspired in him an interest in entering the professional world. Yet, as his high school graduation approached, he found himself unsure about which avenue of that world he wanted to pursue. He liked mathematics but didn't love science, so when people suggested he go to engineering school, he was torn. But then, thankfully, someone suggested accounting. "Though I was interested in ultimately becoming a CPA, I also thought it would be a tremendous baseline for any business I might want to get into, and that it could open a lot of doors," he says. "That's what I've found to be the case."

With this vision in mind, Richard earned his Bachelors and Masters Degrees with honors from Benjamin Franklin University, which was later absorbed by George Washington University. He began working part time at a small public accounting firm to help pay his way through college while gaining valuable experience, and after working hours, he and his employer launched and operated a computer service bureau specializing in punch cards that would make the chads of the future look sleek and sophisticated. "I would sit by the programmer, who would take wires and connect them on electronic accounting machines to make changes I suggest," Richard recalls. "That was the beginning of a lifelong trend—I've never really fit the mold of the typical CPA. I was always out there looking for other areas to work on and thinking outside of the box, with a keen penchant for being an early adopter of technology. I was one of the first people to put word processing into an accounting firm, and I assisted the Information Industry Association in forming their Voice Processing committee."

Richard received his CPA license as soon as was legally permitted, at age 21. Several years later, two friends he had taken a CPA review class with had formed their own small accounting firm, and interested in an entrepreneurial opportunity of his own, Richard decided to leave his post to launch a solo venture in their shared office space. They then decided to join forces to create Aronson West & Greene, which later became Aronson Greene Fisher & Co. and grew to over a hundred employees during his twenty year tenure. Shortly before the formation of the firm, Richard got married, and had three children through its early years.

"I think it's great to live your life amongst different worlds," he remarks today. The following years were indeed a conjoining of many different worlds. From five years of power boating on the Chesapeake Bay, to playing basketball with nuns, his life seemed in a state of constant evolution. At work, he spoke about his interest in the entertainment industry to one of his clients, who ran a small club in Georgetown called The Cellar Door. That client began introducing him to artists like folk singer Tom Rush and groups like the Starland Vocal Band, who later wrote the hit songs "Afternoon Delight" and "Country Roads," for which the group and John Denver received Grammy Awards. Richard became a business manager and accountant for these talents, opening up other doors and leading him to work for political satirist Mark Russell at Ford's Theatre, with its artistic director, Frankie Hewitt, and performers like Red Letter Day. He was also put in touch with figures in the sports world, taking on clients like Bobby Beathard and Russ Grimm of the Washington Redskins.

These brilliant opportunities were overshadowed by the tragic loss of Richard's first son, who died at age eight of a blood disorder. "You never get over that," he says. Still, Richard and his wife were thankful for their younger son, and for the birth of a daughter. They fell in love with the adventure of boating and kept a boat on the Chesapeake Bay for several years, and they picked up biking as well. Though they ultimately divorced, they remain close friends to this day, and shortly after their separation, Richard was lucky enough to meet and marry an outgoing and lovely woman named Miriam, who has two sons and at the time was performing in a Baltimore Dinner Theatre.

The accounting firm, as well, underwent a number of name and cultural changes through Richard's twenty-year tenure. "We ended up with ten partners, and for me, that was nine too many," he jokes. Always interested in the world beyond accounting, he struck out on his own to launch RGA Business Advisory and Venture Funding, ushering in a brand new world of entrepreneurship to explore. "It was a rude awakening to have a hundred people to count on one day, and the next to be ordering my own paperclips," he says. "But I never doubted that it was the right thing for me."

Now, as a business advisor and coach, Richard's leadership philosophy centers upon the passion for communication that has always driven him. He places special emphasis on speaking with people about their interests and earning their confidence, not only because it's a good business and leadership practice, but also because it keeps him young. "I'm still a student every day," he avows. "I enjoy hearing about other people and what they do, learning a lesson in one place and applying it in another to engender new possibilities." To this end, Richard is always looking for ways to utilize his connections and experience for the benefit of others. "I've had my ups and downs business-wise, and I think I've learned from all of it," he affirms. "Communication and reputation are key, and doing what you say you're going to do will take you far. These are principles I live by, and they allow me to lead my clients toward the success they're looking for."

Alongside his work through RGA, Richard continues to a play a role in the entertainment industry as part of a group that utilizes its strategic partner distributors to show operas, ballets, rock concerts, classic movies, and other pieces in over 4,000 movie theaters across the world. "The idea is to expose people to entertainment and sporting events at an affordable price, so that shows that would otherwise be cost prohibitive are instead brought to a larger audience," Richard explains. "Beyond being a positive cultural force, the idea is entrepreneurial in the sense that it's like a Pay-Per-View in the movie theater. Classic movies, for instance, often sell more tickets than any other movie for the week they're showing. This indicates that people want access to these cultural and entertainment events, and as someone who has had a lifelong passion for this industry, I'm excited to help expand this access."

In combining his passion with entrepreneurship in this way, Richard is quick to encourage young people entering the working world today to do the same. "Find something you'd be truly happy to do every day," he says. "I really believe in the maxim that, if you love what you do, you'll never work a day in your life." Invoking one of the numerous sound bytes Richard always keeps in mind, he describes the elements of success by using the analogy of a table that needs three legs to stand up. "The legs are the idea, the implementation, and the marketing and promotion," he details. "Only with all three will the table stand up, and it must have a top, which is made up of the resources, expertise, funding, management, and other pieces you put together. In life, as well as in business, this design applies over and over again. But you can't do it yourself—you need a team that's compatible, with everyone rowing the oars in the same direction and with the same interest and passion."

If one were to read through the individual pages of notes that make up each day in the life of Richard Greene, this is the story that would emerge. It's a story of togetherness and family shared between his two marriages, and a rich tradition of love celebrated between the family as a whole, with four grown children and twelve grandchildren, including the six in Israel. "My wife and ex-wife have become good friends, which makes it so comfortable to celebrate holidays and other gatherings with all of our combined families," he says. It's a story of spirituality and music, hard work and fun. It's a story of connection, innovation, and the success that comes from bringing people together in the pursuit of genuine betterment. And most of all, it's a story of learning, because life is a classroom, and Richard is always taking notes.

Neal Grunstra

The Paratrooper

Neal Grunstra was freshly graduated from college when his life suddenly took a dramatic turn. Like so many other young men of his generation, he was drafted into the U.S. military and suddenly forced to come to terms with a new, much harsher reality. The service was a far cry from his loving childhood home in New Jersey, or his days spent working toward his degree at nearby Fairleigh Dickinson University. "I was shocked at how one is treated in the service," he remembers today. "It was quite an awakening."

Blindsided, but not one to shy away from a challenge, Neal chose to join the paratroopers and began the rigorous physical training required to jump out of airplanes. The decision proved to be a fateful one, for his success there would shape his attitude for years to come. "I was just a 170 pound, 6 foot kid, and didn't have a lot of athletic prowess," he says. "I realized that, if I could get through airborne training,

I could be successful at whatever I set my mind to do." After four years in the military, Neal knew that the business world could be tackled—and conquered.

Now the President of Mindbank Consulting Group, a business he founded back in 1986, Neal's career has realized his prediction. In its 27 years, Mindbank has grown from one man to a company of over 200 employees, and although building the business was complicated, his vision was always a simple one: to supply quality workers to businesses in need. His years of experience in the business world had taught him that capable employees are a valuable resource—perhaps the most valuable—and that such people were always in demand. "I always felt that if you had quality people, work got done on time and usually within budget," he explains. "Whereas, when I employed mediocre talent, I was always explaining our overruns to the client." Neal knew these experiences were common to entrepreneurs everywhere. Thus, he founded Mindbank, a staffing company that sought to recruit the most talented people he could find, usually in the IT field, and create a database of freelance workers which today comprises over 90,000 people. With this exceptional network, Mindbank now excels at finding the right person for every project.

Today, the scope of the business has expanded significantly. 14 years ago, it won its first government contract from the Department of the Interior, and since then has increasingly moved into contracting for various departments of the federal government, mainly on IT projects. A few years after that, Neal opened a new office in Denver, hoping to create a more national presence and explore the emergency radio field.

"Staffing remains a large piece of the firm's business, but over the last decade, our work with the government and with emergency radio have become the other two legs of a three-legged stool," says Neal. "We're proud of the very crucial work we do in both those arenas. Technical problems with emergency radio services across the country have played a negative role in many recent national tragedies, like the shooting at the

Washington Navy Yard and a disastrous fire out in Arizona that claimed 19 lives. In each case, the radio services were not functioning properly, exacerbating the crisis and highlighting the pressing need for improvement." Seeking to address this need, Mindbank audits radio systems to ensure their functionality and speed. The company also works with the government to streamline the production of radio towers, eliminating unnecessary redundancies and saving millions of dollars in the process.

Upon its three legs of exceptional capability, Mindbank has achieved remarkable success under Neal's leadership, thanks to his lifelong entrepreneurial spirit. Growing up in Clifton, New Jersey, he was constantly coming up with moneymaking schemes. Even at the young age of seven, he could be found collecting old magazines from around the house to sell to neighbors. "I didn't realize they were used," he laughs. "It didn't work too well. There might have been one kind soul who would buy a magazine or two." Undeterred, he moved on to shoveling snow, working paper routes, and taking on other neighborhood tasks.

Then, at the age of 12, Neal stumbled into the construction site of a large housing development and found himself a new business. "A couple of the guys working asked if I would get them some soda, so I did, and they gave me a dollar," he remembers. "In no time, I acquired a wagon and a big metal can filled with ice and soft drinks, and I'd wander through the housing development selling sodas. I took a day off one day, and boy were they mad!" That summer, Neal made a few hundred dollars, and the desire to be his own boss never left him.

Neal's father was also a role model in that regard. Although his formal education ended after two years of high school, he ran his own successful home-building business. In fact, neither of Neal's parents attended college, but they encouraged his academic pursuits wholeheartedly, and he became the first in his family to obtain his college degree. Later, he returned to school for a Master's and Ph.D., inspired by advice his mother had given him. "She told me that nobody could ever take away my education," Neal affirms. "That was powerful."

After his years at Fairleigh Dickinson and his time in the service, Neal found himself at a crossroads. It was time to choose a career path, and as he pondered his options, the lessons he learned as a paratrooper came into play. "The field of computer science held a certain interest for me," he remarks. "But back in those days, in the mid-60s, the general impression was that you have to be a real mathematics whiz to do that. I was okay in mathematics, but I wasn't a whiz kid. Before being in the service, I would've abandoned the idea of going into IT altogether. But after airborne training, I had a completely different self-concept. I truly believed that if I set my mind to something, I could probably do it, within reason. So I ended up in the computer field."

Neal's first job was with Honeywell, working at the firm's headquarters in Boston. He then transferred to a Honeywell branch in Pittsburgh, where he returned to school and obtained his Master's Degree in Economics at Duquesne University. With a Master's Degree in hand, Neal then landed a consulting position with Booz Allen in Washington, DC, where he remained for a year and a half.

Though the firm provided excellent opportunities, Neal's entrepreneurial aspirations were ultimately reignited by the atmosphere and culture of the large enterprise. "I was constantly being told to keep my hours up, and I knew that, as a contractor, the business was keeping a portion of my hourly rate," he remembers. All the while, he kept his eyes open for a chance to advance in the IT field, and when the perfect opportunity arose, he was ready.

As fate would have it, the University of Pittsburgh hoped to design and build a central information system that, at the time, was exceptionally sophisticated. They brought Neal onboard as part of the management information system project, and although their ambitions were ultimately unrealistic, the university was so impressed with his expertise and skill set that they kept him on to run a research project. "That project was very successful," Neal recounts. "As a result, a year later, they moved me over to run their computer center." In that capacity, Neal's efforts were met with even greater success. He revolutionized their systems, and while it had traditionally taken the university almost two months to print grade reports for their student body, the implemented technology reduced that timeframe to less than two days.

Neal stayed at the University of Pittsburgh for six years, and during that time he met his wife, Jane, and obtained his Ph.D. in Management. Content though he was, he decided it was time to strike out on his own. "I took over as manager of the computer center at age 33," he remembers. "I realized I could do that for another 32 years and retire, but that I couldn't deny the feeling that there might be something else out there for me." Remembering his time at Booz Allen, Neal wanted to utilize his consulting skills and earn the full value of his work. With that ambition, he founded his own IT consulting business in Pittsburgh. When he sold it seven years later, it employed over 60 people.

With one successful business under his belt, Neal knew his future lay in entrepreneurship. He began exploring possibilities and decided Washington, DC was the best location for his hypothetical staffing company. With that, he packed his bags and drove down on September 15, 1986. "At that time, I only knew three people in the city," he recalls. "I thought it was going to be a little bit of a long putt here, but I intended to do it."

Since Jane and their two children were already settled in Pittsburgh, Neal decided the only viable option was long-distance commuting while he ensured a move would be worthwhile. Successful though Mindbank is today, he had his work cut out for him when he decided to single-handedly found and build it in Washington while his wife and children remained in Pittsburgh. For eight months, Neal would wake up at 3:30 on Monday morning, drive the five hours down to Washington, and be on time to open his office at 9:00 AM. On Friday afternoons he would drive the five hours back home to spend the weekend with his family. Still, he believed in his vision, and as he slogged through the first year, he called upon all the forces of perseverance and resilience he'd learned in the military. "Starting out it was just me, and I would make thirty cold calls a day," he says. "It's amazing how lucky you can be after about 2,000 cold calls!" Finally, when things were secure enough to move forward, Neal's wife moved down with their then 7-year-old daughter and 4-year-old son.

Today, both children have found success in their own respective careers. His daughter, now 34, is an attorney for the Commerce Department, and his son, 31, just completed a graduate degree in Cyber Security. To young people entering the business world, Neal stresses the same thing his mother stressed to him all those years ago—education of all kinds. "The business world today is one of continual learning," he avows. "Don't just blindly decide to be done with school once you get your college degree. You have to continue differentiating yourself. Things are going to change over a 30 or 40-year career. As technologies evolve, so does business, and so must you."

He also stresses ethics as the cornerstone of good business, and credits the golden rule as the guiding force behind his leadership philosophy. He considers his management style to be cooperative, and treating people with respect and embracing participative management. "We take the time to clearly lay out the goal, and if we all agree on it, everybody comes onboard and knows what their piece of that objective is," he details. Neal focuses on finding and hiring the right people rather than micromanaging the wrong ones, and this strategy has paid off in spades; his workforce is self-motivated, using their independence to push horizons and drive innovations.

Self-actualization will certainly be a cornerstone of his lasting legacy, both in the workplace and at home. "I'd like our team to feel they've worked for a quality organization," he says. "And I hope my family is inspired, as well, to take those leaps of faith through life." Neal's own leaps started from a plane and translated seamlessly into bold moves that took him to new industries, new businesses, and ironically, new heights. In leaving the service, he chose to go into IT, at a time when the decision was considered a long shot. Succeeding in the IT field, he chose to quit his comfortable position to go it alone. And even succeeding as an entrepreneur, he sold his first company to pursue an even bigger idea. Neal may have left the paratroopers a long time ago, but in the business world, he never quit jumping out of planes.

BERNHARDT
WEALTH MANAGEMENT

Chip Helme

Making the Grade

Dr. Coffinberger, a professor at George Mason University, called Chip Helme into his office one day to review his transcript. "Mr. Helme, I understand you plan to take the upper level accounting classes next year," he said. "But I want you to know that, unfortunately, it is mathematically impossible for you to get the necessary 3.0 GPA to qualify for taking those classes." Chip, who had been so sure of himself and his ambition, felt the wind fall out of his sails. "But, without the upper level accounting classes, how will I become a CPA?" he asked.

After a moment of reflection, his professor offered him a deal: earn all A's in five classes next semester, and he would give him special permission for the courses. Chip was thankful for the second chance and accepted the challenge, but did not leave the office with his characteristic carefree jaunt in his step. His world had been shaken.

That was the day Chip decided to change his entire approach to life, taking his future into his own hands and vowing to mold it into something powerful. For the first time, he decided to make the grade, steadfastly determined to earn his seat in the upper level classes. He moved into a new apartment, trading his party-going roommates for an Air Force ROTC student, and put his head to the books. "I had rarely gotten an A in any class, but I made it happen," Chip recalls. "I reached my goal and earned all A's. I was able to register for my classes, and I never let my grades falter again. I began treating school like it was a job, and once I did that, all the other areas of my life started to improve as well."

Today, Chip is the Managing Principal of Thompson Greenspon, (T&G), a CPA firm located in Fairfax, Virginia. They offer audit, tax, and management advisory services to construction contractors, nonprofit organizations, government contractors, and professional service firms.

The firm was started in 1956 by Gerry Thompson and Irv Greenspon, who stayed active until they retired in the early 1990's. T&G currently employs around 47 professionals—37 CPAs and ten administrative personnel. It has maintained its status as a leader in the local accounting community for decades—an accolade Chip credits to the firm's "family first" culture. "Our staff is our most important asset," he points out. "To have a loyal and dedicated staff, you need to treat them fairly. If they're worried about their family, they won't be able to meet their full potential at work."

The other factor that has led to the firm's longevity is the variety of industries it serves. "Many of the boutique firms out there specialize in just one industry and can eventually run into issues," Chip says. "We maintain our vitality and stability through diversification."

Beyond diversity, T&G also derives its strength and perseverance through adversity. In fact, Chip believes the recent recession actually strengthened the firm. While many other companies crumbled, the T&G partners seized the opportunity to increase training and get back to basics, focusing on hiring the best and brightest. "That choice engendered loyalty, and the good people who make the firm the great company it is today," he explains.

Along with the great pride he takes in his work at T&G, Chip is thankful for a professional career that has kept him within the same twenty-mile radius that he's lived in since he was a young teenager. His father was in the Navy, so he spent the first fourteen years of his life constantly on the move. He attended five schools in the span of nine years until finally settling down in Northern Virginia to attend James Madison High School when his father retired from the military.

Chip is the youngest of four with a ten year gap between himself and his next oldest sibling, so that once he had turned eight, he was essentially an only child. "All that moving made me mature, especially since my siblings were in college for most of it," he says. "I learned how to depend on myself and overcome my natural tendency towards shyness."

Throughout high school, he worked several jobs, including gigs at Roy Rogers and a scuba shop. Although school was not his biggest priority, it was his father's. He encouraged Chip to earn good grades to ensure a successful future. "In elementary school, when I was struggling with my multiplication tables, he would sit me on the basement stairs and have me recite them over and over again while he worked in his shop," Chip recalls. "Once I learned to enjoy math, my father moved on to emphasizing the importance of English. I didn't understand why at the time, but now I'm grateful because as a CPA, I'm constantly drafting letters and calling upon my writing skills."

Chip and his father were extremely close, so when his father died suddenly of a heart attack, he was devastated. "I remember my mother walking into my room at 1:45 in the morning to tell me what had happened, and all I could think was, 'What do you mean my father is dead? How can that happen?' I was only fifteen,'" he recalls. "I was in a lot of pain, which made me act out for a couple months. I got away with a lot of things my father would have never allowed, and I think I exhausted my mom."

His mother, who was an affectionate and understanding person, helped him through that traumatic time. But when Chip's rebellious ways became too much for her to handle, she would send him to his older brother's house in North Carolina for weeks at a time. "My brother, Bob, is fourteen years older than I am, so he really stepped in to fill that father-figure role for me," Chip says. "We had a lot of deep conversations that really helped me through those times."

As high school graduation neared, Chip was accepted to Catholic University, yet given his wild streak, his mother decided he would do better at Virginia Military Institute. Despite his reluctance, he agreed to go in the hopes that joining the military would fulfill his childhood dream of becoming an astronaut. "Looking back, I'm very proud of that year," he says. "It gave me a lot of self-discipline and taught me to pay attention to details. Both of those skills have really helped me in my career."

Though successful in military school, Chip longed to return to Northern Virginia and a non-military lifestyle. With that, he transferred to George Mason University, moved into an apartment with friends, and spent the following two years having the time of his life. "I had my high school and college friends all in the same place, so I relapsed into having a good time and not working too hard," he admits.

Starting at GMU, Chip also was looking for a better fit than the engineering track he was on, and thankfully, a career interest survey pointed him towards accounting. After taking a basic accounting class, Chip found the material made perfect sense to him. "It was so logical, and it just came easily to me," he says. "I enjoyed it and felt empowered every time I worked out the right answer."

Chip fell in love with the field and, seizing his professor's offer of a second chance, he used his new passion to succeed. He took the accounting world by storm, earning top-notch grades in his last two years of college. His junior year, he landed a co-op position as an auditor with the Department of Defense Inspector General.

After graduation, Chip was hired by his very own Thompson Greenspon. The local firm wasn't one of the large accounting firms he had originally hoped to work for, but when he was interviewed by Irv Greenspon himself, they found a perfect match in one another. Months later, Chip passed the entire CPA exam, all four parts, in his first sitting—a feat accomplished by only 17 percent of CPAs. With such notable success, Chip attracted the attention of a number of firms. "My friends told me I should go work for a larger company to keep moving up the ladder, but T&G hired me for who I am. I have incredible loyalty to them for that," he says.

That was in 1985, and Chip has been with Thompson Greenspon for the entirety of his professional career. It has been a career of fulfillment, growth, and satisfaction. Only briefly, nine years in, did he waiver. Feeling that he was ready to be made a partner, he became frustrated by a lull in his advancement. To get to where he wanted to be, he felt he needed to bring in more clients and work more hours, but he and his wife, Mary, had three small children at home. Working more hours would come at the expense of home life—a sacrifice he wasn't sure he could make.

Looking for a solution, he turned to June, his older sister and a social worker by training, for advice. "Having worked in a hospice for ten years, she had sat by many deathbeds and listened to patients speak of their lives. Never once did anyone say they wished they had spent more of their time working," Chip recalls. "They always wished that they had spent more time with their families. Her words stuck with me, so I decided to be patient. I continued with T&G, working the same amount of time but being more focused and intentional. Staying the course turned out to be the best decision I could have made because I was able to keep family first, and within a year, I was made partner."

Five years later, Chip was voted in as the managing partner. While he found it strange at first to make decisions for the older and more experienced partners around him, he takes confidence in the fact that he was voted into the role by his fellow partners, and thus trusted by the people he leads. "When our previous managing partner was ready to retire, we brought in a consultant who had us vote for who we thought was right for the position," he says. "When it came down to it, they decided I was someone they could trust, so ever since, I've put all my efforts into making sure that the partners feel heard."

Chip's open door and consensus-building approach to leadership served him well as a partner. And since taking on his new role at the head of the company, he has noticed his management style continues to evolve in subtle, significant ways. "I've had to learn this the hard way, but you just have to make a decision and not be afraid of making the wrong choice or upsetting someone," he affirms. "More important than futilely trying to make everyone happy all the time, is the ability to be definitive about your decisions and move on. As CPAs, we are very cautious and risk-averse, but sometimes you have to make hard decisions, try something new, and deal with the outcome. As long as you are able to look yourself in the mirror at the end of the day and know you did what you thought was best for everyone, you're making progress."

This steady determination, reflective of his unyielding pursuit of his CPA dream, has allowed him to make the grade in the professional world just as he did back in college. Since 2009, Chip has been named a Super CPA in *Virginia Business Magazine* in the category of Government and Nonprofits. In 2013, he was appointed to CPAmerica's Board of Directors as Vice Chairman, and he will serve as its Chairman during 2015.

Additionally, Chip is the Treasurer of the Fairfax County Crime Solvers and a board member of both the George Mason University Accounting Advisory Council and the Northern Virginia Building Industry Association. But his real passion for community service lies with the Boy Scouts of America. He was President of his explorer post as a young man, and he has served as Scoutmaster and Cubmaster for his three sons' troop.

"I love spending time with my kids and teaching them the lessons I've taken my whole life to learn," Chip says proudly, echoing the advice he would give to any young person today. "When they get discouraged with school, they say they think it's stupid and they don't want to do the work. I say: You may think that, but it's just like a sport: there are rules, and you have to abide by them if you want to play. I'm thankful to my old professor for helping me see that. I doubt he was even aware of his impact, but I left his office realizing that I had the power to determine my own destiny. I think that's an invaluable lesson to learn at any point in your life—that making the grade is about making your future. It's all up to you."

Doris Johnson Hines

The People Behind the Professional

"It was like being struck by lightning," Doris Johnson Hines remembers. She had just been offered a clerkship by one of the coauthors of the 1952 Patent Act—a judge widely regarded as the father of modern patent law. The year was 1993, and she had a job she loved at the firm of Finnegan, LLP, but Dori knew it was an opportunity she'd never get again. With that, she accepted and spent the next several years working for a trailblazer.

One might imagine it was from this clerkship that Dori cultivated her own abilities as a leader, but in truth, she had found herself leading the forefront of change before. In her upper level electrical engineering classes at Rensselaer Polytechnic Institute (RPI), she was often the only woman in the class. Later, she would become the first woman at Finnegan to make partner in the largest group of the firm. It wasn't long before Dori became head of the firm's litigation section, and under her leadership, it won *American Lawyer*'s biennial award for Best IP Litigation Department in 2012.

Winning the award was about more than the firm's practice of excellence, however. At the award dinner in New York City, Dori and her team were seated at a table with the man who had been charged with interviewing them, assessing their candidacy, and summing them up in a profile article. "He told us that one of the things that really struck him about the interview was how we were genuinely nice people—people he'd want to practice law with," she remembers. "It was incredibly gratifying to win and to be profiled in an article in the publication, but to hear the comments about our character made it even better. So much of the 'why' I do what I do is people-oriented, and we're really a firm that enjoys working together and working with our clients."

Ever since her childhood growing up on the south shore of Long Island, Dori's life has been not about defining moments, but about defining people. Her father worked as a repairman for the New York Telephone Company, while her mother stayed home with her two older children and the twins, Dori and Danny. Both parents impressed upon them the value of hard work in everything they did. "Dad often worked overtime and weekends so we didn't have to want for anything, and mom was a constant presence," Dori reflects. "She taught us how important it was to do things the right way, without cutting corners, and she could always say down to the penny how much money was in their checkbook. She managed with a lot less than a lot of other people, and she did it successfully."

As a girl, Dori had a genuine love of academics that left her crying herself to sleep after the last day of first grade, simply because it was summer and she wouldn't be able to go to school the next day. "I was really blessed to have some fantastic teachers along the way that made me want to go and do well," she says.

Dori's natural inclination toward education was augmented by a freedom to wander outside of school that has largely become extinct today. "In our neighborhood, parents sent their kids out to play and to come home at dark," she remembers. "You rode your bike everywhere—it was idyllic, really. We didn't have the boundaries that kids have now." The family lived several blocks from a beach club, and though women's presence in sports did not have the foothold then that it does now, Dori relished her time on the swim team in the summers.

Along with school and play, Dori's character was also strengthened through work and early lessons in fiscal restraint. As a girl, she had a paper route and would deliver the news by bike, and she babysat routinely. When she turned 16, she got a job in the supermarket across the street, delighting in the additional responsibility and saving up enough money to eventually cover the last two years of her college career.

Dori had always had a natural affinity for math, science, and problem solving, but she hadn't considered applying to RPI until she and Danny were filling out applications at the kitchen table together. "So much happens through serendipity," she laughs. "He had an application for the program but decided he didn't want to go there, so he handed it over to me."

Having never had the opportunity to earn college diplomas themselves, Dori's parents were insistent that their children pursue degrees with clear links to marketable job skills, and RPI fit the bill. Though she could have opted for a public school that would allow her to graduate debt-free, she felt it would give her better options and opted to enroll. After taking several classes in computer science, a cutting edge field at the time, she transitioned over to electrical engineering, which felt like a better fit.

By her junior year, however, she felt that something was missing. With that, she decided to enroll in several writing courses, which strengthened her writing skills while also allowing her to escape the male-dominated world of electrical engineering for a few hours each week. "My professor, Annette, was interested in students as people, and always encouraged us to try something different," Dori recalls. "In some subtle way, she's the one who first opened my eyes to the possibility of law. I was studying such a narrow, focused, specific, and technical field at that time, and my classes with her were crucial because they brought me back up for air and compelled me to look at things from a broader perspective."

As she finished up her studies at RPI, Dori began interviewing for jobs, but nothing really clicked until she serendipitously received a postcard in the mail, announcing that the patent office in Washington was hiring. After her classes with Annette, she felt she wanted to channel her finely honed problem solving abilities away from engineering and toward law, which would allow her to interact more directly with people. The federal patent office would be a fine place to test the waters and see if she liked the subject matter, so Dori called the phone number to get an application, had a phone interview, and was offered the job. With that, she hopped in the new car she had just bought with her own hard-earned money and headed to D.C.

After working in that capacity for a year, Dori knew law was the right field for her. She took the LSAT, applied to law school, and enrolled in a four-year night program at George Washington University in 1987. She continued working in the patent office until 1990, when she took her first job with Finnegan, and her willingness to work while going to school allowed her to complete her degree without taking out any additional loans.

Dori married her husband, Rod, in 1993, just before she began the clerkship at the federal circuit appeals court. Prior to the court's establishment in 1982, there was tremendous variation across America in how patent cases were handled, and people could essentially shop by region of the country," Dori explains. "To ameliorate that problem, Congress created this special court and gave it jurisdiction over patent, veteran, and tax case appeals."

After a tremendously enriching experience there, Dori returned to Finnegan in 1996 and began in patent prosecution, helping clients receive patents from the patent office. When she worked in litigation for the first time, however, she felt an immediate affinity for the practice. In that capacity, she had the opportunity to observe Steve Rosenman, a partner at the firm with incredible passion and dexterity. "I was so impressed by how much he enjoyed what he was doing, and by how good he was at it," she remembers. "I knew I wanted to stay right there and do it too."

Dori then had the opportunity to work with a partner by the name of Liam O'Grady, now a Virginia district court judge. "I was so inspired by the way he solved problems and crafted arguments," she says. "He also went about teaching in a very effective, hands-off manner, giving opportunities and guiding without being forceful. From him, I learned that I wanted to be an advocate."

Founded in 1965, Finnegan remains a specialty firm dedicated solely to intellectual property law, with a team of around 400 attorneys spread amongst its D.C., Palo Alto, Atlanta, Boston, Shanghai, Taipei, and Tokyo offices. "While most IP-only firms have merged with other practices in the past decade, ours has not, and has never wanted to," Dori affirms. "We do one thing, and we do it with excellence. We can handle cases big and small because we have such a deep bench of technical expertise."

Today, 60 percent of the firm's practice is geared toward litigation, where Dori's work is now focused. The remaining 40 percent is comprised of noncontentious work like obtaining patents and trademarks or doing opinions and due diligence. Dori's group focuses on electrical and computer-related cases, which entails semiconductor and communications work. The firm also has chemical, pharmacological, and mechanical groups, with substantial overlap between the sections that led Dori to represent the patent holder for technology used in a groundbreaking hemophilia drug. "That case ended up going to arbitration, and we successfully argued it," she says. "It was one of the most interesting cases to work on because it was so far outside the field I usually practice in. It seemed foreign at first, but really, it was a matter of not being afraid to learn the vocabulary and the technology, so I did it, and loved it."

Dori made partner in 2000, and as such, was given the autonomy to develop her own practice—a responsibility she has shouldered with proficiency and grace, thanks to the careful honing of her craft. "As I was coming up, I tried to work with as many different people as possible so I could learn from them," she avows. "I'd knock on people's doors to see if they had anything I could work on, and I'd get feedback from as many people as possible. I wanted to get real breadth of experience, see what I liked, learn what worked for me, and incorporate that into my own practice."

Fortunately, Finnegan is structured to foster an atmosphere in which this style of collaborative growth is truly celebrated. Profits aren't allocated by the work each partner brings in, so partners feel free to call each other if they think someone else's expertise could benefit a case. "It's one fundamental reason our firm has been so successful, and why we're able to engender such positive interpersonal relationships," Dori says.

In advising young people entering the business world today, Dori acknowledges that college graduates are often required to make professional decisions divorced from the reality of what those decisions will look like. "As such, don't be afraid to completely change course if you get a couple years of experience and feel that a different path is right for you." Dori's watched her older brother do just that, graduating from Marine Academy and working on ships for years before deciding to go back to school to become a history professor. "It takes courage to make a choice like that, but it's important," she affirms.

Equally as important is taking the time to give back. Through Finnegan, Dori does pro bono work for veterans and sits on the board of the National Veterans Legal Services Project. Under the Equal Access to Justice Act, the federal government covers the payment of attorney fees for successful veterans cases, and Finnegan donates those fees to veterans charities, making it one of the top five highest charitable donors in D.C.

Just as Dori hoped when she switched from engineering to law, her profession has allowed her to connect with people and truly serve them in ways that are as genuine as they are critical. Every time she sets foot in a courtroom to serve others, however, she is reminded of the most important connections by a small pendant she wears around her neck—a Mother's Day gift given to her by her two children. Routinely required to take long trips to Japan to continue her work at the forefront of the U.S. innovation industry, and often working long hours, Dori's professional success would not be possible without the support and love of her husband and children. "A colleague of mine, Barbara McCurdy, has three children and helped show me how to be a caring person and an accomplished lawyer at the same time," she affirms.

In this sense, as in all aspects of her life, Dori's professional journey is powered by the people behind it. Whether it's the people she's learned from, the people who have learned from her, the people she's advocated for, the people who have inspired her, or the people she's inspired, she makes not a solitary line of footprints, but an extensive web of impact that spans in all directions, and with incredible strength.

BERNHARDT
WEALTH MANAGEMENT

Michael Jacoby

A Winning Philosophy

Michael Jacoby has always had a penchant for winners. But winning, to him, has very little to do with who actually comes out victorious in a game, and everything to do with how the game is played. "Losers in the conventional sense could be winners in my eyes," he explains. "Taking risks sometimes means failing, and to me, that's not a bad thing. To me, winning is all about being positive." With this philosophy, Michael tends to gravitate toward people much like himself—people with an insatiable drive, a fighting spirit, and a winning attitude.

Having also cultivated the belief that people are able to achieve much greater things together than they can on their own, Michael has always been drawn to the idea of finding common ground with others. Even as a young boy growing up in the inner city of Philadelphia in a row house, cohesion and team-orientation were hallmarks of his approach to life. "There were 75 kids on my block, and at any given time, I could walk outside and there would be ten kids to play with," he reminisces. "It was fantastic. And I came to feel that, when people come together to build something bigger than themselves, one and one can combine to equal four."

Michael's teambuilding skills were further honed by team sports and summer camp. To all who knew him, he was a carefree kid doing what kids do best, but beneath it all, he was laying invaluable groundwork for success later in life. Michael is now the co-founder and CEO of Broad Street Ventures, LLC, a commercial real estate firm in the Washington, D.C. metropolitan area that buys and develops commercial assets, as well as its fully-owned subsidiary, Broad Street Realty, LLC, a firm specializing in property management and commercial brokerage. And it's his ability to unite people in win-win situations, forming genuine bonds and teambuilding to achieve results, that has brought his entrepreneurial ventures to success.

Broad Street Ventures, LLC was founded by Michael in 2002 with his partner, Thomas Yockey, and has since distinguished itself as a D.C. metropolitan area market leader in the purchase and development of commercial assets, including shopping centers, office buildings, warehouses, and condominiums. Six years later, in 2008, Michael started a brokerage firm, Broad Street Realty, LLC. This subsidiary represents businesses, helping them find their space or solve a real estate dilemma.

"Managing equity is part and parcel of what we do. Commercial real estate is competitive, and we try to pursue vertical growth by finding niches," Michael states. "Our physical footprint is now growing beyond the D.C. area as we take on the management of assets from Philadelphia to Richmond, and we just opened an office in Denver, Colorado. We've had real success with value-oriented necessity retail, or shopping centers in densely populated areas, and have bought nine shopping centers in the past two years." What started as a group of four people has now turned into a team of over 50 employees—a true testament to Michael's determination to build a successful business amidst the worst economic climate this country has seen since the Great Depression.

Professionally and personally, Michael loves to help people, and that instinct remains at the heart of the company's mission today. Indeed, the cornerstone of Broad Street Ventures's mission is helping people achieve the results they want. "Universities often get donations in real estate, and there was a case where a university got a farm but had no use for it," says Michael. "So we explained their options and helped them make the best decision possible."

Michael's father, a high school football coach and summer camp director, taught him that leading the team to a win equals a win for everyone on the team, and this kind of positive and cooperative mentality has served as a catalyst for his own prosperous career. His favorite memories as a kid all included being part of something wonderful and successful, whether that was a sports team or a classroom. Raised in inner city Philadelphia, Michael didn't want for much and was most content playing sports with his buddies. "I practically grew up in the locker room," he explains. "And I spent every summer at my Dad's summer camp in the mountains of Pennsylvania, which was like an extended locker room."

Both his mother and father were academics with multiple advanced degrees, earning respectable livings in the field of education. His mother was an inner city school principal and moonlit as a college professor, while his father was a college professor, educational administrator, high-school football coach, and summer camp director. He was also the leader of several Jewish organizations, and eventually became the deputy superintendent of the Philadelphia school district. Michael inherited his father's commanding presence and his mother's tendency to speak her mind. "I've had to tone down my outspokenness a bit in business in order to be more diplomatic," he laughs.

Michael played several sports during his adolescent years, his favorite being football, where he played center. True to form, he was known as the person who called the huddle and as the commander of the line. Required to be efficient in this position is the desire to take responsibility and ownership, which came rather naturally to Michael, laying the groundwork for what was to come as an entrepreneur.

Michael also spent his younger years waiting tables, parking cars, and working construction. In his freshman year of high school, his football coach and mentor saw great potential in him but knew he needed some direction. His coach sat him down one day for a pep talk and spoke to him about dedication and commitment. "That was a notable turning point for me because I realized that I didn't just want to be well-liked," he remembers. "I also wanted to be a good man." The change did not occur overnight, but little by little, Michael went from an average kid to being very serious about his commitment to excellence.

For college, Michael attended Washington and Lee University in Lexington, Virginia and graduated with a degree in biology. He spent summers at the beach, where he made decent cash working in restaurants—enough to secure payment of his fraternity dues and car fees for the upcoming school year. Upon graduating, he received a half dozen job offers and ended up taking one at a hotel in Washington, D.C. He started as a trainee and then became the nighttime controller, where he was responsible for accounting in the business operations. Michael wasn't too fond of the graveyard shift from 11:00 PM to 7:00 AM, but he succeeded in negotiating a 35 percent pay raise. After four months, Michael went to the General Manager and bluntly asked what his career trajectory might be. The GM replied that it took him 10 to 15 years to get where he was, so Michael quit the next day knowing he did not want to follow that track.

Just barely 22 years old, he landed his next job at Merrill Lynch Realty in residential sales and enrolled in night school to obtain his real estate license. Through networking and hustling, he quickly became Rookie of the Year at Merrill Lynch. Not long after that, he met the woman who would become his first wife, and her father was in commercial real estate leasing. "He hired me and handed me a phone, phone book, pen, and piece of paper, and said to make it so," Michael recalls of his future father-in-law. Michael was heavily self-taught in sales tactics by that time, having read everything on the subject he could get his hands on. He connected with top internet technology people via networking, and his efforts won him a blue-chip client. "This client had an internet company and taught me about entrepreneurship at it's grittiest level—how to bootstrap a company, how to make a big pitch at a high level, and how to sharpen my pencil on financial models. He's one of my best friends today," Michael says.

Michael's blue-chip customer was the catalyst for jumpstarting his first development company, which he sold in 2001, and Broad Street Ventures came about the following year. He and his partner launched Broad Street with a no-travel policy so that he would get to see his kids, who were 5, 7, and 9 at the time. Michael is now married to a beautiful woman named Nathalie, who has two children, making a family of seven altogether. "She's the yin to my yang," he avows. "I operate at a very high energetic level, running at full-speed from 5:00 AM onwards and often having to force myself to slow down. My wife is the perfect opposite of me—calm, quiet, relaxed, peaceful. We balance each other beautifully, and being a father to our children has really made me want to be better in life so I can take better care of them."

Just as much a family man as he is an entrepreneur, Michael is of German ancestry and stays grounded in his roots. His great-grandfather was executed in the Holocaust and left behind a gold pocket-watch with his initials on it—an heirloom that continues to guide Michael's efforts today. "What it means to me, is that I should never stand for allowing anybody to feel the way my family felt back then," Michael describes. "I don't judge any book by its cover. I give everyone a chance. The watch is a reminder of where I came from, and of my duty to never stand for injustice."

In leadership, Michael surrounds himself with people who share a common strain of honesty and true dedication to their work. "I'm very focused on making sure I have the right people on the bus," he points out. Above all, he honors respect and communication and emphasizes these things as critical in developing a strong team at work. "Sure, I want to be profitable, but the focus of my day is on making the people I'm working with feel successful and reach their potential," Michael says. "If a team member is having a family issue and we're in the middle of a big project, I tell them to go take care of their family. The project and customer can wait, and if the customer can't wait for something like that, maybe we're not the right fit for them." This inclination to put his people first stems from those earliest days playing with neighborhood friends and on sports team, and is part of what makes him the extraordinary leader he is today.

Michael's altruistic stewardship of others' needs extends beyond the scope of his business and into the charitable endeavors he prioritizes. "I believe in being an involved member of society, and that human beings have a duty to participate and be aware of the world they're living in," he affirms. With this in mind, he served as the Chair of Fundraising for the first annual 5K run for Columbia Lighthouse for the Blind and Visually Impaired (CLB), a D.C.-based organization. Visual impairment is a major problem for war veterans, and Michael proudly supports the local CLB in their efforts to not only raise money, but to find employment for veterans as well.

In advising young people entering the working world today, Michael highlights the significance of bringing passion into whatever they do. "If you don't care, no one else will," he counsels. "And don't be afraid to break the rules. To develop a unique and effective leadership style, one must make their own rules, to a certain degree."

If Michael's success is built on the foundation of teambuilding skills he laid as a child, each brick of his success is a different relationship he's fostered, and the mortar between those bricks is communication—not the impersonal communication of the social media age, but the old-school methodology of simply picking up the phone. "It's hard to build deep, meaningful relationships with human beings via tweet, text, and email. Those are great tools, but an email has no emotion," he conveys. "Pick up the phone, go for coffee, or go to lunch with someone. Face-to-face communication is undervalued and underestimated in this day and age of technology, but it's a tried-and-true method for genuine connection, for which there is no replacement."

Michael's relationships and life philosophy are also fortified by the concepts as simple as the Golden Rule, which he's reminded of each day by his great-grandfather's watch. "It's important to me to treat each person the way I'd want to be treated," he remarks, proving that a simple and principled way of being brings much happiness and success. "I'm also a firm believer in the idea that life is a marathon and not a sprint, and I consider it an ongoing learning experience to discern when to slow down and when to pick up the pace." As a competitive triathlete who has completed several half Ironman triathlons, he lives this idea both figuratively and literally. "It's as true now as it always has been," he affirms. "You're only as good as the guy next to you, and it's as much about the process and performance as it is about the end result. So if you can make that other person better, you're all the better for it, and if you play the game with integrity and heart, it's a win no matter what."

BERNHARDT
WEALTH MANAGEMENT

Greg Kundinger

Proving Yourself

It's never really easy to point a finger at the exact moment someone decides to strike out as an entrepreneur. It's a process—sometimes one filled with a lifetime of experiences that prepare the entrepreneur to go it alone. For others, it is a singular idea so unique that there is no one to share the risk. In other cases, there are simply those who want to be their own boss.

Today, two decades after founding HomeFirst Mortgage, Greg Kundinger has no regrets about deciding to go it alone. His story is about someone who wanted to work for himself. That goal has kept him true to his vision in spite of the many obstacles that present themselves to the entrepreneurially-inclined.

Growing up outside of Detroit with his two brothers, Greg got an early start on learning to work for someone else. Reflecting on the job he held in his father's company at age 14, he laughingly remembers working in the warehouse for fifty cents an hour. "Frankly, upon reflection, I may have been overpaid, since having fun on the job was as important as filling orders," Greg recalls. Nonetheless, his time working for his father taught him the value of a job. His summers working in the family business also allowed him to witness firsthand the challenges and rewards of his own father's entrepreneurial efforts. While eventually his brothers decided to join their father in the family business, Greg could not see a time when, as the middle brother, he would ever be in a position to run the company. So, despite the fact that he would never join the family business, Greg is proud to acknowledge the very things that would enable him some day to strike out on his own—the many lessons he learned over the years from his father.

While Greg's work ethic and determination have ultimately proved to be powerful forces throughout his life, just as potent, if not more so, has been his ability to engage in a kind of motivational judo—the process of turning positive and negative feedback alike into more driving energy. This essential skill was exemplified early on by encounters with a high school coach and his personal and academic counselor, each presenting Greg with two very different evaluations of his potential.

On the positive side was his track and field coach. An award winning coach, he was remarkable for bringing out the best in his athletes and for getting them to work together for the success of the team. During Greg's senior year, the coach led the team to a state championship. Incredibly, the team won without a single first place finish. Greg's coach's concept of team and shared goals elevated his programs and made him beloved by his charges. Greg, as one of the only triple-varsity athletes in his high school, was never going to be one of the most talented members of the team. "I certainly was not one of the four fastest quarter mile runners on our team, but coach made sure I was one of the four members of the award winning mile relay team," Greg recalls. "He let me know that my inclusion on the team was out of his respect for my triple sport efforts, my hard work, and my attitude.

His faith in me and his success in teambuilding have inspired me and guided me throughout the years. He let me know that, with hard work and honest effort, all things are possible."

On the negative side was Greg's high school guidance counselor. Though Greg was a member of the National Honor Society, a class leader, and a regular member of the Honor Roll, the counselor was a study in the art of discouraging the possible. At one point, in a conversation with Greg, the counselor had the temerity to criticize him for the notoriety Greg had received for his athletic endeavors. Greg was simply dumfounded. He felt the criticism was undeserved, as he explained to the counselor that his teammates knew that they were a very integral part of his success. Over time, Greg continued to receive discouraging advice from this counselor, including his suggestion that Greg lower his expectations for his college choices. "Fortunately, I have never discouraged easily," Greg affirms. "His comments to me at the time certainly had a profound impact on me. Who knows—perhaps that was his true intent? All I know is that the word 'can't' is simply not in my vocabulary. Clearly, the relationship with this educator still resonates with me."

Between these two contrary influences, Greg quickly realized that both forms of feedback, if channeled properly, could be a powerful motivator. The lessons learned from each of them would prepare him for the challenges ahead. From then on, he would forever use affirming support to embolden him and doubts to motivate him. "As I grew up," Greg says, "my size left me feeling, as an athlete, that I was an underdog. I actually loved overcoming people's doubts. Frankly, I still like being underestimated. It certainly keeps you humble. Channeled properly, it can also serve as your motivation. One of the very special satisfactions in life is proving people wrong."

After college came enrollment in law school. After a year, however, Greg decided to leave to work on a political campaign in Washington, D.C. "My heart was not really in law school," he admits. "The University felt, and I agreed, that I should take some time to make sure that a career in law was what I really wanted." With the nation in the middle of another presidential campaign season, the timing was perfect. So, seeking adventure, off he went to Washington to join the re-election efforts of the President of the United States.

Over the course of the campaign Greg would work with some of the preeminent politicos of the day. As is the custom in political campaigns, campaign aids dream large. The mere thought of victory filled him with tantalizing thoughts of a position with the administration, eventually a lucrative post-White House career, and perhaps someday, a political office of his own.

But, as happens in every election year, someone loses. In this case, it was Greg's candidate. Left without a preeminent position in the White House, he took the next best opportunity available to him at the time—a job as a busboy and waiter in a restaurant in Georgetown. As luck would have it, on the night of the new president's inauguration, a toilet overflowed. When his manager told him that it was his job to clean it up, Greg took stock of his situation and simply said to himself, "What on earth am I doing? We need to reevaluate." Using the incident to motivate him, he returned to law school, this time with a renewed commitment. "Some of these crazy experiences have certainly served as moments of clarity. They have shaped me," he affirms. "If I had never had these experiences, I am not sure my success would ever be as durable or as satisfying."

After successfully completing law school, Greg returned to working political campaigns in Washington, D.C., and later in New Hampshire. Still, a victorious campaign eluded him. When the unsuccessful candidate in New Hampshire offered him a position with his new company, a business on the cutting edge of the agricultural biotechnology industry, Greg jumped at the chance to join him. Over time, from delivering a litter of pigs in a three-piece suit, to working in tom turkey barns in the southeast and hog farms in the Midwest, he found his experiences with the company were as enlightening as they were exciting. But, after a few years of fits and starts, the future of the biotech firm remained uncertain. It was time to return to Washington.

A fortuitous conversation with a developer friend set him on the path that sustains him today. Upon mentioning to his friend that he wanted to resume a career in real estate, which he had started while in law school, he was instead encouraged to investigate the nascent field of wholesale mortgage banking. After a brief introduction to the industry with a local mortgage company, Greg settled on a position with a small mortgage origination startup. Seven years later, after a successful tenure that included promotion to president and exponential growth in mortgage originations, it was time to realize his own dream. Greg resigned his position to start his own company.

With that, in 1993, at age 40 and with two minority partners, Greg launched HomeFirst Mortgage Corp. He took with him the lessons learned over a lifetime, and through the ensuing years, those lessons have helped him persevere in an industry and an economy that have experienced unprecedented volatility. "Upon reflection, to be an entrepreneur is to live a life of incredible highs," Greg said, "and sometimes some pretty frightening lows."

The housing debacle is a prime example of this. "After spending our first ten years building a strong origination sales team, a rock solid reputation, and a strong balance sheet, we suddenly began to see storm clouds on the horizon. Our company grew, as you can imagine, along with the rest of the market," Greg says. "At one point we had 125 people working with us. While the easing of credit standards helped to fuel the explosive growth of the mortgage industry, since it allowed marginally qualified buyers into the market, it became pretty clear that the housing market was becoming a house of cards. It was apparent that we were playing a game of musical chairs. Increasingly we became concerned for the 'last' person in. What was going to happen to that person if the music suddenly died, if they could no longer sell their home? And believe me, the music certainly died. The housing debacle started as a trickle in 2007. When sellers could no longer find buyers, the 'house of cards' began to crumble. Suddenly, it seemed that everyone wanted to sell, but there were no buyers. Values had peaked and were now falling—fast. Within a year, the housing sector crash was reaching catastrophic proportions. No one could have imagined how far and how fast the economy would fall. We certainly hoped that we had prepared our company for the turmoil that was sure to follow."

As the markets collapsed and foreclosures became commonplace, HomeFirst was fortunate to escape the fate of so many other mortgage origination companies. "Fortunately, we had never been much of a player in the subprime markets," Greg says. "We never really tried to push the envelope to provide financing to unqualified homeowners. In the end, we weren't faced with fateful calls from our lenders requesting that we repurchase loans for clients whose homes had gone into foreclosure. We had always been very, very conservative. In fact, our loan originators were very much aware that we had a zero tolerance policy for the doctoring of a file. Fraud perpetrated by an employee could easily put the company at risk of repurchasing a loan originated by the company. An enforced repurchase request could amount to a corporate death sentence. Our policy was very simple—if we found fraud in a file, we would fire the employee and refer them to the government for prosecution. This explicit policy served us very well, for in the early aughts, when lending standards were eased and home values soared, the lure of big, fast money brought a lot of ethically challenged people to the industry. Clearly we were not the right fit for those inclined to take short cuts, so we avoided many of the problems that subsequently besieged our industry."

For Greg, the most brutal financial crises in his memory simply provided another opportunity. While there remain a host of talented competitors, many more fled the industry during the crisis. He considers his company to be a survivor—battle-tested, more efficient, considerably more experienced, and better prepared to compete in the marketplace.

Today, HomeFirst is a company of 60 people. It closed a third of a billion dollars in mortgage originations last year. In continuous operation since 1993, HomeFirst is headquartered in Alexandria, Virginia.

In discussing his survival, Greg is quick to point out that the credit does not rest on his shoulders alone. "We are still here today because we have wonderful people working for the company," he affirms. "The average length of employment here is between seven and ten years. Some of our key employees have been with us for over eighteen years. Attracting and retaining exceptional talent has been just one of the many ways we've been extraordinarily lucky."

Beyond the quality of the HomeFirst team, Greg's management style has enabled some of his own best qualities in his workforce. "What I have tried to establish over the years is an organization that is simply an umbrella with a lot of quasi entrepreneurs under it," he describes. "I'm really committed to passing along the idea that you, as the employee, are in control of your own destiny. My philosophy, drawing from a lifetime of experiences, is to create a company where ideas flow up as well as down, where the success of the one can create success for the many, and where teamwork and individualism can find a home together. If we can foster an entrepreneurial atmosphere and limit the risk to the individual, I believe the employee will enjoy much greater job satisfaction. It's not my habit to simply tell them what to do—rather, I lead by example, support them, and create a productive and creative environment. The fact that people have stayed all of these years could be considered a testament to our philosophy and is one of the things I'm most proud of in my professional life."

Greg's management style is an extension of his family—especially his parents. "I think the most important thing in life is your value system," he says. "And my parents' values were just unbelievable. I certainly learned my values from them. My mother turned 86 this summer. Her values have never wavered. My parents were always honest and fair. We might not always agree, and they didn't always withhold judgment, but they were always fair."

Today, Greg and his wife, Lari Anne, are proud parents of a college-aged daughter, Kelly. And as a father now himself, he echoes the father he learned from so long ago. "When my brothers and I were children," he says, "he bought each of us a telescope. We knew, of course, it was his way of showing his affection, but we also knew it was something more than that. It was his way of demonstrating that there was something larger than all of us. He came from a very poor background. He saw the world as a merchant marine aboard an "oiler" at the end of World War II. Some might say that he could have been excused for failing to dream big. But he did dream big, and ultimately achieved much on his own. None of this was ever lost on me. Today, I still have that telescope—a continuing symbol of how important dreams and family are to me. I hope that Lari Anne and I can pass that vision along to our daughter, too."

With Kelly only a couple of years from graduating college, words of advice to graduates are not far from his thoughts. "Take whatever job you can get and do it to the best of your abilities," Greg implores. "The problem today is that too many eschew the idea of the entry level position. But I cleaned toilets with a B.A. and a spot in law school. I worked the phones for political campaigns and did a stint as a fundraiser. I worked with turkeys and hogs, swept floors, and promoted rap concerts. At times I worked for pauper's wages. I didn't let any of it defeat me. None of the challenges I faced along the way dissuaded or discouraged me. Rather, they brought clarity, purpose and motivation. They taught me perseverance. Don't be afraid to take that entry-level position. Prove that you are dedicated, a team player, and willing to work hard at the task at hand, whatever it may be. Make yourself indispensible. My own company is a perfect example. We typically promote from within. I like the idea that I have been able to get to know someone's strengths, attitudes, and philosophies. And perhaps most important of all, when hiring from within, I know that we can trust them to protect the integrity of the company."

Success in business can be the result of many factors, but as Greg's story demonstrates, it all starts with you. Proving yourself is ultimately not about proving yourself to others. "Rather, it's far more important than that," Greg affirms. "In the end, it's really about proving something to yourself."

BERNHARDT

WEALTH MANAGEMENT

Juli Anne Callis Lawrence

Life Without Limits

"If you had no limits, what would you do?" This was the question posed to Juli Anne Callis Lawrence by the man interviewing her for the position of VP of Emerging Technology and Business Development at the American Electronics Association Credit Union's Silicon Valley location. The organization, founded in 1979 and later to become KeyPoint, was designed to serve the banking needs of individuals working with companies in the technology industry. The Credit Union was growing at warp speed just as the technology sector was beginning to see significant growth. As an early Apple and internet fanatic herself, Juli Anne had a feeling she had come to the right place, and when her interviewer posed that question to her, she knew the answer immediately. If she had no limits, she'd do exactly what she had always done, because Juli Anne was raised believing there were no limits. It was a certainty ingrained in her throughout her charmed childhood, and which life's inevitable hardships have only served to strengthen so that, today, she lives as limitless as ever.

Juli Anne's parents were both brought to America from Europe as small children, and they grew up fully embracing the possibility of their new country. Nothing was taken for granted, and anything was possible. "They rejoiced in the potential and opportunities of life, and they breathed that into their children," she recalls. "That excitement and belief in America and in life without limits is the common thread that has shaped every choice I've made. I had an exceptionally rich childhood that gave me a solid intellectual and emotional grounding, and which allowed me to launch at a young age, and that's exactly what I did."

Born and raised in rural Long Island, Juli Anne was the middle of three children. Her father, a scientist at the Brookhaven Laboratory on the Atomic Energy Commission research team, walked with the steely character that only the GI Joe generation could engender, and as his namesake, Juli Anne absorbed his strength of will. "The lab was a big part of our lives growing up," she recalls. "It would throw family events and picnics, and that atmosphere really inspired in me a love of science and math." Her mother, a homemaker for most of Juli Anne's childhood, was a chairwoman for the League of Women Voters and contributed a civic influence to her daughter's upbringing when she held young Juli Anne up on a stadium chair in an arena where John F. Kennedy was speaking.

Beyond the sciences, Juli Anne's childhood was shaped by art and music, in which many members of her extensive family tree excelled. Her grandfather owned a beautiful summer home near the water, and she would join dozens of her cousins in running around and rejoicing in "the wonder of it all." Spunky, strong-willed, insatiably curious, and tirelessly vibrant, she fished and climbed trees, seeing no reason why girls should behave any differently than boys—a blindness to culturally imposed gender limitations that she never grew out of. She was also her father's shadow, accompanying him to the lab to watch him work on projects or into the city to see museums and matinees. She dreamed of one day becoming an astronaut, flying where she belonged—high above the earth and the artificial limits society so often imposes.

Amidst this charmed childhood, Juli Anne's father didn't feel his whiz kid daughter was being challenged enough in public school, so he sent her to the most rigorous parochial school he could find at that time. Academically, the sisters pressed their students to be all they could be, and Juli Anne thrived in that environment. "One of the nuns told me I was a social butterfly with a big brain, and that it was her job to make sure I used that brain and didn't just flit about," she laughs. "As a child, I had embraced the idea that learning was fun, and my teachers really encouraged me to continue that narrative. I had a ball with my classes—so much so that I finished high school within three years."

By the summer she was 16, Juli Anne was selected to begin college studies in oceanography at Stony Brook University with hopes of transferring to Virginia Tech with her family after her father finished building a new family home in Blacksburg. All of that changed, however, when he collapsed one day near Thanksgiving when Juli Anne was 17. Years of radiation exposure had caused tumors to grow around his brainstem, and at the age of 49, he became permanently disabled and was never quite the same again.

The effect on his adoring daughter was equally profound. Five days after his diagnosis, she was in a serious car accident that totaled her 1968 Mustang and left her in and out of hospitals for months afterward, and while she was lucky to be alive, the trauma launched her into a rebellion against the cruel twists of fate that seemed to threaten all that mattered to her. Having lost some of her scholarship money for college, and with the dynamics of her family reeling from the vacuum left by its incapacitated patriarch, she dropped out of school. "Let's just say the world flipped, and my orientation changed," she remarks today. "I needed to escape the pain of what had happened to Dad, and I wanted to discover new things about life. I needed to show myself again that life has no limits."

With that, Juli Anne went on a journey in both the spiritual and temporal sense, heading around the globe to live overseas and work at Citi Bank in Guam, where she enjoyed utilizing a platform that allowed her to flex her math muscles while processing loan applications. "This journey at such a young age connected me to the sense of possibility as I worked with people from the Philippines, Japan and Thailand," she remembers. "I recommend all young people find a way to journey out to other lands before they settle into their formalized path in life."

When she returned to the U.S., she decided to continue her studies and enrolled in East Carolina University. "I had learned by the time I got there that life happens," she says. "A *lot* of life happens. I started to think about things pragmatically, and I realized that I especially loved the content of the Community and School Health Education degree program at their School of Allied Health and Social Professions. I thought I'd get a Master's in Public Health Administration and do my piece of good work in the world through that."

To pay for her education, Juli Anne fell back on a skill she developed in secret at the age of 15: waitressing. When her 16-year-old friend Karen got a job serving at IHOP, Juli Anne had been eager to follow suit, but her parents had told her to instead focus on academics and family. With that, she took the job in secret, only to be discovered when an uncle came into the restaurant. She was obliged to resign, but she came to think of waitressing as a fun mental game that she eagerly picked back up to earn money while working toward her degree.

Charles Callis, the assistant manager of the family restaurant where she worked, didn't know what to make of the brash waitress who wouldn't use a pad and pencil to write down orders as he instructed. Instead, she'd whisk around the room, taking as many orders as she could fit in her brain at once before dumping them at the counter. He couldn't deny that she worked the floor faster, made more money, and impressed the customers better than any of his other servers, nor could he deny the power and pull of her spirit. It wasn't long before the two were married, and that's when Juli Anne got serious about growing up.

Upon earning her degree, she landed a job as Director of Aging Services for Greene and Lenior Counties in North Carolina because she achieved the distinction of Outstanding Woman for the School of Allied Health and Social Professions and was subsequently named Outstanding Young Woman of America. As the Director of Aging Services she set up and directed Meals on Wheels, in-home care, and other social programs for over 1,000 seniors throughout the rural, needy region. Passionate about health and wellness, she found the job to be among the most fulfilling positions of her life, as it allowed her to help people embrace a fuller life and a better future, just as she and Charles were doing. They bought a house in Greenville and had a son, Adam, followed closely by their daughter, Lisa Anne. Both pregnancies were fraught with medical hazards, with Juli Anne herself facing a brush with death during Adam's birth and Lisa Anne a 26-week gestation baby requiring extensive treatment in the neonatal intensive care unit. But the spirit of the growing Callis family couldn't be broken, and though their children were little, Charles encouraged Juli Anne to continue her education. "He really gave me wings," she remembers. "He said I had the brain and the talent to do it, so I needed to. We've always had each other's backs like that and been incredibly supportive of each other through everything."

They hardly had time to sink into the rhythms of life, however, before Juli Anne's mother was diagnosed with cancer. Juli Anne was allowed a year-long leave of absence to return to New York and stay by her mother's side as she fought for her life. When that year was up and it was clear the fight was far from over, Charles left his family's grocery store and farm businesses to join his wife and kids in New York. Looking to turn the prolonged hiatus into a productive experience, Juli Anne began selling some real estate, enrolled in graduate school, and then began working for CitiBank again. "I had no intention to go into banking," she remarks. "But I ended up in marketing and marketing segmentation for those three years, until my mother finally recovered enough that we could return to Murfreesboro, North Carolina and pick back up the life we'd left behind."

Finally back home in North Carolina and looking for something meaningful to do with her time, Juli Anne spoke with a headhunter, who found her a job in Norfolk for the U.S. Navy. It was 1983, and the military was downsizing, turning nonessential jobs into civilian billets. A man by the name of Admiral Wilson was running the Navy resale system for the entire globe, utilizing a big business model to create a field support office by dividing the world into seven regions, each with a civilianized billet with its own specialty. Equipped with the consumer research, market segmentation, and statistical modeling experience she had picked up at CitiBank, Juli Anne was hired as the Executive Director of Sales Coordination for the Mid-Atlantic Region of the U.S. Navy, which covered Iceland, Bermuda, Europe, and the Mid-Atlantic States. In that capacity, she was responsible for over $500 million in annual sales and personnel operations, and was instrumental in introducing McDonalds into Naval Hospitals and Ship Stores afloat. While at the Navy, Juli Anne was also the recipient of the Superior Accomplishment Recognition Award, the highest honor a civilian can earn from the Navy. She was living life true to her spirit, without limits and with great plans for the future.

"But while man plans his path, God directs his steps," she avows now, reflecting back on what happened next. Juli Anne was traveling for work as she often did, and Charles was on his family's farm with the children, when Adam suddenly lay down and could not be resuscitated. At the age of ten, he suffered sudden death from an undiagnosed genetic cardiac disorder, marking the single most transformative event of his parents' lives. "The truth is that the rubber met the road, and through that first year after Adam left, I really had to determine if I wanted to stay on this planet or not," Juli Anne remembers. "One of the most tangible mementos we have of him is an audio recording of his voice from when he was dressed up as a shepherd. On the tape, he says, 'And I will live in the house of the Lord for ever and ever.' I know that's where he is now, and I find that divinely comforting."

As it had done when her father fell to the ground so many years earlier, life folded in on itself and called into question the deep faith and tireless spirit that formed its very roots, but Juli Anne reflected back on what she had learned since then. "My father lived through that, and he and my mother actually embraced a very full life afterward," she remembers. "My mother became an RN in her forties because the experience had engendered in her a desire to change the world for the better. And as soon as my father could walk again, he began working with the VA to help others. There was no sitting down or holding back—as long as they could breathe, they were helping others. They really showed me that, when something strikes, you rebound and go forward, and life becomes good again. Charles and I would both walk forward in life, but not without embracing tremendous transformations inspired not only by our son's departure, but also by the wonder of his presence while we had it."

With that, the family that had once been country club Christians began a pursuit of genuine meaning—and they didn't waste a moment. As they left the gravesite of their son after the funeral, Charles told his grieving wife that they were going to do something meaningful with their lives. He left the family businesses and enrolled in Wake Forest Seminary—among the most freeing and fulfilling moves of their lives— and Juli Anne left the Navy to spend more time with their daughter. When Charles graduated several years later, he was taken on as a minister in one of the biggest Baptist Churches in Virginia Beach, and the couple embraced the opportunity. At the same time, Juli Anne was put in contact with Jean Yokum at Langley Federal Credit Union, who had just created a VP of Marketing position and was looking for an innovative mind to fill the spot.

Juli Anne, who hadn't even known what a credit union was and had certainly never intended to work for one, went into the meeting wary of how one might balance faith with business, and couldn't have been given a better example. From humble roots in West Virginia, Jean was now a successful CEO and a fifth grade Sunday school teacher with strong faith and an open heart. Juli Anne took the job and spent the next four years learning, growing, and soaring—most literally when she was given a civil leadership award that included a back seat ride in an F15 Eagle at Langley as thanks for her work to gather and send personal supplies and cards to the troops in the first Desert Storm. When the troops were suddenly mobilized via the air force base, Juli Anne had instinctively jumped into action, working with radio and other media contacts to raise awareness and collect personal care items for the brave service members. "That ride was one moment in life that so far surpassed my wildest dreams," she recalls. "We flew over the Chesapeake Bay, rolling the aircraft. It was incredible."

Juli Anne was given more conventional but no less impressive recognition of her work as well, particularly when she won the Bank Marketing Association's Best of Show award over competing companies like Chase and CitiBank. "I had really hit my stride," she remembers. "I was excelling at my work, and with Charles pastoring at a church, everyone knew and loved us. We were going along merrily, and Charles had taken his first pastor in Virginia, serving there for 14 months when he suddenly collapsed in a Gloucester, Virginia parsonage at age 43 and was diagnosed with the same cardio myopathy that had taken Adam's life."

Thankful for Charles's life but concerned that the condition was expected to kill him within three years, the Callis family wasted no time and relocated to Stanford, California, per the best medical recommendation. There, he was placed on a heart transplant waiting list and program via California Pacific Medical Center in San Francisco. "We waited over two years, counting each day as a blessing and possibly the last day of his life," Juli Anne recalls. "In the early hours of the morning on August 15, 1998, we finally got the call, and four hours later, he was being prepped to have his heart removed as we received the miracle of a heart donation by the family of a young man who had died tragically in a Colorado climbing accident."

The operation went well, but the heart rejected multiple times, and all stops were pulled out by the doctors. They used rescue measures to save Charles's life, including Total Lymphatic Irradiation, massive infusions of test drugs, and ongoing protocols, some of which were not yet approved by the FDA. "Our medical team are the real heroes that God worked through over a post-transplant battle that lasted over a year," Juli Anne says. In the end, Charles rebuilt his strength, and the doors opened for him to return to full-time ministry. With that, he took on the challenge as Senior Pastor of a church in inner city San Jose.

Juli Anne was hired as the first VP of Emerging Technologies and Business Development at the American Electronics Association Credit Union, where she was immersed in the cutting edge frontier of the internet and set up one of the first platforms for accepting mortgage applications over the web. "No one thought it would work, but we did it with CGI scripting, and it started to catch on like wildfire," she recalls. The company exploded from about $320 million to $860 million during the ten years she was there, and Juli Anne was honored with a distinguished Woman in Industry Award, recognizing the success of the top 50 women in Silicon Valley. Life was good again, and the Callis family had regained its strength, ready to face whatever might come their way next.

That's when the same genetic disorder struck Lisa Anne, who, at the age of 28, was already married with two children and working as a bio scientist at St. Jude Hospital near Virginia Beach. She had worked in clinical studies at Stanford and at LifeNet managing a research lab, and at the time the disorder struck, she was working on teams putting cardio devices in patients much like the one her father had prior to his transplant, and much like the one she now needed herself. Her first defibrillator had to be extracted, causing damage to her heart that meant she had to get an experimental external defibrillator instead. Thankfully, Lisa Anne is now doing well in San Diego, working with new surgical products for Stryker. "I'm amazed at her resiliency and her faith," Juli Anne avows. "She was the premie baby we were told to abort. She fought for her life from the moment she arrived on Earth. Even when she was nine years old and watched her brother stop playing and lay down beside her to go to Heaven, she kept her faith. She's our little miracle baby, and the reality is that my life is shaped by two walking miracles, and by a third person who's now in eternity," she says, of Charles, Lisa Anne, and Adam. "Because of them, every moment matters, and every decision is made with them in mind."

That's why Charles and Juli Anne decided to make the move back to the East Coast to be near their daughter, and with the help of a headhunter, Juli Anne was put in touch with the National Institutes of Health Federal Credit Union. The Credit Union was seventy years old, had a $2 million loss in 2008, and was looking for the kind of transformational leadership and limitless vision that Juli Anne had become known for. "That was just as the Obama administration's banking reforms were taking place, shaping the destiny of every financial institution," she remembers. Under her leadership as President and CEO, the credit union rebuilt its infrastructure with a focus on strong technologies and sound services, growing from $380 million to $580 million during her tenure from 2009 to 2013.

"I don't know exactly what the next chapter will be, but I want to give my time and talent—both vocationally and non-vocationally—to things that matter," she says today. "My work at GW is leading a global initiative in compassionate care, and I'm also thrilled to be working with Johns Hopkins University graduate students in a new degree program for bio tech and entrepreneurship. There are so many doors opening up to help nurture the efforts of bright young minds, as well as budding initiatives as a consultant." This next chapter may begin at the George Washington Institute of Health and Spirituality, where

Juli Anne serves on the board and has been asked to take on the role of chairwoman. As such, her passion and focus is now engrossed in meeting with global health leaders, building a sustainable business model for the organization, and exploring avenues to bring compassion back into healthcare. "I don't know what adventure I'm on, but I have a very strong sense that something's happening here," she says.

This unrelenting, brave openness characterizes the advice she gives to young people entering the working world today. "Embrace the opportunities in life," she urges, echoing the refrain of her childhood. "Just go for it. When you're going through hell, keep going. Run for it. Just run full throttle. And through all that, remember that the most valuable thing to attain in life is contentment. Don't miss a moment. Treasure the lessons from your parents and the butterfly kisses from your children. Play more and worry less—that's the way to live a full, meaningful, limitless life."

BERNHARDT
WEALTH MANAGEMENT

Stephan Little

One Life

At 72 years of age, Judy's life hadn't turned out quite the way she planned. Her grown children had lost their jobs during the 2008 recession and moved back in with her, and her Social Security check could only stretch so far. She didn't want to just sit by and lament her situation; she wanted to *do* something. But what?

Enter Stephan Little, whose life's purpose is about creating to make others' lives better. "I'm a strong advocate of people really having a clear connection to their purpose," he says. "I think we're all ordained with a purpose of some sort. I think we're here for a reason, and our purpose will be accomplished with or without our cooperation, so it's better if you can get in line with it and enjoy the ride rather than struggle with it. But you need to explore it. It might not be what you think at first, but once you find it, you should really latch on and make it part of all that you do."

Steve understands this struggle and search for purpose so well because he went through it himself. After garnering tremendous success in the technology and startup space but ultimately finding himself disillusioned by its nuance, he decided to do what he does best—he got creative. With the help of an incredibly effective friend and mentor, Steven Feinberg, he held a retreat at his ranch home in California, inviting venture investors and CEOs he had developed relationships with over the years to come for a weekend of music, wine, and brainstorming about his next move. "The idea was to bring together all these perspectives, cull them out, and generate something meaningful in the form of a compass point," he recalls. "The key realization was that, instead of being systems- and executing-oriented, I'm always wanting to generate and create something new, and the real driver behind that is helping other people get to a place of joy and satisfaction. But how?"

As ideas were shared and mapped out, the group shot down one after another until finally, a collective chorus of "That's it!" was sung. Steve had a visionary knack for seeing and navigating through the complexity of business success. If business was a chess game, Steve would know, within five seconds of first looking at the board, every possible move and exactly who would win. If he could find a way to encode that, he could help millions of people.

Steve quantified this realization in 2008 by creating The Perfect Biz Finder, a self-paced home study program based on the principle of creation through destruction—that is, creation of business success through destruction of the mental models that prevent people from seeing the opportunities around them all the time. "As human beings, we form belief structures that filter what we see and how we translate our experiences," he explains. "I think there's a whole generation of people, including the Baby Boomers, who don't have enough money to live out the rest of their lives without an income, and have been encoded with a limiting mental framework that makes them feel they don't have other options. I saw enormous opportunity in helping people develop the thinking skills that allow them to peel the lenses away so they can see opportunities that were previously invisible to them. It's about helping people break down those old ways of thinking so they can reframe what's possible for themselves and find opportunities they can really ignite themselves with."

Judy was one of those people who came across the program, but after several sessions, she still didn't feel ignited. She had a passion for knitting but was unclear about how to translate it into business success. "Stick with the process and it will be revealed to you," Steve assured her. "It's going to be exciting, I promise you."

Several months later, he answered a call from an unknown number. "I just have one question for you," came Judy's voice over the phone. Steve thought she sounded angry and was ready to refund what she'd paid for the program, when she instead said, "What on earth am I going to do with all this money?" The grandmother had launched a membership site teaching people how to knit, expecting to accrue a few dozen members and charging $97 a month. But by the time she called him, she had 2,900 members—and a system, a method, and a belief in her abilities.

Steve's approach also revolves around dispelling the belief that people have "lives" that are distinct and separate from one another, like a work life, a home life, or a love life. "We compartmentalize everything, but that's really just another inaccurate mental model," he points out. "We borrow time from our families to invest in our work with the bizarre expectation that somehow it will pay a dividend back to the family, but that's not how it works. The truth is that you have one life, and you have to design it to incorporate all the aspects of what you're here to accomplish. What are your real intentions? You need to actually map time for these concepts into your calendar. I wanted to help people recognize that they have one life that they are free to design according to their ultimate goals."

Judy's is one of about 3,800 businesses launched with the help of the Biz Finder, and once the program had become automated, turn-key, and stable, Steve began exploring ways to translate his approach to bigger, established businesses that were being held back by the presence of limiting mental frameworks in their leadership teams. "So many businesses have the old-school perspective that, if you work your life away, someday it'll pay," says Steve. "But that kind of thinking kills businesses."

Once he began advising and consulting with these types of companies, Steve noticed the startling trend that very few of them had solid exit strategies. In fact, few of them had exit strategies at all. He also found that 80 percent of the business owners he consulted with were disappointed when he showed them their company's first valuation, thinking it would be worth more. "The value driver of your business is determined by your buyer, not you," Steve affirms. "If you keep this in mind when you're first starting your business, you have a clear road map of where you want to go. If you can really understand the kind of company you would want to sell to in the future and what they would value in your business, that defines your business model and tells you exactly what you need to do to get the best exit possible." Thus, Steve created Zero Limits Ventures in 2010, a growth-oriented consulting and investing firm that teaches business owners and CEOs how to begin with the end in mind.

Though this idea is a fundamental cornerstone of his approach now, Steve certainly didn't begin life thinking he would end up where he is today. Born in Syracuse, New York, his father worked for General Electric and moved the family down to Daytona Beach, Florida, to work on the Apollo Space Program. He then transitioned into information systems, so they moved to Pennsylvania when Steve was 13. There, they had a creek running through their property where he and his older sister would play and catch crayfish, and his mother, a homemaker, always took good care of them. "She was very social, and from her I learned to talk, listen, and learn from people, which became important in sales later on," he remembers. "And from my father, I got a sense of the importance of breaking away from material aspiration and the debilitating effects of mindlessly climbing up a ladder. He succeeded in escaping that mindset and then regenerating himself so that now, at the age of 80, he hiked Mount Everest and then the whole length of England."

One of Steve's most profound shifts in perspective came when he was 14 and, like any other kid, wanted to earn some money cutting lawns. Within several weeks, he noticed that he could either toil under the hot sun and make $8 a lawn, or he could hire someone else to do the work for $6 and earn $2 himself. With this model, he accrued 30 customers and would ride his bike from house to house each week asking if his neighbors wanted their grass cut.

Toward the end of the season, however, he noticed people turning him down more often and realized there might be a better way to do business. With that, he drew up quarterly, semi-annual, and annual contracts agreeing to varying levels of service, with the longest terms incorporating other lawn care services for the same flat rate. Almost everyone took the long-term contract deals, and Steve was able to scale his business, growing incrementally rather than having to return to each house each week to sell the same deal.

Two years later, his father was transferred. Only then did he realize that his son had amassed a garage full of equipment and a book full of business. With his father's help, Steve looked up nearby lawn care businesses in the Yellow Pages and ended up selling his modest company for $200,000. "It was such a significant inflection point for me because I learned about value drivers," he remembers. "The value of my company wasn't in the customers or the equipment or the employees, but in the book of contracts I had put together. That single entity is what made the business valuable. Now, whenever I enter a business, I look for their 'book'—that thing that's driving their value. Most businesses don't know what that is."

Steve's early entrepreneurial ventures continued thanks to the shop class he took in high school. The instructor, Gene Koons, was a grumpy old man who only took to students that proved they were truly committed to the work, which Steve did. The two developed a rapport and would do special projects together, which led Steve to develop a summer scheme to make and sell grandfather clocks. "But I hated the finishing process—staining, spraying, buffing, sanding," Steve remarks. "By the end of the summer, we had a room full of unfinished grandfather clocks, and Mr. Koons convinced me I was better off selling clock-making kits rather than the completed clocks themselves."

Steve was never athletic in high school, but that all changed when he enrolled at the University of Richmond and put his mind to getting in shape. He began training with the wrestling team and befriended a champion body builder, which got him interested in the sport himself. "I got pretty big and won first place in several regional and national contests as a teenager," he remembers. "Being a champion athlete was certainly rewarding, but even more gratifying was earning the credibility to help others become champion athletes later."

Steve intended to major in mathematics and was excelling with a 3.95 GPA and a course load of 21 hours a semester, but he decided to quit school after two years because he didn't see the value in it. He had figured out how to become the official beer distributor for the campus fraternities and was making money that way, but he was far more interested in launching businesses than he was in classes and campus life. Free of the burden of school, Steve started a cabinet shop doing high-end work for law firms, which led to residential cabinetry and soon attracted the attention of George Tuckwiler, the owner of a light commercial construction company. The two began working together on various projects and developed a close friendship, until George suffered a massive heart attack and passed away soon thereafter. He left the business to Steve along with a note expressing his belief in him, so Steve ran the company successfully for several years.

"During that time, I became enamored with the idea of moving aggressively into the large commercial space, but I had no idea how to do it," he remembers. He decided to call one of the big names in the industry and set up a lunch meeting. Steve showed up in his work clothes, but the executive showed up in a suit, setting the stage for the conversation that followed. After hearing his story, the man across the table said, "There's not a single person I can think of in our entire executive suite who's ever punched a nail in his life. The path you're on doesn't lead there."

"The problem," Steve says, "is that I believed him. In that moment, I decided there was no path from that construction company to what I envisioned. That was a big mistake. I don't regret it, but looking back now, I know I could have accomplished all that and more."

Steve ultimately sold the business, finished up his degree, and decided he wanted to move into a professional job, so he utilized his father's contacts at GE and landed a position in Rockville with their information services group as a performance specialist. In that capacity, he performed the arduous work of building statistical models of performance to help decision makers predict outcomes, launching him into the world of technology. "Our office was right next to Jack Welch's office, and we got to spend time with him while he was in town," Steve recalls. "I learned a lot from him. He taught me that professional advancement isn't about what you do; it's about who you are. You have to be clear about what you want and then become the kind of person who has those things."

From there, Steve went on to GTE Spacenet to supervise their satellite operations center. The operation was experiencing a technology problem that prevented them from seeing satellites in their system, so he brought in a small startup from Boston, Xyplex, who believed their technology afforded a solution. "In the process of getting to know that company and meet the founders, I realized that what I really wanted to do was work for a startup," Steve says. With that, he became a sales engineer for Xyplex and began focusing on network management. Then, by chance, he sat next to Jeff Case and Marshall Rose on a plane, who created the simple network management protocol that became the TCPIP standard for managing devices on a network. They were having trouble getting device manufacturers to adopt their protocol, so the three decided to join forces, and Steve was able to show stakeholders that the microcode made their devices more manageable.

Before long, pieces of their microcode were deployed every time someone bought a new router, terminal server, or switch. The partners began writing programs that could read that code centrally, pulling performance and alert data from remote devices. This success brought Steve to Silicon Valley, where their first company made $147 million in less than three years. "We would pitch an idea to venture capitalists, put together an engineering team, develop a prototype, get funded, build a company, sell it, and start again," he recounts. "I also helped launch the Desktop Management Task Force, which became the standard for all desktop management. That was the beginning of what is now a $100 to $200 billion industry."

After selling companies to Seagate, HP, and Microsoft, Steve shifted his focus to more localized applications like software distribution, building and selling three companies to Microsoft in rapid succession. "We had a really good run and a lot of success, and I earned the reputation in that community of being someone who could figure things out, but it was time for me to retire and move on to something else," Steve says. "After years of building successful software companies for venture investors, I realized I never really loved it. Looking back, I was making those decisions because I felt I had to, because I was boxed in by a mental model that said that path was my lot in life. In a sense, I was a lot like the very people I work to help today. I was driven by fear of not succeeding, rather than by a core sense of motivation."

Steve was making tremendous amounts of money but was the unhappiest he had ever been in his life. He traveled so much that he missed his oldest daughter's childhood completely, and he had been divorced. "Ultimately, I was a mess and really needed an answer, and thankfully, I got one," he remembers. "I went through a sort of spiritual transition in my life where I felt like I connected with God in a very transformational way. I believe there are no coincidences in life and that we all have the experiences we have by design. Going through all of that allowed me to find the path I'm on today, creating opportunities that truly help others understand how to put themselves in a position to win."

Transitioning out of a fear-based life and into an empowered life couldn't have happened without the help of Steve's wife, Kimberly, who was instrumental in helping him let go of his former existence. "I was feeling a tremendous amount of interpersonal tension about letting go of a stable corporate lifestyle for something that wasn't a sure bet. Then, one day, while doing my daily devotionals, I had a very clear feeling that it was going to be okay, but I had to stop standing at the edge and just jump," he remembers. "I talked to Kimberly about it, unsure about how she would react because it was her and our daughter's security at stake too, but she just looked at me and said she was so excited about it, and that I should just do it. In doing that, she eliminated a big piece of the fear that was holding me back. She's truly incredible and a wonderful partner."

Today, Steve operates at the 50,000 foot level, leading Zero Limits Ventures around obstacles and creating an environment where his employees can flourish in a unified direction. With a focus on open and clear communication channels, each team member is not concerned with *being* right so much as *getting* it right. Once they have a good vision of who a client is and where that client wants to go, they tap their extensive network of strategic partners, investors, and merchants to find the highest valuation potentials for that client.

Alongside work, Steve designs his own life to prioritize time with Kimberley and to foster good relationships with his daughters, Emily and Madeline. He's also returned to bodybuilding, recently taking second place in a national contest. "There's a certain discipline that comes with being a champion athlete that's mirrored in being successful in business," he says. "It takes a level of commitment that only comes with a true awareness of one's purpose, and an awareness of the influences of advisors and the people you surround yourself with. It's important to fill your life with people who make you a better person and don't drag you down."

This focus on being mindful of both physical and mental states is echoed in the advice he gives young people entering the working world today. "It's true that you can do anything you want to do," he insists. "The important thing is to get the wiring between your ears right. Read as much as you can, from business books to the Bible, or whatever resonates with you. If you invest in fueling your mind with good brain food, everything else will take care of itself. You have to exercise your brain like you'd exercise your muscles. You become a better thinker with better quality outputs, both for work and for relationships."

Beyond this, Steve's example demonstrates the importance of recognizing and surpassing the mental frameworks that hold us back in life. "It takes courage to commit to changing and evolving as a person—to give up the status quo in the hopes of attaining a better life," he affirms. "But it's worth it. Every time I'm there to help Madeline with her homework, I know it's worth it. Every time I see clients overcoming roadblocks and achieving the success they deserve, I know it's worth it. Every day I remind myself that I've got one life to share with my family, my community, and my work, and knowing that I've designed it to be the kind of life I want, makes it all worth it worth it."

Raymond F. Lopez, Jr.

Promise and Purpose

Raymond F. Lopez, Jr. was an E4 Third Class Petty Officer in the Navy during the Vietnam War, and his division had just gotten back from a cruise in the Western Pacific, when the leading chief aboard the ship received orders to send one officer back out. Nobody wanted to go, but Senior Chief Snyder had an incredible command of authority, and when he pointed at Ray, the young sailor thought it was settled: he'd be the one to go. But much to Ray's surprise, the Chief had something else in mind. "I want to keep you," he said, "because you have promise."

Ray had never considered himself a model sailor, but those words planted a seed of ambition in his mind that began to grow over the coming years. When he was an E5, he decided to apply to the Naval Enlisted Scientific Education Program in the hopes of studying ocean-ography at the University of Washington. To apply, he had to retake his college boards and send for transcripts from his parochial high school. When they arrived, he reviewed them and noticed a note from the nuns he had overlooked before. "Although quite popular socially, Raymond shows a lack of purpose," it said.

Promise and purpose. He knew he had both, and he resolved to bring them out by applying for the officer program. With that, he started attending night classes at St. Leo College at Fort Eustis. He took challenging courses, and his wife, Carol, would stay up late to help with his accounting homework. The Lopezes decided they were going to get through it together, and the promise that Chief Snyder had seen in Ray began to transform his career. Now, after retiring from a phenomenal career in the Navy as a commander, Ray is the founder, President, and CEO of Engineering Services Network, Inc. (ESN), continuing to bring his promise and purpose to life by providing mission-critical services to the military and federal government.

Ray launched ESN in February of 1995 after rising up through the enlisted ranks as a Chief Sonar Technician and retiring in November of 1994. "I didn't know anything about business, but after spending almost three decades in the Navy, I felt I was uniquely qualified to help sailors and make their lives a little easier," he recalls. "When Space and Warfare Systems Command and Naval Sea Systems Command were still located in Crystal City, I'd walk the halls, talk to people to get a sense of what was going on, and then go home at night to figure out how I could help."

After he began closing deals, he then had to actually solve the technical problems at hand, but thanks to his affinity for technology like radar, sonar, communications, and computer networks, things continued to fall into place. Within the first year, he had five employees. The following year, he got involved in the 8(a) Business Development Program, which helped put ESN on solid ground and develop its infrastructure as a professional engineer assignment company. ESN then got involved with the Department of Defense (DoD) Mentor-Protégé Program, which changed the course of the company's future.

As part of the program, ESN was mentored by Anteon and won the Nunn-Perry Award for outstanding mentor-protégé teams. "The program helps you see what you need to do to move your company forward," Ray explains. "By putting together action diagrams, hiring a contracts officer and a quality manager, and implementing consistent and standardized forms and procedures, we landed a contract in 2000 and did the work with enough efficiency and innovation that we have won it each award year since."

Today, the company has over 250 employees and four divisions, preserving its culture despite its growth and maintaining a 91 percent employee retention rate. Its Maritime Division is the largest in the country and consists of their Coast Guard, Navy, and Submarine Corps work. Their Air Land Division serves the Army and the Air Force, which they knew little about until Ray hired a two-star general, who in turn hired the A6 and CIO of Global Strike Command. "It's a different mentality, but by hiring the right people, we were able to really build that program out," he affirms. ESN's Federal IT Solutions division serves agencies like the VA, while its final division handles DoD work that is specifically D.C.-focused.

Broadly speaking, ESN delivers trusted solutions that support national defense, working shoulder to shoulder with sailors and troops to improve mission readiness. Through one contract, its employees serve as Combat Systems Maintenance Coordinators, working on teams with government workers and maintenance manager contractors to handle daily communications, electronics, command and control systems, and computer network problems on aircraft carriers. They also map out the availability of the ship's workforce and what needs to be done to prepare a ship for redeployment. Through another contract, ESN has focused on the consolidation of multiple commands, saving tens of millions of dollars for the Federal government. "The Navy was my mistress for a very long time, so it's been important to me to take everything I've garnered throughout my career, both technically and morally, and use to help current servicemen and women," Ray explains. "I was a rowdy kid when I started, but I had a successful command tour before I retired. I worked hard for the Navy, and the Navy worked for me, so I wanted to pay that back in some way."

Working hard wasn't always at the forefront of Ray's thoughts through his unruly youth, but it was written in that inner promise of his from the time he was a young boy growing up in Atlantic City, New Jersey. His father, a product of the 1930s who joined the service when he was 16, had an incredible work ethic. He worked in a hotel as a master chef, and Ray can still remember the day his father hired him on to help in the kitchen at age thirteen. He placed a thousand pounds of potatoes in front of his son, armed him with four potato peelers, and instructed him to make oven browns. "That was day one," Ray recounts. "The oven browns had to be shaped a certain way, and laid out on the baking trays like so. I worked for my father for four years, and I knew I wanted to pursue something different with my life."

The oldest of five children, Ray played baseball and football, sang in the choir, and swam competitively in high school. To earn spending money, he bagged groceries at the local Acme Supermarket for tips and caddied at the country club. He worked at a deli, and as a pool boy and a lifeguard at the High Ho Silver Motel. But work was as much about respecting his father as it was about earning money. "I inherited my father's work ethic and my mother's compassion, and I always treated both with respect," he remembers. "She was tough, and he was quiet. They were like yin and yang."

Ray wasn't really interested in school, but the stern approaches of the nuns and priests prepared him for boot camp. His mother was from a well-to-do family but didn't finish high school, and his father had been a ward of the Catholic Church as a child, so college was not talked about. Upon graduating from high school, he considered Morningstar and Tulane, and was nominated to the Merchant Marine Academy at King's Point, but he ultimately chose the Navy like his father. He spent his first eleven weeks stationed in San Diego, where he met Carol, the woman who would become his wife. "I had actually gotten kicked out of the Navy's electronics school and was sent to a ship overseas," Ray recalls. "When I came back, I met her. She was in town on a trip for legal secretaries, and we hit it off. For the first time, because of her, I began wanting to do more with my life."

Thanks to Carol's stabilizing love and support, coupled with Senior Chief Snyder's belief in him, Ray began to grow by leaps and bounds socially and professionally. The first time he applied to become a Limited Duty Officer (LDO), he didn't make it, so he tried again, and was ultimately among the 200 out of 2,000 candidates to be commissioned. The year was 1977, and John Disher was the Commanding Officer at Naval Station Roosevelt Roads, later to retire as the Naval Chief of Personnel. John had never worked with a former enlisted like Ray, but they got along well. "I'm very fortunate," he says. "Most of the people I've worked for were excellent leaders who did the right thing."

Through his Naval career, Ray developed a leadership style that balances firmness with compassion for the experiences people have been through. He couples passion with discretion and is careful not to act rashly. "I remind myself that the first report back from the battle is not necessarily the full and correct report," he says. "I try to get all sides of a story, and then I take action by making a decision. I don't wait things out, but instead confront them head on."

Toward the end of Ray's Navy career, he and Carol moved their family to a rural town in West Virginia, where he grew passionate about coaching at a local high school. He might have liked to stay there to teach and coach after retiring from service, but Carol was tired of driving 42 miles through the mountains to the nearest large full-service grocery store. He had learned during his last tour that there were many military personnel, civil servants, and contractors in Washington, D.C. who wanted to do the right thing for the military and the country, so the Lopezes decided to move to the nation's capital and try their hand at starting a business. "We didn't have time to worry—we just jumped into it, so we had to make it work," Ray remembers. "We had to build the company, pay off our debts, and succeed. I spoke to everyone in the Navy, from seamen to admirals, and it was almost like I never left. I was willing to help out with anything."

In imagining ESN, Ray wanted to build a company the size of a destroyer—between 250 and 380 people—because it would be big enough to have the kind of impact he envisioned, but small enough to maintain the company culture borne from his experiences in the Navy, with his family, and through life. "Our company is like a ship," he says. "It's a culture of interdependence, in which the mission isn't successful unless everyone pulls together and works together."

Ray originally thought he'd grow ESN and sell it for $10 million, but his goals evolved as rapidly and unpredictably as the company itself. Its revenue rose to $52 million several years ago, but has fluctuated somewhat due to contractual changes, the unique challenges of mid-tier companies, and uncertainty stemming from sequestration and the political climate. Now, Ray aspires to organically grow the company to $100 million, and though ESN continues to evolve, Ray is confident it will retain the culture that has landed it on the Fairfax County Chamber of Commerce list of finalists for its Contractor of the Year GovCon Award in 2012. That same year, Ray himself was a finalist for Executive of the Year.

Even with the challenges of leading a mid-tier company through constantly changing terrain, Ray makes time to give back, whether he's mentoring others or talking to groups of service-disabled veterans about how to succeed in business and give back to the service they came from. As a company, ESN believes in working for the betterment of the nation while also making a positive, intentional impact in the local community, so every organization in the company supports charitable efforts in its own geographic location. Whether it's supporting the Joy Fund to help supply toys to thousands of children in need in Tidewater, Virginia;

supporting the efforts of charities working with battered mothers and children in Arlington; or helping veterans; the company is focused on its impact at home as much as it works to achieve national and even global results.

In advising young people entering the working world today, Ray emphasizes the importance of asking questions. "If you don't ask, you'll never learn," he explains. "Seek the advice of knowledgeable individuals. Do something you're interested in and have an affinity for." For people interested in going into business, he underscores the reality that no two days are the same. "Expect the unexpected," he avows. "Don't be afraid to take risks and venture into the unknown, but get an idea of what the consequences could be. Make sure those risks are reasonable and qualified."

And above all, Ray's story shows the importance of paying success forward so that others can realize their promise and achieve their purpose in life. It's the arc that connects him back to the Navy and the future sailors who benefit from ESN's help. And, because he and Carol have committed to fund the education of their grandchildren, it's the thread that connects him to future generations of his family. "I believe paying it back and paying it forward is so important because I want to see people succeed," he says. "We live in the greatest country on Earth, and it's important to do what we can to improve society and the worth of our fellow man. There's promise and purpose in all of us, and everyone can use their potential to achieve success and change the world."

BERNHARDT
WEALTH MANAGEMENT

Sandra H. Magnus

A Space of One's Own

When Sandy Magnus read the 1978 newspaper article announcing that the astronaut class would include women for the first time that year, she breathed a secret sigh of relief. Those six women had broken a mold, shining a light in darkness to show that there was, indeed, a pathway between young girls like Sandy and outer space.

A freshman in high school at the time, Sandy had known since middle school that she wanted to become an astronaut. Like many of her peers, she loved the idea of space exploration and wanted to do it herself one day; unlike many of them, she latched on to that dream and didn't let it go. Soon after the 1978 women astronauts showed her that a path was possible, Sandy began forging one of her own.

Though chemistry was typically a junior class at her school, she took it as a sophomore so she could take physics and advanced chemistry as a junior, and then advanced physics as a senior. She had a plan:

she would major in physics in college, earn her masters and PhD in the subject, and become an astronaut. Now the Executive Director of the American Institute of Aeronautics and Astronautics (AIAA), Sandy spent sixteen years as an astronaut, but the path that got her there was actually much richer and more fulfilling than the homogenous route she thought it would be.

Born and raised in Belleville, Illinois, a small town idyllically straddling the line between rural cornfields and bustling St. Louis, Sandy grew up the oldest of four children. Her mother was a nurse who became the coordinator of a medical assistant program at a community college, while her father worked in insurance. She was five when her parents woke her up late at night to watch the televised broadcast of Neil Armstrong walking on the moon, but it wasn't a particularly defining moment for her. Rather, her character was forged in the perpetual string of questions she posed to her parents. She always wanted to know how things worked, to the extent that they bought her a book containing two hundred answers to "why?" questions.

Sandy took breaks from reading and exploring the world around her to play soccer starting in fifth grade. Her high school didn't have a soccer team, so her father coached Sandy and her two sisters on a recreational team. She also ran track for two years and helped manage the boys' soccer team, all the while remaining steadfastly focused to the rigorous science and math curriculum she had mapped out for herself. As a young lady excelling dramatically in STEM courses at a time when such intelligence wasn't considered very cool, Sandy was quiet and introverted through high school, keeping her astronautic aspirations to herself except for a demure sentence in a journal assignment for junior English class.

All that changed, however, when she got to college at the University of Missouri-Rolla, now the Missouri University of Science and Technology. Her father decided to get his bachelors degree when she did, and without a firm guiding hand through the college selection process, Sandy landed at the prominent engineering school largely by chance. "Illinois and Missouri had a cooperative agreement that allowed me to enroll at the school and receive an in-state tax credit, which helped make the tuition more affordable," she remembers. "There was no big scheme or plan behind any of it. I didn't even know what engineering was at the time."

With the start of her freshman year, Sandy decided to dispel the social anxieties that plagued her in high school. She was who she was—an engaged, somewhat geeky, passionate student of science and technology committed to understanding how the world works and pushing the boundaries of what's possible—and people could either take it or leave it. Thanks to her father's coaching, she was also an excellent soccer player, landing a spot as a starter on the varsity team all four years of college. "As a Division Two school, academics were our primary driver, but we were able to engage full-time in sports activities as well," she explains. "It was a spectacular experience and taught me a lot about leadership, teamwork, discipline, and work ethic. It was also a big factor in helping me achieve my dream, as the Astronaut Office looks for well-rounded applicants."

Sandy had planned to pursue degrees only in physics simply because she thought her only other options were chemistry and biology, but her eyes were soon opened to the world of engineering, and she became particularly fascinated in the electromagnetics side of electrical engineering. Upon graduating, she felt burnt out by academia and decided to experience the real world, accepting a job at McDonnell Douglas Aircraft Company in St. Louis. She took night classes toward her masters in electrical engineering at Rolla's St. Louis extension center, earning the degree over a four-year period while working on the A-12 attack aircraft program. Nine months after she finished her degree, the program was canceled amidst the first Gulf War by Dick Cheney, who was Secretary of Defense at the time.

The cyclical world of aerospace contracted, but Sandy had mastered her skills in that capacity and was ready for a change anyway. She enrolled at Georgia Tech to earn her PhD in materials, learning how materials drive design choices in aircraft construction and impose limitations in manufacture and integration. With the work combined applied physics, chemistry, and engineering, offering an ideal blend of her interests.

It was there that she met retired Navy Admiral Richard Truly, head of the Georgia Tech Research Institute and a former astronaut. After making his acquaintance at a campus event, he agreed to sit down with Sandy to talk about the astronaut program, and in the midst of that conversation, he offered to be a reference for her application. "I wouldn't have dared to ask him to do that because I had just met him, but I understand why he did," she reflects. "Now, when I talk to people, I can get a sense fairly quickly sometimes of whether they'd be a good fit in the Astronaut Office."

Now that she was a collegiate athlete with some work experience and escalating degrees in three different fields, Sandy felt ready to apply to the Astronaut Office at age thirty. The interview process is a week-long battery of medical tests on top of a meeting with the Board, and the selection process is highly dependent on the year and context. The demand for pilots, engineers, physical scientists, or medical doctors fluctuates wildly, depending on the demands of the office and the climate of the industry, so applicants are encouraged to apply again if they don't make the cut but are truly committed to the profession.

Fortuitously, Sandy picked the best year in the history of the office to apply, as NASA was in the process of building out the space station. Of 3,000 applicants, 35 astronauts were selected, and Sandy was one of them. Over the next sixteen years, Sandy went on three mission—each special in its own way, and each an occasion for her parents to host a pseudo reunion for her extended family around eighty people to gather and watch the launches. Alone in quarantine, Sandy would reflect on the happy Christmases they'd all spend piled in her grandmother's tiny house, with over a hundred presents around the Christmas tree. On the other side, her parents watched the launch nervously, but were genuinely happy their daughter was doing what she wanted to do in life.

For her second mission, Sandy spent almost five months living on the space station, and her third marked the last shuttle flight of the office. "There's really no typical career in terms of your missions," she says. "It really just depends on the timing of your flights, your interests, your personal situation, and what's going on in the space program during your tenure."

Between missions, astronauts are given technical assignments throughout the vertical office structure. Surrounded by outstanding people with their own strengths and weaknesses, there was no ladder to climb—only roles to fill and jobs to be done. Sandy found herself traveling to Russia for months at a time over several years to help with launches, team building, and defining the operational vocabulary that would allow English and Russian teams to communicate effectively. She worked with Europeans, Japanese, and Canadians, as well as Mission Control. In the wake of the devastating Space Shuttle Columbia disaster of 2003, she led the office's return to flight efforts and monitored investigations into the cause of the accident. All the while, she maintained her proficiency training and flying skills, persevering through grueling spacewalk training sessions in heavy suits designed for body types much larger than the typical woman's.

When Sandy became Deputy Chief of the Astronaut Office, she was still eligible for flight assignments, but her role had largely transitioned to one of management. She was comfortable in the position, so when she received a call from AIAA, she was under no pressure to make a rash decision. "The most important thing to me was finding something that really fit," she recounts. "I wouldn't leave NASA for anything less than ideal. It wouldn't just be a job change; it would be a life change. So I did a lot of preliminary research."

As the professional society for the aerospace industry, AIAA is a 501(c)3 nonprofit organization with about 32,000 members that span the profession but trend toward science and engineering. The community has been around since the 1930s, when rocketry gained momentum, but the institute was first formally recognized some fifty years ago, when the astronautics and aeronautics merged together. "The aerospace community is an extremely passionate and engaged group of people," Sandy affirms.

AIAA is essentially the curator and knowledge base of the industry. It publishes peer review technical journals and puts on conferences on industry issues to provide venues for the community to gather, forge relationships, develop new ideas for programs, and keep the industry alive and advancing. With local sections around the world, student sections, and national level committees focusing on specific technical or programmatic issues, the AIAA staff of 62 people supports a wide array of endeavors. "We advocate on behalf of the industry, but we're not lobbyists," says Sandy. "We're the neutral ground where places like the Office of Management and Budget, NASA, or Capitol Hill can get the perspectives of the technical, scientific, and engineering community."

What do you do when you've already done the only thing you ever dreamt of doing? At 48, Sandy found herself confronting for the first time what most of her peers experienced as they graduated from college and tried to find their paths in the world. She had always known exactly what she wanted to do, but now that she was on the other side of the path she had been focused on so intently her whole life, she wasn't sure. "There's no normal for what an astronaut does after that career is over," she reflects. "Some of us are active duty military and continue doing that, while others retire and become civil servants. Some go to aerospace companies, academia, or consulting. Some retire, write books, or find other employment with NASA. There's really no set path, but when I was offered the position at AIAA, I knew it would open more doors than it would close."

Sandy has been the organization's Executive Director since 2012, running its day-to-day operations while aligning them with the input of the Board, which is comprised of elected volunteer members who set its strategic vision. For the past year, the team has been focused on the fundamentals of updating its processes and finding ways to connect with the younger generation. "The Baby Boomer generation has defined much of the world, the culture, and how organizations operate," she says. "Without abandoning that generation, it's important to shift our emphasis, focus, operations, and identity so that the importance of our society resonates with young people." Through Sandy's leadership, the organization is also transitioning from a siloed mode of operation to a more integrated, vision and strategic plan.

As a leader, Sandy's key outputs are energy and good decision making, which she accomplishes by asking the right questions. "If you follow the logic path in confronting problems, things tend to come to light," she points out. Recognizing that being a good leader means also being a good follower, she pursues a consensus style of leadership and highly values the input of the people around her.

As she hones her management skills, explores the nonprofit space, and advocates for the industry at this critical time when slashes to federal funding of the space program means disinvestment in the nation's future, Sandy still prioritizes her identity as a role model. Through the course of her career, she has talked to every public school in Belleville, as well as many parochial schools. She video-conferenced with students at her old high school while living on the space station, engaged with Girl Scout troops while in orbit, and wrote pen pal letters to various classrooms. "I felt that I could have the biggest impact by connected with the area where I grew up," she says.

Over the years, she's also fought actively against the stereotypes that prevent middle and high school girls from pursuing math and science courses. "It's incredibly important that we counteract that trend in our schools, so I do a lot of outreach to those girls," she explains. "I tell young people to pursue their passions, to never let anyone tell them no, and to never not try. You can only fail if you don't try." It was this determination that ultimately transformed her from a shy young lady growing up in a small town, to a winner of the "40 Under 40" Award given by the

National Sports Group to celebrate the 40th anniversary of Title IX and gender equality in sports. The organization selected forty women athletes who had used their lives to make incredible impacts, and Sandy's name amongst others like Sally Ride and Condoleezza Rice. "I've been surrounded by women in science and engineering through my whole career," she says, "but there should be so many more—and I believe there will be."

Debra Moser

Trying Something New

Worlds away from the rigid and regimented high school curric-
ula many American students are initiated into today, a number
of high schools in the late 1960s and early 1970s were willing to try
new things, and they cultivated this fearless attitude in their students.
In the halls of one such D.C.-based institution, young Debra Moser
watched a world of possibility unfold around her with each lesson and
each assignment, fortifying a lifelong propensity for a grounding self
confidence and an elevating ambition. "I hung with a very creative
crowd, and our teachers encouraged us to try different things in the
classroom, which led me to believe you could try different things in
life," she remembers. "I learned that it was okay to take chances in life
and move beyond one straight and narrow path—that life itself can
be a work of art, and that we have the agency and ability to apply our
creativity to it and forge the kind of path we envision for ourselves."

Debra's creative vision has led her from the art world to the world of business, serving her just as well in her current entrepreneurial ventures as it did in her days as a high schooler who believed in dreaming big and doing good. "I'm a product of the do-good generation," she remarks. "We never talked about making money when we were younger. My career has never been motivated by money, but instead by challenging myself and society to be better. How could I effect change somewhere? How could I impact people's lives for the better? That was our focus." Now the partner and cofounder of MeatCrafters, a boutique meats company in the D.C. metropolitan area, Debra's work is succeeding in opening doors for the local community to try new things simply because she, herself, has always been willing to.

MeatCrafters produces specialty salamis, sausages, and other cured meats. The artisan food company was launched in 2008, the brainchild of Debra and her husband Mitch Berliner. Mitch had long worked to bring specialty and organic foods to the Washington, D.C. area, and when he decided to enact a career change, Debra encouraged him to follow his lifelong passion of making salami. With her business acumen added to the mix, the couple created MeatCrafters, and the new business began to take on a life of its own. Debra and Mitch partnered with Stan Feder, the President of Simply Sausage. Stan now heads up the charcuterie production, and Debra and Mitch have learned how to make salami with equipment purchased from Italy.

Each partner brings something unique to the table. As a chef, Stan perfected the art of making dried charcuterie and salami after studying techniques in France, Italy, and Spain. A fantastic salesman, Mitch has long been passionate about using his entrepreneurial drive to bring high-quality, local foods to the D.C. area, and Debra brings her skills in strategic marketing and planning, underscored by the creative flare she has expressed and nurtured all her life. That creativity proved especially crucial when the team first tested spices for their meats. Thanks to her suggestions and commitment to trying something new, the salamis are now flavored with Middle Eastern, Indonesian, and Spanish spices that aren't found in run-of-the-mill salami. The meats stand out for their unique flavors and the "do good" business approach behind their production are sold at Debra and Mitch's joint farmer's market venture, Central Farm Markets.

Debra holds a pastry certification but had never worked in the meat business before launching MeatCrafters, so at first, she was understandably hesitant to take the leap into something so new, and especially into an industry with such high barriers of entry. Thanks to advice from Mitch, however, she found the courage to go all-in. "My husband encouraged me not to slam the door shut right away," Debra explains. "When someone asks you to do something, say yes, even if you don't know how to do it. Have the confidence in your capacity to learn, grow, and navigate the challenge." Indeed, MeatCrafters has been a learn-as-you-go experience, but Debra's fresh outlook, creative thinking, and willingness to say yes to new challenges have lent the venture a unique edge that sets it apart and has been crucial to its success.

Debra's own success to date stems not only from the fact that she was willing to try new things, but more so because she insisted upon it. This commitment to innovation was nurtured in her from a young age, even before she enrolled in the unconventional high school that brought her creativity to new heights. Born in Albuquerque to an aeronautical engineer father and a schoolteacher mother, the family moved to Silver Spring, Maryland, when she was nine months old, and she's been in the D.C. area ever since.

When Debra was 15 years old, she got her first job working at a dress shop near her grandmother's house. She worked all summer for $1.50 an hour, keeping her eye on a beautiful camel-colored coat displayed in the store. When September rolled around and her time at the shop came to an end, she was thrilled to see that her diligent savings had paid off and that she could afford to buy the dream coat. Hard work and fiscal responsibility have been hallmarks of her approach ever since, thanks in part to the day her father gave her a checkbook when she was 16. He showed her how to balance checks to the penny, underscoring the lessons of self-reliance and wisdom her parents had always modeled for her.

Debra's parents and beloved grandmother also encouraged the creative thinking that came so naturally to their daughter. "My father was a photographer, so I kind of grew up in the darkroom," she recalls. She also still remembers vividly a painting she did when she was five years old, and the feeling she had when her grandmother saw it and proclaimed, "This girl's got talent!" In middle school, her parents enrolled her in art classes at the Corcoran College of Art and Design. Debra loved going to the prestigious school every Saturday morning to paint and draw with the college students, and though her parents encouraged her passions, her decision to follow an artistic route was ultimately her own. She was given the freedom and flexibility to choose a path that suited her passions, with little pressure from her parents to go in any particular direction.

Free to follow her heart and her sense of what was right, Debra entered college at the University of Maryland as a set design major and later switched her degree to graphic design and photography, developing skills she still uses in her work today. Her first job out of college was a graphic design and art director position with Woodward & Lothrop, a department store chain headquartered in Washington. She took the position as a chance to grow her skills by paying attention and thinking creatively, and when she was given the opportunity to hire photographers for the company, she brought in the very best professionals from around the world. "I wanted people I could really learn from," she says.

Debra left Woodward & Lothrop when her first son was born, but after six months as a stay-at-home mom, she found she felt too restless when she wasn't making things happen in the workplace. With that, she went back to the University of Maryland to pursue a degree in secondary education, fulfilling her passion for working with teenagers through teaching photography and computer science courses. "I wanted to make a difference in teenagers' lives the same way my high school teachers had made a difference in mine," she explains.

As Debra transitioned from participating in the arts to teaching the arts, she was surprised to discover a natural affinity for leadership. "I found that I really liked being in charge of something, keeping it running and making things happen," she recalls. "I saw a side of me that was good at managing, networking, putting people together, and building relationships. For the first time, I realized I was interested in business."

With that, Debra enrolled in Johns Hopkins University's graduate business program with a focus on strategic planning and marketing, keeping her job as a teacher on the side. "I was drawn to marketing and strategy because of the creativity involved," she affirms. "To me, it's just like art. You're creating something new—a different kind of picture of the direction you want to take a company." Through that time, Debra found herself teaching during the day, attending school at night, and raising two children.

When she successfully earned her MS in Business, Debra experienced a defining shift in consciousness, realizing that she could probably succeed at anything she set her mind to. She continued teaching at Johns Hopkins for eleven years, and as she pursued more ventures, she found that she most loved jobs that combined teaching and training. She ran a paramedic education program at George Washington University for several years before working in consulting for several more. Then, when the Rockville arts organization, VisArts, offered her a position as interim Executive Director, she agreed to a fifty percent pay cut to pursue a professional path that was highly aligned with the passions she had cultivated since her earliest years.

"The art center was in the basement of a grocery store, and one day, the City of Rockville claimed eminent domain and said they were taking back the space," she recounts. "I said they couldn't do that, and that they should instead help us relocate to the new town center they were building." The center did, in fact, have a 28,000 square foot building with some potential, so Debra set her mind to writing a 100-page business plan. All in all, the venture engulfed over three of the ten years she worked for VisArts, but in the wake of the move, she succeeded in turning the organization around and tripling its budget—thanks, in part, to the tradition of fiscal responsibility in which she was raised. Also during her time at VisArts, Debra married Mitch.

When Debra left VisArts in 2008, she was flooded with letters from people from all over the county, thanking her for the difference she had made in the community and offering her words of encouragement for whatever her career held next. Thanks in part to these kind words, she was ready to put her skills to the ultimate creative test, and after working together on Central Farm Markets, the couple decided to launch MeatCrafters. Debra had always wanted to run her own business and be her own boss. "I had never had the opportunity to work for myself, so I wanted to take all of my career skills and see if I could apply them to something that would be my own," she says. "I wanted to try something new and see if I could rise to the challenge."

Alongside the burgeoning success of MeatCrafters, Central Farm Markets started with 15 vendors in the spring of 2008 and has since grown to over 100 vendors and three locations, with six employees working behind the scenes to run operations as Debra handles marketing and events and Mitch covers much of the logistical work. With a division of MeatCrafters specially geared toward the market, and another division focusing on wholesale, Debra and Mitch are essentially growing three entities, yet these many responsibilities don't discourage her from serving on the boards of several charities and organizations. Her greatest philanthropic passion, however, is having the opportunity to speak to women's groups. "I talk about how your life moments influence your career choices, and what to do when you decide to change your career, whether you're 22 or 50," she says. "I ask people what it is they've always wanted to do, and I tell them to go out and do it."

It's always a challenge to balance career and family, but amidst her professional accomplishments and volunteer work, Debra has managed to devote time to her husband, children, and now, her grandchildren. Indeed, the impact of her work expands beyond the deepening culture and food choices of the D.C. metropolitan area, blazing a trail for others—like her own grandchildren—to take risks without fear and push the limits of their own skill set to create the path that's right for them.

In advising young people entering the working world today, Debra emphasizes the importance of following your passion and being open to change. "Don't focus on the money," she says. "Follow your heart. You'll probably change careers three or four times, and that's okay. Don't be afraid to try something new." From those early days working in the clothing boutique, to teaching college students, to building up an organization, to running her own business, Debra's career has shown that creativity, flexibility, and hard work are the keys to a fulfilling career, and to living life on one's own terms. "In my career, sometimes I'd worry about where I was going," she recalls. "Now I'm in a place where I can see where I've been, and I wouldn't change a thing. And there's still so much for us to do. I can't imagine a life where I'm not working toward something and trying new things."

BERNHARDT
WEALTH MANAGEMENT

Jonathon Perrelli

The Arc of Achievement

"**A**s long as you can sell, you'll be able to put food on the table." This was the advice that Edward Herman gave his young grandson, Jonathon, and the boy never forgot it.

Himself the grandson of immigrants and a child of the Great Depression, Edward and his wife Ruth knew what it meant to struggle, but even more so, they knew what it meant to persevere. Whatever product he sold, he believed in wholeheartedly. "Pop-Pop taught me that, if you believe in something enough and are passionate about it, others will see that in you, and it will really speak to them," Jonathon remembers today.

Edward grew up in a generation where people stuffed money under mattresses, yet through hard work and incredible passion, he built a wonderful life for himself and his family, to the extent that he was able to enjoy his passions, retire, travel the world, and try his hand at a game he could never afford to play before—golf. He found that he didn't particularly like the sport, but he bought an ugly red plaid golfing hat, complete with a green pompom, which he wore from time to time for fun.

Years later, when Edward passed away during Jonathon's junior year of college and the family gathered together to sort through his things, his very distraught grandson noticed the hat amongst his belongings and immediately recognized it as the thing he would remember his grandfather by. "To me, that hat represents an arc of achievement, whether it's financial, cultural, or familial, that connects across generations," Jonathon describes. "It represents the incredible strides my grandfather made in his own life, which echo those made by generations of people who came to this country to build a better future." Now a founding partner of Fortify Ventures, an early stage investment fund that lives side by side with its portfolio companies to provide support along the way, Jonathon surges toward achievement with each professional endeavor he engages in, employing that same infectious and transformational passion he learned from his grandfather all those years ago.

As an early stage technology fund investing primarily in software companies to date, Fortify believes in funding innovators. "Our goal is to inspire and support entrepreneurs," Jonathon says simply. "We invest, syndicate with other investors, help companies put in place the tactical steps to achieve their strategic goals, and most importantly, we let them know that they can do it." This is done in part via direct funding and community support through the Fortify Ventures Fund. Another component of the company, a pitch series called Distilled Intelligence designed to bring founders and funders together, reviews hundreds of companies for a rigorous vetting program. Through this series, Fortify has awarded $125,000 to entrepreneurs in the two years since its inception, and an estimated $50 million has been committed through other investors to companies in the program. Fortify also created D.C.'s first tech Accelerator, a 20-week program created in support of startups that want to grow their teams and bring products to the market.

At the core of these programs is belief. "In the two years since we launched Fortify, we have paid employees, but I haven't taken a salary myself," Jonathon explains. "I've been doing this because it needs to be done, and the payoff to me is represented in more than money. Fortify was a startup as well, and we are growing it like any bootstrapped entrepreneur would. The venture capital landscape is evolving along with how investors engage entrepreneurs, and Fortify is evolving with the market. We operate differently. We don't sit in an ivory tower awaiting founders to pitch and educate us; we engage them directly. There are open, active channels of communication and information so that everyone can learn from each other. We've been referred to as the Jerry Maguire of investors because we care to spend quality time with our companies and see them as more than just a collection of statistical data points." With 34 promising companies in its portfolio so far, Jonathon and his team plan to grow the fund and continue to support and invest in their companies as Fortify lays the groundwork for a second fund.

Jonathon's vision for Fortify reflects a lifelong drive to achieve that was evident even at an early age. He was born in New Jersey but moved with his family to West Germany when he was very young. The Perrelli family then moved to Great Falls in Northern Virginia. "I think I developed an early hunger for success because I grew up in a relatively rural area and saw a lot of lower middle class families that seemed trapped by their circumstances," he remembers. "I once asked my mother what it was that makes kids want to get out of challenging inner city environments, improve their situation, and do better than generations before them. She said that the fact I was so curious exhibited to her that I already had it."

Indeed, young Jonathon did have something best described as chutzpah. The youngest of three brothers, he was a risk taker and early entrepreneur who took his grandfather's lessons on sales to heart. He experienced the value of a dollar early in life when he started selling bubble gum, and when he had made enough money doing that, he could afford to start selling fireworks instead—a more profitable venture. His efforts earned him thousands of dollars each summer which, along with assistance from his parents, he parlayed into investment accounts that ultimately allowed him to purchase his first townhouse in college. "Those early experiences with money helped me understand supply and demand," he recalls. "And I always had cash on hand from the sales, so when banks were closed on the weekends, my parents would come to the Bank of Jonathon if they needed cash in the pre-ATM days, so I was able to return the favor."

As civil servants, Jonathon's parents were hard workers and instilled in their children an extraordinary sense of patriotism and family values. "They're extremely caring and motivational. They taught us that, no matter what your profession is, hard work pays off," he affirms. "It may not be that day, year, or decade, but it will. Hard work pays off for you, your children, and your grandchildren. And above all else, it builds character. My team and I work incredibly hard, and that is in part thanks to their influence."

Fortify is far from the first team that has benefitted from this work ethic. While Jonathon was growing up, there wasn't a lacrosse team in Great Falls, so his parents would shuttle him to nearby Vienna to play. When he started his freshman year at Langley High School, he and some friends decided to start a team of their own, raising the money themselves and with the support of their parents to start the endeavor. Jonathon was the captain of Langley High School's lacrosse team, leading his classmates to an incredible near victory at the regional championship. "We lost by a single goal, but we gained a great deal from the entire experience," he emphasizes. And while the win was not immediate, Jonathon helped to build something that withstood the test of time.

Now, two decades later, the program not only perseveres, but thrives, and the team has won state championships for the last four consecutive years. "To me, that's what business and entrepreneurship is all about," he says. "With Fortify, I see a twenty-year plan that creates value across a variety of fronts and advances entrepreneurship in the region, similarly to how the lacrosse program adds value to the community and helps kids learn the value of team work, as well as earn scholarships. For some reason, I feel like some people have an attitude that if you fail, you'll be written off. But sometimes we learn from failures more than we learn from successes, so failing often leads to more valuable success."

One key failure came during Jonathon's junior year of high school, when he did something wrong and was grounded for the entire school year. "I was a really social kid, so I thought it felt like the end of the world," he laughs. "But I look back now, and it was one of the best things that could have happened to me. For one thing, I got closer to my parents, which I cherish. For another, they brought me along to events where I had the opportunity to meet real captains of industry. One of Ross Perot's right hand men lived in our town, and he shared stories with me about his time in the Vietnam War and about his journeys in business."

Jonathon always had an affinity for business. He would literally cut and paste newspaper articles about the founding of companies like Microsoft, Oracle, and Dell, following the stories of the entrepreneurs and taping them to his walls. He even ended up investing in those companies himself as a teenager. In college at Virginia Tech, many of his closest friends were entrepreneurs, and they would sit around and talk about business and technology ideas. He would pet-sit for Edward and Norrine Spencer, the Dean of Student Affairs and the Associate Dean of the Business School, who encouraged him to apply for a real estate investor scholarship, which he was awarded. "Ed and Norrine taught me the importance of putting on different hats when looking at every situation to understand the perspective of an investor, employee, customer, potential recruit, advisor, competitor, or friend," Jonathon says. "There's a way to do business where everybody wins. Thanks to them, I am always trying to think this way."

After earning his bachelors of science in finance and particularly enjoying his psychology courses, he graduated and took a job with a small consulting firm, where he learned he couldn't work for a company that didn't truly care about its clients. With that, he decided to start his own company, HelpNet. "Many of my parents' friends were professionals with their own practices, but they were not connected and often weren't even aware of the internet, so I'd go into those offices and install modems," Jonathon explains. "I started connecting these businesses to large ISPs and ended up meeting with the sales team of UUNET, once the world's largest ISP and based in Northern Virginia." He believed in the network they were building and accepted a job as a salesperson.

Before long, the UUNET leadership team indicated that their biggest challenge was not scaling the network or winning customers, but instead growing the company by hiring the right people. "I took that as a challenge and transitioned over into recruiting," Jonathon says. He essentially built an online recruiting system that streamlined the application process, revolutionizing the way the company was able to process and hire top-notch team members. UUNET grew from a few hundred people to over 8,000, and from $25 million in revenue to over $5 billion. Thanks to his vital contributions, Jonathon had his pick of opportunities within the company, acting as director of a group in Engineering dealing with tier one VC-backed hardware and software vendors.

In the five years he spent with UUNET, Jonathon had a hand in hiring a former Marine to serve as COO of their engineering group, and the two developed an immediate friendship that revolutionized the way Jonathon viewed leadership. "Layne Hefner made things happen and did it as a true servant leader," he remembers. "On his first day, he wanted to meet the people in every department who really kept things in order. He helped me see that a leader might have the tools, resources, and ideas to get something done, but the power was in the hands of the employees that actually took action to make things happen. At least, he made them feel that way and empowered them to take action, to enjoy their contribution, and to feel like they were a part of something bigger than themselves. Thanks to Layne, I came to appreciate various styles of leadership, management, and sales skills as a powerful trifecta."

After UUNET, Jonathon cofounded a digital media company called e-Tantrum, a Shazam-meets-iTunes vision that ultimately became a dotcom tragedy, but from which Jonathon learned a great deal. After taking a motorcycle trip with his brother through the Himalayan Mountains to refocus his mind, he returned to the U.S. and became more involved as an angel investor. As a co-founder and investor in Plesk, Jonathon continues to enjoy the success of a hosting automation software platform now known as Parallels that has over $150 million in annual revenues and is poised to go public.

While Jonathon had failed with e-Tantrum, he made the most of the situation by re-hiring some of the e-Tantrum security engineers to do perform security posture assessments for ISPs, including UUNET. "Make the most of your network and try your best to make lemonade out of lemons," he advises. "We had an incredible team and everyone needed to put food on their tables, so I went back to what Pop-Pop had taught me. I sold our capabilities, and it worked!" This effort evolved into a business called The Shadow Group, which was sold within six months. Jonathon was also involved in the founding of cyber security companies SecureSoftware (acquired by Fortify Software and subsequently by Hewlett Packard) and SecureForce, the latter of which is entering its tenth year. After seven years as President and CEO of SecureForce, Jonathon moved on to Chairman.

The fabric of Jonathon's career is woven with mind-expanding ventures, influences, and accomplishments. He was an early employee at the world's largest ISP, co-founded companies whose products are now sold all over the world, and exchanged thoughts and ideas with some of the best venture capitalists in the country. But one of the most life-defining of those experiences was the day he met a venture coach named Chris Bradley. As Chris helped out with marketing, product messaging, and sales at SecureSoftware, Jonathon found himself telling Chris, "Someday, I would like to do what you do."

That's the dream Jonathon accomplished when he opened the doors of Fortify Ventures in May of 2011, and that's what continues to drive him today. "In startupland and as an angel investor, I learned that I'm more effective at being a coach and cheerleader than a quarterback," he affirms. "I've cofounded and run my own companies, but I'm enjoying being effective at driving and motivating others, helping them to achieve their dreams. I'm driven by innovation, disruption, inspiration, and vision. That's why I love coaching—it's all about helping someone who dares to innovate in the face of obstruction. It's about shaping a dream into something others believe in and invest in, bringing in the capital to actually make that dream come true. The backbone of our economy is entrepreneurs and the creation of jobs through the growth of individuals, and I hope to be able to support both in my role at Fortify."

And as Jonathon's own childhood indicates, this is a dream that can start even at a very young age. "I believe innovation and entrepreneurship is something that every child has within them," he remarks. "Its creativity and the urge to think about something new, and I try to support that as much as I can." This encouragement is not only professional, via his involvement as the Executive Producer of a documentary series called 'Startupland', as a mentor aboard the inaugural Millennial Trains Project, at a variety of Startup Weekends, at The Founder Institute, as a Mentor at Thomas Jefferson High School for Science and Technology, with the Network for Teaching Entrepreneurship, and at a number of universities in the region. It's also personal, via his own children. At home, he plays a version of Shark Tank with them after watching the show, in which they pitch entrepreneurial ideas to him which he in turn actively engages them on. "Whether my children become entrepreneurs, scientists, teachers, public servants, athletes, artists, or any career path that they choose, I want for them to be exposed to a variety of options," he says. "And most importantly, I want for them to be happy."

In advising young people entering the business world today, Jonathon reminds us that it's easier than ever to start a business. "In the past, you'd have to spend millions of dollars to build corporate communications systems with your own server infrastructure, along with hiring professionals at every turn," he says. "Now, all of that is virtual. It has never been this easy and cost effective to start and manage a business, and it can be done from your smart phone. So pursue your passion and take action to make things happen. The world of angel investors, accelerators, and incubators needs innovative young people with great ideas just as much as those young people need it. I believe that the main goal in life is to be happy, so why accept a job doing something that you don't enjoy? Ask yourself what you're best at, and what you love to do, and find a place within that intersection." And as he stands at that intersection today, making dreams into reality and fueling future generations of entrepreneurs, Jonathon never forgets that the arc of achievement extends backward as well, connecting him to those past generations of dreamers that paved the way for today.

BERNHARDT
WEALTH MANAGEMENT

Peter Rogers

Climbing Every Mountain

At the age of 10, Peter Rogers chose to leave his childhood home in Connecticut to attend a boarding school in New York. Although both parents encouraged him to go, the decision was left to Peter, and at first he declined the offer and remained home as his 5ᵗʰ grade year commenced. But during the Thanksgiving holiday, his two older brothers, both already students at the school, urged him to reconsider. Ultimately, Peter put aside his concerns and resolved to take advantage of the opportunity, enrolling in his class late and setting to work catching up on everything he'd missed. That decision was his first major defining moment—one that set the stage for a life of self-reliance, independence, and many adventures to come.

Today, Peter is the Senior Advisor to FrontPoint Security Solutions (FrontPoint), a business he co-founded with two partners. FrontPoint sells home security and home automation services utilizing top-of-the-line technology, with systems that are both modern and affordable. Customers can control their system remotely, and those with a credit score of 600 or better receive significantly discounted equipment. But it's their business model that truly differentiates FrontPoint from their many competitors in the alarm industry. While fewer than 5 percent of alarm systems on the market today are Do-It-Yourself, Front-Point systems can easily be installed by the end user in less than an hour.

According to major industry metrics, the company's success is evidenced by its low cancellation rate and low costs per customer added, and by the fact that all of their customers have been added organically. "Everyone that we talk to is someone who was searching online for an alarm system," Peter affirms. "We're not direct mailing or cold calling. It's not push marketing, but pull marketing, lessening our acquisition costs and attracting better customers." Thanks to this approach, business has taken off since FrontPoint's founding in 2007. Once comprised of Peter and his two partners, the company now employs over 400 people. The entire operation has been self-funded, with almost all of the equity remaining in the hands of the three founders. Success on such a large scale, without limited outside investment, is practically unheard of in the alarm industry.

Peter has long been clearing his own path, professionally and personally—a character trait he's been known for since childhood. His father died ten days after his birth, but his mother remarried three years later, and she and Peter's stepfather always encouraged their children's independent spirits. In fact, after their children had finished with school, Peter's parents had to track their various whereabouts on a world map full of pushpins, with one brother sailing the Pacific, another motorcycling through South America, and Peter working his way across Asia and the Middle East. Along with Peter's two brothers, his mother and stepfather had two daughters, and all five children were exposed to travel, music, the outdoors, and reading of all sorts. Peter developed a lifelong love of nature that paralleled his stepfather's love of hiking, and between junior and senior year of high school, he spent time at Outward Bound cultivating a passion for climbing and exploring. His interest in music also played a major role in his formative years, compelling him to sing with boys' choirs through his grade school years and to later consider majoring in Music when he enrolled at Harvard University.

After his sophomore year at Harvard, Peter travelled with the men's glee club to Europe for a summer trip, but unlike his classmates, he didn't return home when the summer ended. Instead, he chose to remain in Europe, determined to explore his passion for singing and then decide if his career lay in music before returning to Harvard the following year. It was another foray into the unknown, and well worthwhile, but he ultimately decided a music career was not in his future. "I didn't feel I was on par with the professionals, and I was afraid I wouldn't be able to support a family, even with some mild success in the field," he recalls. "And above all, the future vocal stars I did meet possessed a certain single-mindedness that I did not. The unwavering focus and commitment to doing only singing in my life—I simply didn't have that. I wasn't ready to close all the other doors that were open before me."

Peter's adventure had taught him much, and he returned to his junior year at Harvard with his options open. His major had changed from Music, to Classics, to English. And now, with a year in Europe and German fluency under his belt, he finally settled on Comparative Literature. He didn't have any idea how he might apply his degree professionally, but through his time at Harvard, his passion for climbing had grown. The Harvard Mountaineering Club became his primary interest, and with them he learned to ice climb on Mt. Washington, then travelled out west for more climbing adventures. "When everybody else was graduating and applying to grad school or attending their on-campus recruiting sessions, I was dreaming of Patagonia and the Himalayas," he recalls. "I ended up going to the Himalayas by way of the Arctic and the Alps. I just wanted to travel and climb." Sure enough, when graduation rolled around, Peter took off for Nepal. It was 1976, and these adventure trips were far from common. He considered trying to turn his passion into his occupation, but the odds of making a living through adventuring were even worse than those he faced in pursuing a singing career. Being a guide was a possibility, but it had some of the same attributes as being a full-time opera singer: constant travel and potentially challenging economics.

With these concerns in mind, Peter returned home without any clear direction, but as free-spirited and willing as ever. His brother was running a bee operation in North Carolina and invited him to explore the bee industry, so Peter joined the business as an apprentice beekeeper, learning the trade and spending a summer working with the local Conservation Foundation in Nantucket. "They gave me the rights to a lot of their honey, which I harvested and then sold to natural food stores to fund more expeditions," he explains.

Finally, his then-girlfriend proposed a move to San Francisco. Neither of them had ever been there, and that was reason enough for them to pack the car and make the trip across the country. They fell in love with the city immediately and decided to buy a house there, and Peter found a job with Eddie Bauer. "It seemed like a good place for me to earn a living and utilize my knowledge and passion for the outdoors," he remembers. After a circuitous but rewarding route, Peter had finally joined the business world, and his star quickly began to rise.

During his seven years working at Eddie Bauer, Peter ascended from part-time Christmas help in the San Francisco store to Regional Manager running all the stores east of the Mississippi, managing to find the time to marry and have his first child in the midst of his professional success. In the business environment, his competitive spirit and desire to be productive made him a true force to be reckoned with. "That's where I got the beginnings of my business education," he recalls. "I came in the back door as a mountain climber and left as a retail industry professional."

In 1984, the family decided to move back to Connecticut, where Peter found work with a small manufacturing firm for the next four years. In that capacity, he got an education in operations management and learned about computers, networking, and the efficiencies each could engender. In the process, he automated so much that he worked himself out of a job. Once again, he was eager to start down a new path, now with a whole tool belt of business expertise.

Peter's move into the alarm industry was nothing less than serendipitous. He was looking for work, networking with friends and professional acquaintances, when an HR consultant he knew found him an opportunity at a growing company. In 1989, he joined his first alarm company as a senior manager. The second alarm business he worked for was acquired by a larger one, and he stayed on to work for the acquiring company for a time. In the process, he gained a wealth of information about the alarm industry. "We were a little different from other alarm companies because much of our growth was organic, but we also grew significantly through acquisition," he says. "So we had to understand not only what it took to run a successful company, but also the deal-making and transaction side of the business. Most folks in the industry understand one or the other of those reasonably well, but you won't find a lot of people who understand both."

The thorough business education he received at the alarm companies, combined with the expertise he already had, left Peter confident he could run his own operation business—an idea that had been germinating in his mind for the past 15 years. "I always liked the idea of having my own company, of being my own boss, but the opportunity hadn't arisen," he reflects. Now, armed with experience and knowledge, he decided to create that opportunity himself and set up a consultancy specializing in the alarm industry. His efforts were met with almost immediate success.

Though his first marriage hadn't worked out, Peter remarried in 1997 to the love of his life, Bonny, who from Day One has been nothing but supportive of his goals and work ethic. "I was working with the lenders and investors and the operating companies themselves, mostly on mergers and acquisition activities," he recounts. "Then Goldman Sachs entered the industry as a lender and investor, and I began working with them." Peter and his point person at Goldman, Chris Villar, enjoyed working together and began to explore their shared interest in the alarm industry. "We had met a lot of smart people and seen a lot of good business models, but there was a gap in the market" he says. "It was clear that we had an opportunity to do things other people weren't doing, so we decided to start our own company." With that, Chris enlisted another Goldman employee and a friend from Georgetown, Aaron Shumaker, to join them, and in 2007, FrontPoint was born.

Before FrontPoint, Peter and Bonny had dreamed up a meticulously planned future in which he retired with his consultancy money at age 62. But with the heart of an adventurer that was first kindled when he decided to leave home for boarding school at age ten, the twist in the story has brought the thrill and excitement he's always loved, and Bonny has supported him every step of the way. "She's the angel on my shoulder," he avows. "She's always reminding me to look for the best in people or in a situation, and to have high expectations without necessarily applying the expectations I have for myself to everyone else. She's a great coach." With such a strong supporter, it's perhaps poetic that, when asked what one object he most treasures, Peter references a black, heart-shaped rock given to him by Bonny before they were married. While they were dating, she told him she planned to give the rock to the man she would marry, and he proposed soon after she gave it to him.

"Making the bold decision to start FrontPoint with Chris and Aaron was the smartest thing I ever did for my family," Peter says today. It's only the latest in the series of bold steps that have propelled Peter through life, and the leadership style with which he operates is as honed as the journey that has warranted it. "Whether you're an expedition leader on a wild and wooly trip to the mountains, where people may face serious injury or even death, or the CEO of a company, leadership is leadership," he says. "To me it's a combination of competence and conscientiousness—the ability to lead by example and the willingness to roll up one's sleeves and do whatever needs to be done, which garners the essential element of respect." Peter emphasizes the importance of modeling the behaviors expected of employees, and warns that the best leaders are neither mired in detail, nor singularly focused on the big picture. "It takes a combination of tactical and strategic thinking," he explains. "Good leaders can think on both levels, and the best leaders can move with fluency and speed between them."

To young people entering the business world today, Peter is encouraging and optimistic. "I would say there is more opportunity today than there has ever been, which is the exact opposite of what a lot of people think," he says. "The rate of technological change and advancement is opening a lot of doors. You can either be part of that and engage, or sit on the sidelines and lament the fact that you think all the good ideas have been taken, which couldn't be further from the truth. You've got to get out there, try stuff, and climb every mountain—otherwise you'll never know what's there and what you're truly capable of." From the man who left home at age 10, who left Harvard to travel Europe, who left a comfortable life to climb the Himalayas, and who left a successful consultancy to launch an even more successful business, it's clear that making the effort to explore the unknown isn't necessarily about finding opportunities and success, but about making them yourself.

BERNHARDT
WEALTH MANAGEMENT

Wolf Ruzicka

Citizen of the World

In 1983, Wolf Ruzicka celebrated his fourteenth birthday in a very different way than he had celebrated his thirteenth the year before. To expand his mental horizons, his father had sent him to a school in Peru, and though he was staying with a well-to-do host family, the terrorism rampant throughout the country at the time crept into everyday life.

The most profound of these occasions came one day when Wolf and the family were driven to see an American movie. He will never forget the moment he stepped out of the car, and right onto a dead body riddled with bullet holes. "It was a wrenching shock, gearing up to be transported to a Hollywood environment and then coming face to face with that violent reality," he remembers today. "From that moment onward, when anyone asked me at any given time how I was, I always said that I had no problems. No matter how hard my life becomes, I'll always have enough money to fill my fridge and put gas in my car. I'll always have a job and health insurance. That was such a defining and grounding moment for me that has kept me calm throughout my life, even in times of crisis."

That's why, when Wolf celebrated his birthday several weeks later, he knew he would never be the same. He had left his home country of Germany as a boy who hated that his father had sent him away to Peru, but later returned to the Frankfurt airport as the most thankful son, and as a young man eager to see more of the world. At his first opportunity, he spent half a year in Morocco and then signed himself up to attend schools in Australia, France, and Great Britain.

In a way, Wolf was pursuing a feeling he had seen in his father when the wall came down in Germany. His father had immigrated from Prague into West Germany years ago, where he met Wolf's mother. He had continued running Westward across the Atlantic, only to arrive in Chile and Ecuador, and realize he was in love with the woman he had left in Germany. Soon after, Wolf was born.

The first chance he had after the wall came down, his father put Wolf in the car, and the two drove the autobahn until they reached the hills surrounding Prague. "Once we saw the golden rooftops of my father's hometown, I looked over at him," Wolf recalls. "His sleeves were rolled up, and he had goose bumps on his arms. I realized that he hadn't been there in more than twenty years, yet he belonged there. And I realized that everyone needs to have a place of belonging; otherwise, you're a lost soul in a big world."

Wolf has lived his life traveling the world to find that perfect place of belonging, only to discover key pieces of himself each year and at each stop along the way. "I am a citizen of the world," he affirms. "But I'm a capitalist at heart, and the United States is where I'm supposed to be." Now the CEO of EastBanc Technologies, a bleeding edge software development company that builds game-changing products for large organizations, Wolf's search for that innate belonging has led him to where he is today, leading a company he plans to dedicate the rest of his professional life to.

The streets of Washington's Georgetown neighborhood are so idyllic and charming that one would hardly peg them as the scene of some of the world's most vanguard software development initiatives. Yet behind the understated façade of its offices, EastBanc Technologies' team of 150 top-notch employees are hard at work building products that transform lives worldwide in ways at once simple and elegant.

Each time a gas tank is filled, there's a good chance that the fuel was analyzed with solutions built by EastBanc Technologies for some of the largest oil companies in the world. The International Monetary Fund recently won a design award for a highly sophisticated yet user-friendly mission-critical system that Wolf and his team refined, modernized, and mobilized. They've produced key software components for clients like Microsoft and Comcast, utilized by millions of users worldwide each day. "We are the secret behind some cutting-edge technologies put out by some very well-known companies that may have changed your life one way or another," Wolf says. "That's why I wake up with a smile every morning and feel so proud of the things we do."

EastBanc Technologies was founded in 2000 by Anthony Lanier, a real estate developer, and Stanislav (Slava) Arseniev. From astrophysics, to rocket science, to mathematics, Slava had seen the great scientific talent in his home country and had the idea to bring some of the best and brightest here to the U.S. to see what would happen. "And what happened was magical," Wolf affirms. "Without any nurturing, purely through happenstance and through the value of their work, the company grew to 35 employees."

At that point, the founders were interested in assessing the real potential of the fledgling company, so they got in touch with Wolf, because of his renowned work ethic and unparalleled commitment to success. Wolf, who was living in New York City at the time, made the trip to Washington to analyze the company and give his recommendations.

"I didn't have an agenda to become CEO, as I was too young at the time," he laughs. "But as soon as I returned to New York, they called and asked if I wanted to run the company. I didn't even have to think about my answer—of course it was yes."

Since Wolf came onboard in 2007, the company has grown because of its uncompromising commitment to the quality of the team members it hires. Thanks to their highly selective hiring process, their chief concern becomes keeping those employees engaged and happy, which results in an employee turnover rate of virtually zero. And thanks to the resulting enthusiasm of their work force, EastBanc Technologies has never had to invest resources in any kind of marketing or sales effort. "Our customers talk about us in their inner circles, to the point that I was cold-called by a major stock exchange when one of their IT systems malfunctioned," Wolf remarks. "They had heard about our little swat team through word of mouth. It all boils down to reputation."

But how did a young boy born in Nuremberg and raised in Ingolstadt, Germany, come to sit at the helm of EastBanc Technologies? "Along the way, life throws you some very strange curveballs," he remarks. "You can either let them go sailing by you, or you can reach out and catch them. It's the ones I decided to catch that led me to where I am today."

Wolf's parents had been raised in relatively wealthy families, but when communism swept over Europe, their assets disappeared completely. As a young boy, Wolf would fill buckets with coal in the basement of their apartment building and then climb five stories so they could have hot water for bathing. Thanks to the unrelenting entrepreneurial spirit of his mother and father, however, the Ruzicka family fought their way back from poverty to a modest lifestyle. His mother ran a delicatessen with hundreds of different cheeses, while his father was an air conditioning, sanitation, and heating systems engineer. He had a number of opportunities to grow his business over the years, but having had and lost so much in the past, his top priority was spending time with his son, giving Wolf the unconventional childhood that cultivated such strength and soundness of character.

His grandfather, by turns an archaeologist, artist, racing team owner, and factory owner, taught Wolf to focus on the things that most interested him. Those interests spanned math, geography, and English, bleeding into different cultures and countries as well, so the young boy began reading scientific and educational magazines and materials much earlier than his peers. As a result, he excelled in school without trying. "For a period of about three months one year, my father would knock on my door each morning and ask if I wanted to go to school that day," he recalls. "If I wanted to go to the swimming pool instead, he'd simply write me an excuse note. I'd show up to school to take tests, and I'd get great grades. This unbelievable laissez-faire fathering allowed me to discover my true self. I flourished."

The town of 20,000 people where he grew up had 10,000 American soldiers stationed in barracks on a hill he could see from his bedroom window, but Wolf never understood what they were doing there. When he was ten, he began playing basketball, and since most of his European peers played soccer, he would play with the Americans on the courts nearby. He learned English by counting baskets and free throws, growing especially close with a 17-year-old soldier named Kevin. It wasn't until Kevin showed him a piece of paper he kept in his uniform, detailing the estimated number of nuclear warheads pointed at their small town at that moment, that Wolf understood the tenuous severity of the Cold War he was growing up in. "When it dawned on me that I was on the front line of that shadow war, I got the very clear sense that I had been quite sheltered," he remarks.

It was true. And though he was number one in his class, his father worried that he was missing out on the world and becoming too narrow-minded as a result, so he decided to take matters into his own hands. When Wolf came home from school one day, his father asked, if he had started studying Spanish yet. Wolf was confused, so his father

said, "Did I forget to tell you? I signed you up for Spanish classes."
Several months later, his father asked, if he had packed his bags yet.
When Wolf was confused again, he said, "Did I forget to tell you? You're
studying in the German School of Peru next year."

After the ensuing years of transformative world travel, Wolf graduated at the top of his class and decided to go to business school because
he wasn't sure what else to do. He would soon come to realize, however, that the business education he received from religiously reading
the *Economist* and the *Wall Street Journal,* paired with watching and
learning from his own entrepreneurial parents, was the best education
he could have had. Japan seemed to be a dominant global presence in
business at that time, so he participated in a student exchange with
a university in Tokyo, but was quickly disillusioned. He then sat in
on several lectures by the business school at Columbia University in
New York City, where he quickly realized that the core of business
was simply common sense. "At that point, I decided to just suck it up
and work my way through a private business school in Germany as
fast as possible, picking up jobs along the way to gain the real world
experience that would be most valuable."

Upon finishing his MBA, Wolf had just put together his English
resume for the Japan External Trade Organization where he had interned
previously, when he noticed a recruiting poster for a young American
company called MicroStrategy. The company's ambitious spirit captivated him, so he faxed his resume and was invited to interview in their
newly established German office, where he was among their very first
hires. The company sold software, but Wolf wasn't clear on what that
software accomplished, so he attended an intensive 6-week technical
boot camp at their headquarters in Vienna, Virginia. "With no prior
technical experience, it was grueling day-and-night training, but I
came to understand the value of the technology, and I fell in love with
this country in the process," Wolf reflects.

Wolf became infamous at MicroStrategy as a jack-of-all-trades. After
a year in the technical field, he diversified into management and was

then put in charge of the company's internal operations center, keeping tabs on every piece of data that traveled through the business. "I was like the company historian," he laughs. "I was the only one who knew every sales cycle, when we won, why we lost, every competition that took place, and what value our projects delivered to the respective enterprise customers."

Throughout that time, the company had grown from 300 to 2,700 employees, but when the bubble burst in early 2000, MicroStrategy had no choice but to lay off hundreds of its employees. "I still remember exit interviews with a guard sitting outside the office, waiting to escort that friend of mine, who had virtually gone to war with me, out of the building with a shoebox with their belongings," Wolf says. "I promised myself I would never go through that again, which is why, at EastBanc Technologies, I consider myself more of a risk manager. I'm always certain that we're insured against all eventualities. We experiment enough that we don't miss out on opportunities, but we never risk the future of the mother ship."

As MicroStrategy struggled, Wolf, being the stubborn German that he is, resolved that he'd ride the ship out and do whatever it took to stabilize it. "It cost me half my hair, but we made a comeback," he remarks. Part of that comeback involved his transition to the sales side of the business, where he became the right hand man of the VP of Worldwide Sales and Services. "Every dollar the company generated went through us—everything from licenses, services, consulting, education, technical support, and maintenance," he remembers. "After that, I realized that the ability to sell was a key component of running a company that I hadn't mastered yet."

Sitting around the table one day, the MicroStrategy team realized the company was healthy again, save for two offices. With that, Wolf was sent to the New York City office to help them adopt the new model and to learn through active participation what sales was all about. "We started from scratch," he recounts. "I called every single customer to introduce myself and set up meetings. One by one, over the years, we turned dissatisfied customers into satisfied customers."

Wolf's efforts culminated one day as he waited for an Amtrak train at a New Jersey station. A potential customer called him on the phone with "one final question" before they announced their decision. Fearing the worst, Wolf braced himself for a disappointment, but the voice over the phone asked what fax number to which they should send the signed purchase order, worth hundreds of thousands of dollars. "In that moment, I felt like I had finally come of age professionally," he reflects. "Meeting someone who isn't onboard with your product at first, building a deep relationship, and then convincing them to put their trust in you, attaching value to your product through your personality in that way—it gave me this sense that, in this capitalist country, I had done something great. I still have a copy of that first commission check."

Looking back, Wolf can't put a finger on any one time he failed at business, but he remembers with regret when he almost missed the birth of his first child, Lucas, because he was on his Blackberry working to close a deal with Citibank. "It hit me in that moment that my priorities were absolutely wrong," he affirms. "The only way to save myself from myself was to hand my Blackberry back to MicroStrategy and take a long sabbatical, which allowed me to be truly present for the birth of my second child, Siena." Though he had every intention of returning to MicroStrategy, it was during that time off that he received the call from EastBanc Technologies, and the rest is history.

As that history continues to unfold, Wolf makes a point to sit down on an annual basis to reflect on the moments during his expansive journey that should never be forgotten. "I take the time to mine out the gold nuggets from the previous year that really are worth remembering," he says. "I add them to the string of memories that define me—a string that grows longer and richer each year." Whether it's the moment he heard the muezzin's call to prayer in Marrakesh; when he married Barb, his perfect match and an entrepreneurial, yet caring woman with exceptional emotional intelligence; reading bedtime stories every night with Lucas and Siena; the profound influence of mentors like George Moore, the founder of TARGUSinfo; or being personally invested in the lives and futures of his employees; Wolf empowers the blessings of his life each time he makes a point of remembering and honoring them.

In advising young people entering the workforce today, and speaking as a true citizen of the world, Wolf reminds us that the world is our playground, and not to be limited by what we see in front of us. "Engage your imagination, as it may not be nurtured enough by society," he says. "Turn off the video games and the TV, and instead fall back on the things that you can't wait to do when you have a free moment. See if you can build a career out of those things. My passion was to build and create something that flourishes long after I am gone—to become a CEO and run my own ship. I wanted to be responsible and accountable for something meaningful, and to make that something truly incredible. And as I actively engaged in the development of my character and my professional journey, I left enough leeway for the wind to blow me, as it will blow anyone, to exactly the right place—that place I truly belong."

BERNHARDT

WEALTH MANAGEMENT

Chris Schroeder

The Drive Home

A ll through grade school, Chris Schroeder was a solid C student—
not because he couldn't do the work, but because he lacked the
motivation and drive to be exceptional at school. Without a passion,
what was the point? He preferred to spend his time playing sports,
working paper routes, and lifeguarding at the local pool. "I remember
knowing that, at some point, I'd need to pick a career because that's
what people do in life," he says today. "But I had no clear vision of what
I wanted to do. I felt like the need to define my future was extrinsically
motivated, and not my own."

Having worked on his high school's newspaper and the yearbook,
Chris went to college thinking he might as well become a photojour-
nalist major. As luck would have it, however, he attended a job fair
during his first semester, where he had the opportunity to speak with
people who had pursued the profession. When he asked what a typical

career path looked like in that field, they laid out a long road with a series of gates that would need to be opened before he even began to see any real success. "I realized that, at the end of the day, my ability to advance forward would depend on the subjective criteria of taste, over which one has minimal control," he remembers. "I wanted to have a sense of control in the process, so I began to rethink my options."

Chris had dabbled in computer programming in high school and appreciated the fact that, unlike the art world's subjective standards of good and bad, the world of technology was much more objective. "If your work doesn't function, that means you did it wrong," he says. "But if it does work, you did it right." Working in technology promised tangible measures of success that linked directly to one's skill levels, and that resonated with Chris. He decided to declare a computer science major, and with that decision, it was as if the floodgates opened. The uninterested student transformed into a driven, determined, passionate individual poised at the brink of a real future, marking one of the most defining moments of his life. Now the cofounder and CEO of App47, Inc., a startup that specializes in systems management for mobile apps to the enterprise, Chris has used entrepreneurship to expand the impact of that transformative realization so that, now, he builds businesses that allow others to achieve life-changing experiences of their own.

After unlocking his passion for computer science, Chris's success could have taken any number of forms. He could have easily found a safe, stable, secure career working with the federal government or at a large corporation, if it weren't for the drive home at the end of the day. "At the end of the day, on my drive home, I always ask myself, did I move the ball forward today?" Chris explains. "When you work for a large company, even if you're putting in 80-hour weeks, the probability of your actions having an impact on the public stock price of your company is so negligible. I enjoy smaller, entrepreneurial startups where I can have an impact on a daily basis. As I go through my list and get through the day, I know I make a difference in moving the company forward, and that matters to me. There's a lot of risk that comes with that, but at the end of the day, you have to believe in yourself and your ability to bounce back, even if things don't go as planned."

This willingness to take risks stands in contrast to the approach taken by Chris's own father, who was a helicopter pilot for the Navy. Chris was born in Norfolk, Virginia, and the family moved once before settling in Virginia Beach when he was five years old. "It was important to my parents not to uproot my older brother, younger sister, and me," he remembers. "So my father would go on deployment and rotate through the various jobs, squadrons, and roles, all while stationed in the same place." After 22 years in the service, however, his father found he couldn't progress any further because he hadn't engaged in the hardship tours that are integral to rank promotions. "He made a conscious decision to give us a stable home, and who knows what would have happened otherwise," Chris says, "But I know he would have liked to serve longer, and I was left with the impression that the safe route isn't always the best route."

In Chris's household growing up, family always came first. His mother, a homemaker, was a religious woman, and both parents were extremely engaged in their children's lives and in the community. "Everyone in our town knew our parents, so everyone knew the Schroeder kids," Chris laughs. "If we went out and got into trouble, the news would get home before we did. So, because of that engagement and involvement, and because our parents were so present in our lives, we weren't tempted by some of the things the other kids were doing. We were good kids."

Despite this involvement and support, the Schroeders encouraged independence in their children, which frustrated Chris when he entered high school and found himself faced with bigger decisions that would shape the course of his life. Being forced to make his own decisions, however, cultivated in him a sense of self-reliance and confidence that grew through the years and would become particularly important toward the end of his college career at Radford University, as he struggled through 400-level computer science and mathematics courses. "As I was approaching the end of my studies, I considered the idea of joining the military and flying helicopters like my father," he remembers. "But I had made the decision to invest four years of my life in figuring out this field called computer science, so I stood by that choice."

A professor had told Chris that computer science is a trade, and that he would be charged with going out in the world and figuring out a domain where he could apply his skills and become an expert. Upon graduating and beginning his pursuit of that domain, he hoped to become a user interface programmer, but was lured into accepting a systems management position at a government contracting firm. "It was a blessing in disguise, because the systems management domain is perfect for me," he affirms. "It's relevant and lucrative, and it's something I understand and am passionate about. That was a career-defining twist of fate."

With that, Chris became a systems administrator, and over the next eight years working in the government contracting world, he learned how to manage servers, build and manage networks, and detect and address security intrusions. He built small networks and large network operation centers for three letter organizations, earning security clearances and eventually returning to school to earn his masters in telecommunications engineering.

Chris then left the government contracting world behind when he accepted a position at UUNET, one of the largest internet service providers at the time. In that capacity, he helped build and manage their system manager platforms. "With one of the largest networks in the world, there were tons of devices that needed to be monitored," he recalls. "We needed to collect all the events that were occurring and channel them into a manageable view that would allow us to determine if the network was healthy, and to troubleshoot any problems." Working on a team of around 60 people spread between the U.S., the UK, and Amsterdam, Chris spent four years there, and during that time, he met two people that would change the course of the rest of his life.

One was Kim, the friend of a friend that Chris met one evening at a group dinner at Plaza America in Reston. They were playing word and number games on the paper tablecloth, and someone wrote down a series of numbers that Kim readily identified as a famous sequence of numbers that links directly to the golden ratio. "We always joke now that she had me at 'Fibonacci series,'" Chris smiles. "We got married in 1999, and I couldn't have done all of this without her. She's always been supportive and has focused on what makes me happy."

Also at UUNET, Chris met Sean McDermott, the CEO of Windward IT Solutions. UUNET hired Windward to help Chris's team build its system management tools. Sean was heavily involved in the startup world, and Chris decided to leave UUNET to try his hand at a startup himself. With that, he took a job as the VP of Engineering at Statusphere and was charged with building a new product. "We hit every engineering milestone we laid out—on time, feature complete, fully tested," he recounts. "It was awesome, but we closed the company doors because the sales and marketing weren't aligned with the product. The lesson learned was that engineering is the easy part; it's sales and marketing that are hard, and those areas are where investment dollars should be channeled."

Closing Statusphere's doors marked a particularly poignant time in Chris's life. He remembers vividly standing outside the hospital the day after his first son was born, on the phone discussing who would pay the lawyers to close the company since there was no money left in its bank account. Chris wasn't sure how he would get his next paycheck, but he was coming to understand that stability is the product of one's network and capabilities, more than anything else. What's more, he had been wholly bitten by the startup bug. "Even the late nights, hard work, pain, suffering, and sacrifice of the Statusphere experience was fun to me," he remarks. "I knew I was an entrepreneur at heart."

Chris went on to serve as the CTO of a company called Approva and then left in 1992 to launch Vanward Technologies with Andy Glover, the current CTO of App47. Vanward was a bootstrap consulting company focused on automated software testing and could reduce the platform development cycle of their clients by weeks, or even months. Sean McDermott then asked Chris to come to Windward and help productize a piece of intellectual property, which spun off into its own company, RealOps, Inc. The company automated the troubleshooting and recovery of failed systems and was sold to BMC Software in 2007, resulting in an exceptional exit that generated a three-fold return for its investors in less than three years. "That's one of the business ventures I'm most proud of," says Chris, who was the company's CTO.

The day after the RealOps check cleared, Chris and Sean asked, "What's next?" They had had enough of enterprise's software sells and wanted to do something in the consumer market. Chris served on BMC's M&A team until 2009, when a severance package became available. Ready to leap into entrepreneurship again, he took his chance, and he and Sean began pitching a number of consumer-based product ideas. "Everyone said we were two enterprise software guys who didn't understand the consumer space, so we decided to figure it out ourselves," he says. With that, they built several mobile apps to serve as testing platforms to understand how the consumer-based market worked. "After making them available to the public and analyzing the data, we concluded that, yes, we were two enterprise software guys who didn't understand the consumer space. But we learned a lot about mobility!" Chris laughs.

The process led to a key realization: it wouldn't be hard to instrument an app to report who was using it, where, and how, as well as how it was performing, where it was crashing, and why. "These are answers I'd want to know for any IT asset," Chris points out. "There were no system management tools for mobile apps, so we returned to a space where we were well-versed. We went back to the Series A investors who had funded RealOps, though we didn't have a line of code written. They funded two guys and an idea."

With that, App47 was born in January of 2011. A product was built by June, and almost three years later, they have just over thirty customers, including the U.S. Department of Agriculture, the U.S. Air Force, Bed Bath & Beyond, and Bristol Myers. The company now sits at the inflection point of any seed-stage startup, poised for the market to take off. With its main office in Reston, and with a team of ten employees, it helps to deploy, configure, and secure apps, moderate their performance, detect their faults, and measure their usage—often for companies who have written the app for internal employee use to streamline business practices.

A pure technologist at heart, Chris aspires to serve as the CTO of a publicly traded company, and as his first CEO role, his experiences at App47 have been a perfect stepping stone toward that vision. From running a sales team, to negotiating partnership deals, to working with lawyers, to conducting federal, Fortune 500, and international sales, his business acumen and technological expertise combine to lend him an intuitive sense of how to provide the best value to the customer at the lowest cost to the company, and how to build the right product at the right time for the market.

But for Chris, the most gratifying aspect of leading startups to success is the creation of opportunity and jobs in an economy where both are lacking. "I love finding people who, based on their resume, are unqualified to do what they want to do," says Chris. "I believe they should have a chance, and I like to give them that opportunity. It's about seeing the character and potential of a person, rather than letting their experience limit them. I love taking someone fresh out of college, or someone who wants to switch career fields, and giving them the support they need to follow their passion. When they fail, we teach them how to correct their errors and watch them grow. I like to build companies that create opportunities for people to come in and grow themselves." In advising young people entering the working world today, Chris emphasizes the importance of finding something that speaks to one's passion, and to be prepared to work hard for it once you find it.

Chris and Kim work to create a similar atmosphere at home for their four children. Beyond teaching them right, wrong, and the nuance of a good moral compass, they've founded a charity called Majomani—a name comprised from the first two letters of each child's name. "We haven't decided whether the mission will focus on education or on more humanitarian concerns, but we've begun to build it as a way for our family to give back together as a unit," Chris says. "To me, family is the most important thing—I don't know what I'd do without them."

Now, on the drive home each night to the family he cherishes so much, Chris doesn't have to wonder if he moved the ball forward that day. For the App47 team and clients, for the people given a chance to achieve their goals because of opportunities he's created, for the children he's raising, and for his own future, it seems Chris continues at a steady jog, keeping that ball in play and never letting it rest.

Mike Sformo

One More

"This much," says Mike Sformo, casting his eyes toward the millimeter separating his thumb and index finger. "The different between winning and losing is this much."

This observation comes after a lifetime of marveling over the reality that, for the most part, people are born with the same faculties, but achieve wildly varying outcomes. Some people are positive and happy, while others are negative and vicious. Some are able to create jobs, businesses, and wealth while building wonderful families, yet others are left homeless and begging for food. "Why do some people make it while others don't?" Mike asks. "I think of this as the success struggle. Everyone goes through heartbreaks and failures in life, and the difference is what you do with them. So often, the difference is just one more try."

Mike's life philosophy is reminiscent of the Japanese concept of Kaizen, which means "change for the best" and entails continuous, daily improvement. It's about laying one brick after another until you feel you've depleted yourself completely, and then challenging yourself to lay just one more, one more, one more. "It's impossible to reach ultimate perfection, but with each step you take toward it, you get closer," he says.

Thanks to this philosophy, Mike is now the founder, chairman, and CEO of Operation Backbone, a nonprofit dedicated to providing crucial brain and spine surgical treatments to active duty and veterans around the world. A U.S. Navy veteran who recently suffered a non-military injury for which he sought care, Mike launched the venture in 2012 after finding himself snagged in a web of bureaucracy and red tape for requests that should have been simple. His injury was minor, but the experience was a window into the tremendous burden placed on some service members and their families when they suffer more traumatic experiences.

"Our overall goal is to be able to extract any service member or veteran suffering from a brain or spine injury anywhere in the world and integrate them into the Operation Backbone pipeline by bringing them into one of our facilities around the nation and providing them the treatments they need, followed by post strength, nutrition, and mental rehabilitation services through the National Hockey League—Buffalo Sabres (NHL), which we're partnered with," Mike explains. "The surgeons on our team provide their time at no cost, and we work with insurance carriers and our generous donors and sponsors to eliminate any monies coming from the soldiers or their families once in our care. We aim to provide the best surgical treatments available on this planet today at no cost to the solider or the family." By taking into account the needs of the soldier or veteran's family as well, Operation Backbone is also about showing spouses and children that there are people who care about making a difference for them. In this way, the organization expands its impact to make the success struggle less of a struggle, producing positive results that reach more people through a transformative ripple effect.

Now that he's set the vision and begun drawing together the team it will take to get there, Mike sets his mind each day on confronting the learning curve before him. One day finds him working with top spine surgeons on stenosis. Another finds him working with world renowned brain surgeons on brain aneurysms. He might begin the week working on cadavers or on research and discovery in the high tech MRI, CT, and FMRI fields of radiology, discussing a multitude of business, finance, personal, and professional matters with his advisory and board members. He might end the week with his focus shifted to developing his partnership with the Buffalo Sabres, or working with the Pentagon to streamline Operation Backbone's processes, or promoting the organization through interviews. "The people I work with have so much knowledge that it's mind blowing," he exclaims. "The key to my success so far has been my willingness to jump into these uncomfortable situations where I'm truly challenged, because my options are to either quit or learn, and I don't quit. Brain surgery? I'll try it. Back surgery? I'll try it. I give it hell and make it happen."

Mike's fearless attitude and unconventional approach to learning stems from a lifelong resistance to traditional academic styles of education. Though his father was a school teacher and principle, and his mother taught school before becoming a homemaker, Mike was the wild child of the family and preferred to be out in the world, learning by doing. Born and raised in Corfu, near Buffalo, New York, his Italian and German parents were well-rounded and encouraged him to try art, music, woodworking, clay, kayaking, camping, reading, and math. A talented athlete, he was the only kid in his ninth grade class to make the varsity baseball team, where he played catcher. "I never understood the point of school, but I had an unbelievable childhood," he says. "I had very little structure and loved running around with my high school sweetheart, Maria. I also loved working on the farm down the street and still go there to bail hay sometimes when I'm visiting home."

Having spent his childhood dreaming of becoming a professional bodybuilder, Mike knew college wasn't for him and instead enrolled in the Navy, where he was introduced to a highly structured program that actually resonated with him quite profoundly. Serving from 1991 to 1995 during the Gulf War, Mike traveled the world and remembers it as one of the greatest experiences of his life. "It didn't change me that much or calm me down," he remarks. "If anything, it lent more fuel to my fire because I got to see how big the world is, and how much there was for me to do."

Stationed in California in his early twenties and working on contracts for the military, Mike first realized that business is done on golf courses far more than it is done in offices or meeting rooms. "I thought people won contracts based on the quality of their product and the competitiveness of their prices, but I was wrong," he remarks. "It's more about investing your time in the right people."

As Mike continued to work his way through the military, he began to realize that the more he learned, the less he knew. "When I was young, I thought I knew how everything worked, but as I got to know people who had achieved incredible personal, professional, and financial success, I realized how much I didn't know," he says. "I looked at the things people had created, and I was completely in awe of the sacrifice, passion, and tenacity they displayed as they reached certain levels of success, surpassed them, and then went back to help others along the way. I decided that's what I want to do, too."

Despite his love of service, Mike readily noted that the pay structure of the military left much to be desired and decided not to reenlist. Thanks to his experience and network in nuclear technology and the rigging he had done on fast-attack and Boomer submarines, he was immediately snatched up by a civilian group called American Rigging, a San Diego company interested in entering the submarine field, where he assumed blue-collar work. "The hours were long and dirty, and when I got my first set of stitches, I said there had to be an easier way," Mike laughs. "So I kept pushing, and I was finally allowed to apply my industry knowledge to sales."

Thanks to his unflagging persistence, Mike succeeded in creating his own department within the company for working with the military, and then had the opportunity to branch out into other fields, including training and work with Sea World. The dynamics he learned on the golf course in the Navy remained relevant as purchase decisions were based on how well a buyer liked a seller, and people were drawn to Mike. "I learned more and more," he affirms. "When you find yourself in front of someone, and you need them, and they're willing to give you their time, you don't waste it."

After a number of years working in that capacity, Mike went to work for a competing firm and ended up in Atlanta, where Maria was working as a schoolteacher. Mike hadn't seen her since 1993, and she was engaged to be married, but when the two reconnected, it was as if they had never said goodbye. They married in 2007 and decided to move home to the Buffalo area, where he was invited to be a guest on a radio show. Mike was so invigorated by the experience that he created a show of his own, which focused on entrepreneurship and overcoming setbacks in life. "We talked about the real stuff, like debt and repossession," he says. Over time, the subject matter shifted to cancer research, and Mike became acquainted with the complex interplay between politics and progress. "My work brought me down to D.C. and Congress," he explains. "I was stunned to see the obstacles put in peoples' way as they work to develop new treatments."

The urgency of Mike's work was underscored later when his own father was diagnosed with Stage 4 pancreatic cancer in 2011 and died just 49 days later. Mike's family was blessed to be in the room when he took his last breath, and today, Mike wears his father's watch as a reminder to keep pressing forward with all he's got. "I have a beautiful wife and three incredible kids," he says. "The third hand on that watch is ticking away, and when I reach my last breath, I want to know that

I did everything I could to put them on the right path and to blaze a trail that will help others in the future."

Mike didn't have a job when he and Maria moved down to Washington, but his interest in entrepreneurship and in clearing the obstacles that stood in the way of progress and treatment spawned another radio show. People from all over the U.S. would speak on during his segment, and he began doing consulting work. It was around that time, in 2011, that Mike went to the gym and decided to squat 500 pounds for old times' sake. Though he hadn't squatted in years, he was feeling good—until he lowered the weight on his second repetition and heard a sound like the snapping of a dry twig. A horrible, cold sensation shot through his body, and it wasn't until several hours later, in the emergency room, that his spine cracked again and his senses returned. "I realized I was okay, but I was terrified," he remembers. "It was my sign from God that my days of loading it up and just doing it in the gym were officially over. He made it clear, so I never look back. I just moved forward and was incredibly thankful I could walk."

In moving forward, however, Mike was shocked by the confusing and often arbitrary stipulations that determined the quality of care he could receive and how difficult it was to access that care through the VA system. Expressing this concern to Maria, she challenged, "What are you going to do about it?" Thanks to the example set by his father's stern commitment to follow-through, and by Maria's unwavering insistence on the importance of finishing what you start, he knew he had to be sure before committing to action. "I saw the journey ahead of me that would become Operation Backbone, and I thought, Oh God," he remembers. "It would be a career- and family-altering tour for the rest of my life, but I decided to do it." With that, Mike quit his job and embarked on a journey to change the way medicine is delivered to wounded soldiers around the world.

Mike had no paperwork, no business plan, and no large amounts of money, but when he began asking people to get involved, they agreed without hesitation. From Johns Hopkins physicians to Pentagon officials, everyone wanted to help, and many of the people he had interviewed on his radio show have since reappeared to help the Operation Backbone mission in some way. "I'm proud to say that, two years later, it's been an incredible journey for me mentally, physically, spiritually, and financially," Mike affirms. "I wouldn't change it for anything because, to me, this is what it's like to really live. This is going out there, knocking on doors, introducing yourself, and communicating to people how important it is that they're a part of this vision and that they have a role to play. It's been a lot to spearhead, but it's like taking a chunk of clay. You have all the tools and ingredients, so you just have to keep shaping and molding it."

The success of the venture thus far rests on the solid foundation of the leadership skills Mike has cultivated throughout his life, which hold steadfast to a philosophy of candor, passion, faith, and persistence. "Candor is the number one thing people lack today," he remarks. "It's important to have a clear vision of what you're trying to do, and to be able to communicate with others in a direct and honest way. You also have to have passion, because people don't want to invest in someone who's only pursuing a hobby. And for those who aren't won over to the cause initially, it takes true tenacity. You just have to keep pressing forward and pressing forward, no matter the obstacles."

Despite the strong character traits that have guided Operation Backbone's development to date, Mike readily admits that the organization would not exist today if it wasn't for Maria. "It's been a miracle to have her around," he avows. "On my own, I would have accepted an easy way out, but she was insistent. Because of her, all of these troops and their families will benefit. The soldiers and their families are the heroes, and the Operation Backbone team is the true driving force."

In advising young people entering the working world today, Mike likens the experience to looking into a forest packed full of trees and obstacles. "Pick the tree you want, block out everything else, and aim," he instructs. "Once you take your eye off that target, you're done. To this day, I still have to redirect my gaze when I realize I'm eyeing too many targets. Just focus on the mission at hand and don't get distracted." More than anything else, however, he stresses the importance of reaching beyond one's self in one's life goals. "I believe we're put on this earth to provide a view, or an option, or even a roadblock for others," Mike affirms. "I think that's the true secret to success—something that's often lost when we look in the mirror and say, 'What about me?' That kind of mindset only magnifies our problems. But when we focus on helping other people, our own problems seem so irrelevant, and life takes on new meaning."

Integral to this effort is an element of faith—faith in something beyond your immediate perception, faith that your efforts will pay off, and faith in your vision. "I remember being in the Navy and going out on deck one night, where it was pitch black," he recounts. "You couldn't even see your own hand in front of your face, but after five minutes, your eyes would adjust and you could finally see the world around you. Faith is trying to see in the dark like that. People are terrified of the dark, and terrified of looking at their own shortcomings. The really successful people are those who try to see—those who get up every day and say, how can I change to be faster, stronger, or better? It's those who say, what's one more thing I can do to make this happen? Just one more?"

Kimberly J. Shanahan

Reaching for More

Even when she was fresh out of college, Kimberly Shanahan was never one to leave the office at 5:00 PM. She would watch peers and even superiors clock out as soon as the technical end of the work-day rolled around, and would find herself wondering, shouldn't there be more? "I yearned for the kind of work where you're really tied to what you're doing," she remembers now. "I wanted to be staying late because of some deadline—something important that couldn't wait. I learned I really needed to reach for more."

Thanks to this lifelong drive to push the envelope of success, Kim was promoted three times throughout her first four years in the professional workforce. That drive and determination have carried her throughout her career so that now, as the Senior Client Partner and Managing Director of Korn/Ferry International's Human Resources Center of Expertise, she has accomplished exceptional things, both for the organizations that have turned to her for help and in balancing her flourishing career with her flourishing young family. "I'm tied to our mission and extremely passionate about it, which is what I need to succeed," she remarks. "And I work with incredibly smart people who want to have an impact as much as I do, which truly allows us to do great things."

As part of the Korn/Ferry team, Kim places executives in organizations with the full business, personal, and industry impact of those placements in mind. A publicly traded company launched in 1969 as an executive search firm, it has evolved into a broad-based talent management organization specializing in executive search, recruitment process outsourcing, succession planning, assessment, diversity and inclusion, and other human resource strategies. It is now a 3,700-employee global force that garners $812.8 million in 2013 annual revenue, with Kim running its 19-person Virginia office from a P&L standpoint and the HR center from a high-level strategy standpoint. Making critical placements in companies like Western Union, Humana, Macys, and Under Armour, she thrives on the diversity and challenge of the work. "Having to learn the nuance of each business we serve really feeds my intellectual curiosity," she says.

Kim has thrived off challenge since she was a young girl growing up in Northern Virginia. In elementary school, she ran for student government and launched an enthusiastic campaign, only to be met with unexpected defeat. In middle school, she was bullied. "I hated middle school, but you get through it, and it makes you so much stronger," she remarks. "I was always compassionate and kind, but it made me even more so."

Kim ran for class office again in high school, and again, she was met with defeat. "That was tough," she recalls. "It's not easy to put yourself out there, especially at that age. But I later ran for class treasurer during my freshman year of college and won. I ran for office again during my junior year, and won again. My personality certainly evolved during that time, but I also just learned from things. I didn't give up."

Through her grade school years, Kim always held odd jobs—not because she had to, but because she liked making her own money and the independence that came with it. "When I was in elementary school I always had little businesses," she recalls. "I'd make flyers for car washing, babysitting, and weed pulling services and then deliver them around the neighborhood." One year, Kim and her friends put together a small amusement park in the neighborhood, where kids would pay a quarter to play a game or ride a ride. Her first job was in high school at Herman's Sporting Goods, followed by stints as a waitress and at a clothing store. The self-reliance afforded through earning one's own income became even more important to her when she watched her parents divorce at age 17. Her mother had been a homemaker, and it was hard for Kim to see her struggle to adapt to a new life of self-sufficiency. "That's one reason I'll always work," Kim says now. "It's risk mitigation, if nothing else."

As she grew up, sports, school, and art became her main interests. "I played tennis and soccer and loved the great highs and learning lows you experience as part of a team," she explains. She developed a strong work ethic on the field that helped her in the classroom as she took AP classes. She felt she had to work harder than others to excel and was shy in academic settings, but she loved her courses and the challenge that came with them.

What she loved most of all, however, was art. She even had her own art class in high school and won the gold key award at the Corcoran, developing her creative side to be just as strong as her analytical skills. With the dream of going into advertising, she was admitted to Vanderbilt but declined so she could attend Virginia Tech instead, believing that a liberal arts education wouldn't take her where she wanted to go.

Her father, who worked his way up from Staff Director of the Senate Armed Services Committee to Acting Secretary of the Air Force, was upset with her for giving up an Ivy League school, but after seeing how much she excelled at Virginia Tech, he agreed it had been the right choice. Kim connected with the school and the people there instantly, transforming from a shy introvert to an outgoing student with a large circle of friends. "Tech was a perfect fit for me, and I have zero regrets," she says.

The school didn't have an advertising major, so Kim instead majored in communications, and although she found some of the courses less interesting than expected, she wasn't going to give up. Instead, she added a finance major to her curriculum. It meant she would have to retake several math classes, spend a couple summers studying, and stay an extra semester, but she graduated as a double major and was hired immediately by the NRA, where she excelled in financial operations and took the initiative to implement some financial planning strategies that hadn't been tried there before.

After four years garnering incredible success in that capacity, Kim decided to switch tracks and took a position at DFI, a management consulting company in D.C. There, she worked on market entry strategies and the commercialization of defense products, starting as a research analyst and moving through the ranks to become senior associate. "I loved the diversity, but I was the only person in the company who had started a family and was living in Virginia," she says. "One year, they discussed using participation in social events like softball as a factor for bonuses, which didn't make sense to me."

Kim had met her husband, Patrick, while working at the NRA, and the couple got married when she was 26. "I always liked kids, but I never thought that was my path," she remarks. "Growing up, I had had friends with working moms, and they always seemed so cold in their business suits. That was my image of a working mom, and I didn't want to be that. I wanted to be free to always climb and reach for more, but then I had my first daughter, Jordan, at age 27. It was the best thing on the planet, and then we were equally blessed with our second child, Caili, several years later. My kids are absolutely amazing—interesting, beautiful, smart, intellectual, successful. I learn something new from them every day."

Interested in leaving DFI, Kim's father introduced her to Korn/Ferry, opening her eyes to an entire industry she hadn't known existed. "I thought it would be fascinating to take the things I was learning about businesses—where they were going, what the competitors looked like, and where they could go—and blending them with an understanding of people and who would be the right person to take a company to that next level." Kim had grown comfortable connecting with executives at a young age and was offered a position at Korn/Ferry, but she decided to check out the company's competition, Heidrick & Struggles. Heidrick made her the same offer, and she decided to accept because the culture of teamwork it boasted at the time held more resonance with her.

With that, Kim entered Heidrick's technology practice as an associate, and four years later, she was running its telecom practice as a senior associate. "I remember not knowing anything about telecom when I started, and being frustrated in a good way," she recalls. "We were building the telecom practice during that time, and the partner I was working with had a great network and could readily solve searches. I was desperate to find my way to add real value." Thus, Kim built a spreadsheet of every telecom company in the world, allowing users to sort by company name, revenue, state, person, and skills. Thanks to this tool, she was able to quickly come up with top candidates, transforming the practice's business development strategy in the process.

It was in the midst of this success that a senior partner called her into his office. He observed that she was heading down the partner path, which he said would be a very difficult road to travel as a female and a mother. He advised her to really think about whether it was something she wanted to do. "Of course it's important to be conscious of your path and how you define it," Kim says today. "But this negative approach was wrong. Shouldn't I be able to define my path on my own terms? And having seen both men and women achieve balance, shouldn't he have put me in touch with someone who had done it successfully, rather than trying to plant a seed of doubt?"

Shortly after this frustrating conversation, Kim received a call from MCI, which was about to emerge from bankruptcy and needed someone to build out its global executive recruiting function. Kim hadn't yet worked at a corporation, so she accepted and spent the next two years learning and building. Having done some M&A work at DFI, she also talked to the company's strategy team about an acquisition, impressing the leadership team so much that they transitioned her to Director of Strategy, responsible for building out wireless capability. "It was a big fork in the road for me, and while it was hard to leave HR, that move was part of my original plan," she explains. "I had wanted to go into a role I knew well and then move over to strategy or business development."

The company's wireless guys worked out of Jackson, Mississippi, and weren't used to a young female coming in and pushing the envelope, but Kim quickly won them over. They built out wireless networks and tier 2 markets, and Kim got back into financial modeling. "I have this pattern," she observes. "I tend to take big leaps, so my first three months on a new job are brutal. I worry to my husband that I'm not cut out for the work, but then I hit my stride and settle in, and it gets fun again. That's what happened on the strategy team."

When MCI was acquired by Verizon, leadership asked her to stay on the strategy team, but Kim felt the new environment was too big. Turned off by the idea of being a cog in a wheel, she considered her next move and found herself missing the executive search side of her work, in which she had excelled. "I liked the impact piece, the intellectual side, and not feeling like I was trapped in a bubble," she says. "You get to learn so much about so many different things, putting it all together to see the fabric of what's going on in an industry. And beyond that, you develop incredibly deep relationships with people, who become friends and clients. That's when I made a conscious decision to go back in for the long haul."

Kim looked at a number of different firms and chose Korn/Ferry, joining the team in February of 2006 as a client partner. She was immediately struck by how welcoming the culture was, and she was promoted from client partner to senior client partner within a year. Though she had started in the firm's technology area, she saw a considerable need in the HR space and steadily transitioned over, so that before long, it was all she was doing. She made a name for herself and others in the practice, and now, they are considered thought leaders in the field.

In 2009, the head of Kim's office left the company, and the person she was reporting to asked if she had interest in assuming the role. "I said I would be interested at the right point in time, thinking that point would come sometime in the future," Kim reflects. "But they ended up promoting me, which again was earlier than expected. The firm has been good to me, pulling me up to new levels before I even have the chance to ask for them. It's really advanced my aspiration."

Now, Kim brings a boldness and determined spirit to her work that keeps the company's strategy pressing forward. She can step back to analyze any situation, keeping her own concerns off the table to determine the best business move. This steely will is coupled with an infectious enthusiasm for the success of her colleagues that makes for an exceptional team atmosphere. "We all genuinely like each other," she affirms. "We've got a really strong group that helps one another, and I'm seriously passionate about rewarding hard work and watching my team succeed."

This approach speaks to Kim's leadership style, which is more participative today than ever before. "I like to provide direction and then be hands-off," she says. "I love to give feedback, support, and credit where credit's due, publicly and sincerely and in a meaningful way. Some people might say I'm challenging to work for, but it's just because I want people to care. I want good work product, and I want my team to learn. The other side of that coin is the fact that we laugh a lot, remembering that we can only control so much. When we have an off day, we take responsibility as a team and regroup together."

In advising young people entering the working world today, Kim encourages the use of contacts—something she purposefully avoided because she wanted to do everything on her own. "That was silly," she laughs. "Be humble yet confident. Seek healthy mentors early, because people want to help. Be bold but not too fast that you break things. It will all come—just don't expect it too early."

Beyond this, Kim's story demonstrates the power of reaching for something more. "I've always had this compelling drive to understand more, help more, and see more people succeed," she avows. And working for more inspires others to do the same, as is the case with Kim's daughters. Excelling in school, lacrosse, dance, and singing, the quest for betterment mirrored from their mother extends into deeper pursuits of the soul as well, and reflects back to Kim. "Caili is a beautiful dancer and someone who will practice and practice until she is satisfied with the results," she says. "Jordan is an amazing lacrosse player and singer. She has also really connected with God, reading the Bible every night and going to church or youth group two to three times a week. My drive may have inspired her, but she's now inspiring me to ask some important questions about life and what I should be doing right now. It's a journey, and I couldn't be more thankful for the family I'm walking it with and the places it's taking me."

Norma M. Sharara

Figure It Out

Growing up in Pittsburgh, Pennsylvania in a blue-collar family of five children, Norma Sharara knew that going to college meant a better future, but it would be up to her to figure out how to pay for it. Thanks to the example set by her parents, she had been a hard worker all her life, and thanks to her own resourceful, innovative, and tirelessly curious spirit, she knew that the established and prescribed ways of doing things weren't necessarily the best ways. That's why, when it came time for Norma to apply to her dream school, American University, instead of submitting an application form, she asked her guidance counselor for the address of the school's president.

"That's not how we do it!" the counselor protested. "Applications must always be sent to a school's admissions office." But Norma knew what she was doing.

Dear Sir, began the letter. *I would love to attend your school. Let me tell you why it's in your interest to have me as a student.* She went on to describe the energy, enthusiasm, background, and open-minded vigor she would bring to the campus, with her passion for the school's international program fueling her focus. Before long, she received a reply in the mail from the school's president, granting her a full-tuition scholarship and requesting to meet her when she came to campus. "If you follow normal channels in trying to accomplish something, you'll likely get normal results," she says today. "It's so important to be original. You have to figure out your own path in life, instead of settling for the path everyone else is taking just because it's commonly accepted." Now a partner at Luse Gorman Pomerenk & Schick, P.C., a nationally-ranked banking law firm based in Washington, D.C., Norma's philosophy has made for a life rich with character and depth, vibrant in its inimitability and with an arc all its own.

Luse Gorman was founded in 1993 and has since grown slowly but smartly to 24 lawyers. It focuses primarily on financial institutions like credit unions (which are tax exempt organizations with special exec-utive compensation rules), private mutual banks, public stock banks, and transitioning institutions with IPOs. With an expertise in mergers and acquisitions, Luse Gorman's clients are from Main Street, not Wall Street. "Coming from a small blue-collar town, I really relate to the fact that the bankers we serve are the pillars of their communities," she explains. "When a small community bank goes public and is listed on NASDAQ for the first time, it can be one of the biggest events for that community, and I love the opportunity to help that process go smoothly."

Norma joined the firm in 2005 when Section 409A was enacted, generating a plethora of deferred compensation work that would need to be managed at the partner level. It was a sea change in the world of taxation, and Norma was ready to make a change of her own. At Buchanan Ingersoll & Rooney, she had proven that she could work with Fortune 50 companies and go toe-to-toe with Wall Street law firms. The impersonality, however, left something to be desired, and she liked the idea of working for a boutique firm, where she would interact directly and routinely with the people who created and operated the banks. These CEOs and board members genuinely cared about what happened to the people in their communities, and Norma found that she, in turn, genuinely cared about what happened to them. Leaving her position as a cog in a prestigious wheel to have a more profound impact, she wanted to apply her sophisticated background and training in a market where it was sorely needed.

Norma excelled at foreign languages in school, prompting her to study Arabic, French, Spanish, German, and Italian, and in a sense, her career as an executive compensation and employee benefits lawyer is another act of translation. "I enjoy the intellectual puzzle of this exceptionally complex area of law, and I have the ability to communicate the issues in a folksy way that the layman can understand," she says. "I view the law as a helping profession, much like teaching. By translating its language into common, everyday speak, I equip the business owner, retiree, employee, HR director, CEO, or board member with knowledge that makes a difference."

This skill is underscored by the innate passion she brings to her work. In the six years she spent teaching her subject matter at the American University Kogod School of Business to graduate-level accounting students who signed up for her class because it fit in their schedules and not because they cared about compensation and benefits, she worked miracles. "By the end of the class, students actually felt dialed in, connected, and intrigued by the subject," she recalls. "They would leave with the understanding that there is life and logic behind line 17 of IRS Form 5500 with important real world applications. I love helping people see that this subject is alive, and not just some complicated and intimidating aspect of the tax code."

Norma's interest in the field dates back to the earliest days of her childhood, when her mother would lament the fact that she didn't have a job with benefits. As a young girl, Norma had no idea what these elusive "benefits" were, but she knew they were something to aspire to—something almost sacred. Her mother worked as a housecleaner, while her father worked for a financial printer, spending tedious hours printing the disclosures for SEC filings and stock offerings. The family struggled to make ends meet, so Norma got a paper route when she was twelve. She bought the routes on either side of her own route as well and employed her brothers, converting an old bicycle and scrap wood into a cart so they could carry the Sunday papers for all three routes at once. "If you wanted home delivery of the *Pittsburgh Press* anywhere in my neighborhood, you were doing business with me. I realized that 'monopoly' was not just a board game," she laughs.

Having devised a number of strategies to increase subscriptions and tips, Norma earned a princely sum of money during her first year of delivering papers. Her mother had been raving about the latest technology, called the microwave oven, which she had seen while cleaning the houses of wealthy people. Norma knew her mother considered the device only a nice dream, considering its cost, but because the price of microwaves was advertised in the newspapers that she delivered every day, she also knew the paper route had garnered enough money to buy one. She used her natural powers of persuasion and influence to convince her brothers buy in so their parents could have an extra special Christmas that year. An aunt drove them to Sears to buy a microwave for their mother and a snow blower for their father, and on Christmas morning, their parents were stunned. "I had always heard the word '*can't*,'" Norma recalls. "A family with five kids *can't* go to the amusement park, or *can't* go on vacation, or *can't* go out to eat. I wanted to show them that we *could* do things."

Norma's worldview rested firmly on the idea that all people are created equal. She was born in 1963 amidst the Civil Rights Movement and the climate of Martin Luther King, Jr., and her mother underscored the tenets of the time. She taught her daughter that some very wealthy people had low class behavior, while some very poor people had high class behavior, so wealth and class had nothing to do with one another. For Norma, the idea that everyone is equal naturally bore the question, why not me?

The inquiry sparked an innate ambition that was reinforced by the young girl's inclination to read anything and everything she could get her hands on. Late at night, she'd read under the covers with her flashlight, and when the Irish Catholic family attended church on Sundays, she'd study the maps of the Middle East in the Bible. She read the Encyclopedia Britannica cover-to-cover, as well as the dictionary. "It was something to do," she laughs. "While the wealthier students at my school went on summer trips to the shore or exotic places, I read. I quickly saw connections in the material and asked hard questions in school, which got me in trouble a lot. People thought I was being a smart aleck, but I just wanted to learn."

In high school, Norma worked as a country club waitress and at a bakery. Her parents had taught her to never say no to an opportunity to earn money, so she often juggled multiple jobs at once. One summer, she worked as a proofreader in her father's financial printing office, where she observed lawyers playing pool and eating pizza for large salaries while she was hard at work for five bucks an hour. "My parents always demonstrated incredible work ethic, so I've always been comfortable with hard work," she recalls. "But I wanted to see what it was like on the other side of the table, where I had the knowledge and authority to review the work of others."

Norma also thought about her future when she had the opportunity to travel to D.C. for the Cherry Blossom Festival as a color guard with her high school's band. When the students were given two hours of free time, Norma and her three friends took off like jack rabbits, determined to see as much of the city as possible. They got lost for six hours and were thereafter infamous as the girls who delayed the bus home, but they got to know the essence of the city, and Norma knew it was a place where she could truly thrive.

Norma crammed her schedule with AP classes but still managed to finish high school early, and the day after she graduated in January of 1981, she hopped on a plane to Paris. Through housecleaning, her mother had befriended a Dutch woman with connections in Paris, who knew of a family in need of an American au pair. Norma, who had practically lived in the foreign language wing of her high school, leapt at the opportunity to spend a year abroad living with a French family, where she pledged to live life to the fullest and embrace every opportunity that came her way. She hitchhiked to Brussels, spoke Farsi with Iranians soon after the American Embassy hostages were released, absorbed the dynamics of France's election of a communist as president, and was the only one who knew all the words to the songs when Bruce Springsteen came to town. When she returned to the U.S. to attend American University, she was a new woman.

This older and worldlier version of Norma happened to meet a young Egyptian man in an elevator during her freshman year of college, and the two hit it off immediately. In the wake of the Camp David Accords of 1979, Egypt and Israel each sent fifty of their brightest young scientists to the U.S. for advanced studies, and he was one of them. "We were both hardworking people from opposite sides of the world, and we found that the similarities far outweighed the differences," she remembers. They married when she was nineteen—a decision made despite the disapproval of her parents, friends, and community. "While the worldview of my parents tended to vector inwards, mine vectored out," she says. "I wanted to marry this Arab Muslim and raise bilingual and bicultural children in an international city like Washington, D.C."

Having majored in International Studies and launched an international family, Norma was shocked when she graduated from college and found that there were no decent paying international jobs to be had. She had always been told to follow her heart and pursue her passions, but when she entered a harsh job climate with student debt to pay off and no marketable skills, she vowed to never earn an obsolete degree again. With that, Norma set about doing what she does best—figuring it out. Perusing the want ads in the *Washington Post*, she saw a posting for a human resources position at the Insurance Institute for Highway Safety. She wrote in saying she was qualified for the position because she was human and resourceful, and they got such a kick out of her willingness to jump in that they offered her the job.

In that capacity, Norma was the assistant to the HR Director of the seventy-employee research organization. She was horrified when she was told that one of her first duties would be to handle the COBRA, but she soon learned that it had to do with health insurance and not snakes. She was eager to learn, and her boss was eager to teach her all about the benefits her mother had praised all through her childhood. She also learned how to talk to boards and get CEO approvals. "The experience really hit home that I could do anything I put my mind to," she says. "Whatever the opportunity was, why not me? I was as capable as anyone. That's how I saw myself, and that's how I found my way."

Through that experience, Norma gave birth to her daughter, Amira, and earned her masters in linguistics. Her husband had come to the U.S. on a J-1 visa, which meant he would have to return to Egypt to teach at the University of Alexandria for two years. When the young family moved to the 5,000-year-old city in 1987 to fulfill the obligation, Norma visited the American Cultural Center to see if they had any jobs for English teachers. When she was informed that they only hired teachers with linguistics degrees, she proudly held up her master's degree. Thus, she began teaching and fully immersing herself in the culture. The Egyptian Supreme Court was preparing to send several district attorneys and judges to the U.S. to learn about the American legal system, and as Norma was considering law school herself, she volunteered to help prepare them. The Chief Justice of the Supreme Court was her student, and while everyone else treated him as a superior, she treated him like all her other students, earning his respect in the process.

While most Americans in Egypt lived in compounds with walls, guards, and housekeepers, Norma walked the streets freely with her daughter. Because she could speak Arabic, and because she was married to a local, the community was protective of her and treated her as one of their own. It was a good life for the Shararas, but when the two years were up, they decided to return to America, where there was more opportunity to succeed and evolve. With a PhD in mathematical statistics, Norma's husband became a professor at the University of Maryland and worked on projects at the Goddard Space Flight Center and Jet Propulsion Laboratory. Meanwhile, Norma decided that, if she wanted to go to law school, she had better investigate first to see what lay on the other side.

With that, she landed a job as a legal secretary in the compensation and benefits department of a mid-size law firm, where she observed paralegals, associates, and partners. "I realized practicing law wasn't magic, and that I could do it," she recalls. "Since I had a young child, people suggested I settle for being a paralegal, but I saw those attorneys' offices with windows and discussion tables and thought, why not me?"

Norma attended the University of Maryland Law School in Baltimore, where tuition was discounted thanks to her husband's professorship. She had been told that she shouldn't hold outside work during her first year because her early grades would determine the caliber of job she landed for her second summer, so for the first time in her life, she was unemployed. "I was married with a daughter and a mortgage, so I related more to the professors than to the other students," she recalls. "They would fret about being called on in class, but after being shot at in Egypt, I didn't get worked up over that kind of thing. With eight years of life experience between college and law school, I had a very different perspective."

Few people go into law school with the intent of studying compensation and benefits, but Norma was sure it was the field for her, so she mapped out her coursework in tax, securities, labor, family law, bankruptcy, and corporate business issues. Most of her classmates planned to focus on a single area of law, but she wanted to do it all. Once students paid for a certain number of credits, they could audit additional classes for free, so she sat in on as many courses as possible, just to let the knowledge wash over her. She was there to be a sponge and absorb as much as possible, treating knowledge as a buffet that was there for the taking.

For her second and third year, Norma found a paid compensation and benefits internship with The Rouse Company, a publicly-traded real estate development firm headquartered in Columbia, Maryland, with 62,000 employees nationwide. It was 1992, and the company needed someone to work twenty hours a week on the new proxy disclosure rules that had gone into effect. Norma grew tremendously over the next several years, addressing the SEC executive compensation disclosure work, ERISA, and securities, as well as 401(k) and health plan issues. After she researched and solved a given problem, the general counsel told her to check her work with the firm's outside counsel, Piper & Marbury. Her capabilities were so impressive that the law firm—one of the largest and oldest in the area—offered her a job upon graduation. "It was a recession, and a very difficult time to find a job," she explains. "I was so shocked by their offer that I asked them to put it in writing. I hung it on my refrigerator to remind myself that it was real."

Piper & Marbury wanted her to start immediately, so she began making the 84-mile round-trip commute from Bethesda to Baltimore each day, all the while balancing her obligations to her family with the weight of studying for the bar exam. She passed with flying colors and, over the next three years, continued to excel at the firm. Eventually, however, she decided she wanted to work in D.C., spending less time in the car and more with her fifth-grade daughter. After a headhunter call, she accepted a position at a small tax boutique called Silverstein and Mullens, which was later acquired by Buchanan Ingersoll. The national firm was headquartered in Pittsburgh, and she found herself traveling to her childhood home for work, attending functions at the very country club where she had waitressed all those years ago.

Despite Norma's incredible success, the Sharara family fell on hard times when her husband was diagnosed with leukemia, passing away in January of 2001. She was up for partner the next year, but was held back a year because of the loss and its aftermath. Despite the hardship, Norma found herself achieving that large office on K Street she had set her mind on as a legal secretary, complete with a discussion table and windows. She did well there, but when a headhunter called about the opportunity at Luse Gorman, she recognized the chance to do better for the community and stretch her skills further. "I love discovering new things, whether they're 15 minutes from my house or 15 hours by airplane," she remarks. "It's why I love traveling the world, from Thailand, to Peru, to Fiji, to Brazil, to Cambodia. It's why I see complicated rules as interesting puzzles and perfect opportunities to bring value to my clients. I love discovering new things—I want to know what I don't know."

Now, Norma approaches her work at Luse Gorman with the same resolve she saw in her parents as a child growing up. Her parents taught her to stand by her decisions, follow through on her commitments, and never break promises to the people who were counting on her. She also strives to help young people who not only go the extra mile, but take the path that is less traveled and more true to their natures. Norma has mentored and trained several successful lawyers over the years who began as determined, enthusiastic kids who boldly went out on a limb to pursue their dreams, and she's proud to watch them succeed. "You can't teach hunger for knowledge, or attitude, or how to have a fire in your belly," she points out. "Those are the raw traits with which true success is built."

Norma's own success has landed her the John Nolan Award, a prestigious recognition given by the American Bar Association's Tax Section to future leaders in the field. She accepted the award wearing hot pink sandals and a colorful scarf, standing in stark contrast to the other dark blue suits on the stage and proving that she excels at what she does not in spite of her personality, but because of it.

In fact, it was her indelible character that led her to enter a contest when she was a freshman at American University, in which the best lip print on an index card won an all-expenses-paid trip for two to Acapulco. Everyone else kissed their cards with typical pink and red lipstick and promptly submitted them, but Norma found out when the contest would be judged and returned that night with harlequin-designed lip prints in vivid colors, like ice blue and silver. The judges went wild and awarded her first, second, and third place. They went even wilder when she gave the trip to her parents, hoping to bend the trajectory of their worldview outward, ever so slightly. "In life, do you want to be one of those pink or red lips?" she asks. "Those won't get you to Acapulco. You have to be different, independent, and strategic. And most of all, you have to be you. If you take the time and make the effort to figure it out for yourself, you'll get there."

BERNHARDT
WEALTH MANAGEMENT

Andrew J. Sherman

An Educator at Heart

In a world that trends toward instability when left to its own devices and often switches gears when we least expect it, knowledge is something we can hold onto. It's a spark that leads to big ideas and better futures, and Andrew J. Sherman is committed to catalyzing that spark.

As the author of 26 books, a professor at the University of Maryland Smith School of Business for almost three decades, a coveted lecturer, a partner in a major D.C. law firm, and a devoted husband and father, his time is divided amongst an array of important roles, yet in each setting, he remains an educator at heart. "Every day, I live my life hoping to spread knowledge about the things I have experience in to help others get to where they want to go," he affirms. "It's about helping people through education and sharing good, transparent, agenda-less knowledge. That's why I do what I do."

Perhaps Andrew's innate commitment to education is born from the transformative power it has had over his own life, though the route he took to get his diplomas and degrees was far from traditional. Born and raised in Philadelphia, his family often had to make do on a very modest income, so he was always looking for creative ways to make money as a kid. Among other things, he ran fruit stands, lemonade stands, a lawn mowing business, and an NFL sticker business. Perhaps his most entrepreneurial venture involved cutting school and taking the bus into the city, where he and a friend would rummage through record store garbage bins for the beautiful displays they would discard after exhibiting them in front of their stores. The boys would then sell them the next day at school.

Life took a sudden and dramatic turn for the worse, however, when his parents divorced when he was 16. Less than a month later, Philadelphia was hit with a record snowstorm the day his house caught on fire. Frantically, Andrew got his mother and two younger sisters out and then phoned the fire department a mile down the street. Because of the snow, it would be an hour before they could dig out their truck and arrive on the scene, so Andrew ran back into the house to salvage what he could. "In a situation like that, your adrenaline is pumping and you think you're made of Teflon, so I kept running back in," he remembers. Thankfully, the family's dog was saved, but most of its mementos were lost—a heavy blow to suffer just after the divorce.

It wasn't the first time a fire had touched Andrew's heritage. His maternal great grandfather, Samuel M. Goldman, was a true patriarch, having built a hugely successful business manufacturing wooden produce baskets for farmers. Tragically, a prison escapee burned the plant to the ground, and as most businesses didn't have insurance in those days, most of the family's wealth was lost in an instant—a blow that echoed through the next several generations and left Andrew determined to do better. "People ask me where I get all my energy from," he says. "It's from a fundamental instinct to be a good provider for my family and a core value to take nothing for granted. I was determined to be a patriarch and achieve a level of financial success that would allow me to give my children a better life."

When his home life dissolved in 1978, however, the right way to accomplish that vision remained opaque and elusive. His mother and sisters moved to California, but his East Coast blood led him to Baltimore, where his father had relocated. Having only completed eleventh grade but wanting to get the ball rolling faster, he arranged a deal with his previous high school and the University of Baltimore Maryland County (UMBC) that, if he completed a year of college and maintained a B average, he would be awarded his high school diploma retroactively.

Andrew accomplished his goal and was awarded his high school diploma, but by his sophomore year he had decided to drop out of college to run the tennis fitness and training company he had launched with a friend the previous year. Around that time, the Baltimore Sun ran a story on the company that referred to Andrew and his partner, Lewis, as entrepreneurs. "I had to look the word up in the dictionary," he laughs. "Was it a good thing? A bad thing? Little did I know, I'd spend the rest of my life representing and supporting entrepreneurs."

The business took off quickly, garnering attention from press and major TV channels and landing its founders on the cover of *Baltimore Magazine* when it featured a story on the 81 people to watch in 1981. At age 17, Andrew found himself living the life of a 35-year-old. The company was recognized by the U.S. Tennis Association, and he was a guest speaker at the U.S. Open in 1981. "I believed I didn't need a college degree and that I'd be an entrepreneur for the rest of my life," he remembers. "But then harsh reality hit when President Reagan took office and loan interest rates were high. People could get 18 percent and a toaster for opening a CD, and nobody was going to invest in some punk kids trying to start a business."

As things began to devolve with his tennis business and the bright future he thought was so certain began slipping away, Andrew returned to that catalytic spark that he must have known, somewhere in his gut, was the only sure way to security: education. He re-enrolled at UMBC and took night classes to finish his degree, but because his business wasn't earning any money, he had to go to exceptional lengths to make ends meet. As he finished his junior and senior year of college, he would go to class from 6 to 10 at night. He would then return home to the group house where his friends were often partying and sneak in a couple hours of sleep before going to work from midnight to 6:00 AM—usually at some sort of security or maintenance job. He would then catch a few more hours of rest before putting in a day of work at the tennis company.

Through the daily grind of those grueling two years, Andrew's belief in the power of education coalesced around a very clear goal for his future: he wanted to go to law school in Washington, D.C. "I had the epiphany that I would be better as a coach than as a player," he remembers. "Instead of being an entrepreneur myself, I wanted to be a lawyer who helped entrepreneurial companies grow." With that vision in mind, after completing his undergraduate degree after five and a half years, he cobbled together a patchwork of scholarships, student loans, and money from part time jobs to fund his enrollment in 1983 at the American University Washington College of Law. It was there that he met his wife, Judy, and finally saw the light at the end of the tunnel as he felt himself closer and closer to establishing a stable life with a steady income.

Sometimes, the greatest burdens can turn out to be the greatest blessings. As Andrew again found himself looking for ways to work through school, he stumbled upon journalism. "I had never written formally before, but I realized I had a skill for it, so I began writing freelance articles and generating good income from that," he explains. "That led to publishing my first book, an aggregate of articles supplemented with new content, in 1988, just after I finished law school. That was probably the first time I really connected with the concept that I'm an educator at heart.

Writing is just another platform to share knowledge and experiences with others in a way that can be helpful to them."

As Andrew started his law career at a one-man firm called Scott G. Smith & Associates, his career as an author and thought leader took off in tandem. One book quickly became two, and when he left that small firm to start a firm of his own, the brand recognition garnered by his writing attracted the interest of new clients and big law firms alike. His practice hit the tipping point and went global in the late 1990s, and his clients ran the gamut from startup enterprises to Walmart. "In 2007, I realized I might be better suited at a large firm with offices all over the world," he recalls. "The global footprint of Jones Day was very attractive to me because I knew I'd be able to collaborate about my projects with partners in Amsterdam, Beijing, London, France, Cleveland, Los Angeles, and a number of other places."

More alluring than the network of invaluable information and experiences inherent in the architecture of the firm, however, was its culture. The firm was founded in Cleveland in 1893 and imbued with strong Midwestern values. Now, at a time when the legal profession is experiencing tremendous upheaval and the advent of a cutthroat ethic, and when many formerly vibrant firms are faltering, Jones Day owes its stability and success to the culture of teamwork it fosters amongst its partners, associates, and employees. "Many of our firm's core values are modeled after Notre Dame football," Andrew remarks. "It's a very egalitarian, fair place where everyone is a player but no one wears their name on the back of their jersey. It's about the team's success, and I'm very proud to work at a firm that still values and celebrates people and the unique contributions they can make."

To date, Jones Day's transactional practice is the largest in the world, and they ranked number one globally in Mergers & Acquisitions for 53 consecutive quarters as of late 2013. In this context, Andrew continues his commitment to offering excellent guidance to clients through Mergers & Acquisitions, corporate growth, exit planning and strategic advisory work. "But these days," he says, "more of my time is spent on strategic planning and marketing development projects where the legal work is almost secondary to the strategy. For many of my day to day corporate engagements, I play more of a strategic sounding board role, which is a perfect match for what really drives me. I love being a catalyst in the growth of companies and helping entrepreneurs succeed. It all comes back to educating and helping people take their companies where they want to go."

In perfect symbiotic fashion, helping others get to where they want to go has landed Andrew exactly where he had dreamed of going himself. After growing up fast at the age of sixteen, he knew he wanted to reestablish the cycle of patriarchy in his family that had been broken by the factory fire that decimated his great grandfather's wealth, but without mentor figures of his own along the way, he drew lessons from his great grandfather's memory and from the examples of other business leaders he believed were doing the right things with the right focus and dedication. "My great grandfather was a boxer and a very street-smart guy who had a physical and mental toughness that seemed to go hand in hand," Andrew explains. "From him, I learned the value of walking softly and carrying a big stick. You don't have to use it, but it's there if you need it."

Success also took an incredible amount of patience and persistence—two qualities that Andrew encourages young people entering the working world today to cultivate and utilize. "Things don't happen overnight," he says. "Success takes a long time, so you can't get frustrated or complacent. Stay with it and be proactive about keeping progress moving. This is easiest when you find something you truly love, because so much of your success will be driven by the degree of genuine passion you exude in the workplace."

With over two dozen books published so far and more to come, Andrew's impact continues to move the needle with the power of education that was so transformative in his own life. One of those books, entitled *Harvesting Intangible Assets,* is designed to urge business leaders to think about assets like their brand, relationships, systematic approaches, or byproducts in an agrarian way. If these assets aren't harvested while they're ripe, they spoil or rot. "Like Dunkin Donuts used to throw away its donut holes before it realized they could be marketed as one of their most popular products, every company can apply the principle of recycling and creative use of intangible assets in the corporate atmosphere to maximize shareholder value," he remarks, hearkening back to his days of record store display retrieval and resale at school.

Conceptualizing, developing, and ultimately publishing this knowledge revolves around the fundamental idea that, in life, we must play the cards we've been dealt and make the most of our hands. For Andrew, life is about helping others make the most of the hands they've been dealt as well. Indeed, for the mentors he lacked in his own life, he has made ardent strides to mentor others through each of his various roles. "I've had the opportunity to help hundreds of entrepreneurs grow their businesses," he remarks. "In 1987, I helped the Young Entrepreneurs Organization file its articles of incorporation, and in 2012, they honored me in Istanbul in 2012 for 25 years of service as outside general counsel. In that time, I've watched them grow to 10,000 members worldwide, which has been tremendously rewarding." Andrew also founded the Small and Emerging Contractors Advisory Forum, which has grown to around 400 members spread across the Mid-Atlantic region. In 2000, he was named by *Fortune Magazine* as one of the ten smartest minds in business, and the homage was echoed by *Inc.* Magazine several years later. "The biggest professional honor I've had, though, was the opportunity to launch new organizations," he affirms. "I was one of the cofounders of the Association for Corporate Growth's DC Chapter." He also speaks regularly at events held by the National Association of Corporate Directors—yet another avenue through which he has the ability to educate and empower leaders and those who govern.

Looking back over the course of his personal and professional development, Andrew has never taken a traditional route, and perhaps that's what allows him to live today as he does—taking nothing for granted, and deeply grateful for everything he's been able to accomplish. Unendingly dedicated to his wife of almost thirty years, their children, and their children's friends, as well as to his students, former students, neighbors, and friends, Andrew's example shows that being an educator at heart builds the kind of wealth that no fire can burn down—genuine relationships with others that create a catalytic network of people willing to give for each other. "If you can give more than you get and with a clear heart and mind, the results are powerful," he affirms. "They're so powerful that I pinch myself every day to remind myself to acknowledge and enjoy every minute."

Jonathan B. Smith

The ChiefOptimizer

Many parents encourage their children to find part-time work from an early age. Some kids do yard work around the neighborhood, while others might apply for a paper route or work in a local shop. Jonathan Smith, on the other hand, found himself swinging hammers and wielding drills as he helped his grandmother rehabilitate properties for one of his family's many businesses. From the age of seven, he lent a hand down at his grandfather's liquor distribution factory. And, young though he was, he understood entrepreneurship at an age other children might have had trouble pronouncing the word. "I would always think it was okay to be at the board table, or to be part of a business conversation," Jonathan recalls. "I'd say I have a lot more business experience than a traditional person my age, and at this point, it almost feels like entrepreneurship is part of my DNA."

Since childhood, Jonathan has witnessed the way entrepreneurs successfully—and, at times, unsuccessfully—assemble their teams, handle their financials, provide intelligent leadership, and establish respected core values. Today, he is able to manage and quickly improve the myriad workings of complex operations by drawing on his deep understanding of the way businesses succeed or fail to promote the former and avoid the latter. And now, as a high growth business strategist known as an EOS Implementer, and as the founder and CEO of ChiefOptimizer, LLC, he's created the perfect avenue to make this experience available to the businesses that need it most.

When a business can't achieve its desired level of growth, is in need of restructuring, or simply doesn't have a clear vision for the future, Jonathan and his team are there to provide guidance and leadership skills. Generally, they're businesses who who want to "Make It Big." They aren't start-ups, but instead have existing structures that ChiefOptimizer can observe and mold as necessary. "I work with second-stage entrepreneurs because there are more levers to pull," Jonathan explains, "They have cash flow, they have the people in place, and they have some strategy. But oftentimes they don't have a clear vision of where their business is going."

These emerging-growth businesses range in size from $2 million to $50 million and typically have teams between 10 and 250 employees. All of the companies are growth-oriented—in other words, they are businesses that are well off of the ground, but in need of assistance as they climb to the next level. "I show up when someone's hit the ceiling," says Jonathan. "They say, 'I have a $10 million dollar business, and I want to have a $20 million dollar business. The market's there, but my people aren't right, or I'm not profitable enough, or my processes aren't in place properly.'"

In these situations, Jonathan helps management teams analyze their structure, clarify their goals, and establish a long-term vision using the Entrepreneurial Operating System, a set of management tools that can be implemented over a two-year period. Originally developed by Jonathan's friend Gino Wickman, the system helps management teams communicate, prioritize, and make impactful changes, with the goal of ultimately "graduating," and running their business on EOS without the need for Jonathan's input. "My ultimate goal is to successfully graduate my clients so everyone can celebrate," he says. "When a company gets to that point, it's not only great for them. We've achieved what we initially set out to do, and I have another great referral source. It's deeply gratifying to create significant value for my customers and help them be their best."

The type of progress Jonathan aims for can only be achieved with a comprehensive understanding of the organization and its group dynamics. This aspect of his work distinguishes his skill set from that of an executive coach. Rather than working with individuals, he focuses on understanding the business as a whole and implementing a system that involves the entire leadership team. In many cases, confusion and inefficiency in an organization is the product of breakdowns in communication, so this comprehensive approach proves exceptionally effective. "Oftentimes employees don't have a clear vision of where they're going," he says. "If I sit in a meeting with a leadership team, I often find that the CEO, the COO, the CFO, and the President all have very different ideas of where the business is going. They also often aren't clear on their objectives for the next 90 days, which we call traction."

Providing clarity in such scenarios is crucial, and developing strong and consistent values is another important piece of the overall success puzzle. "If true accountability doesn't exist in the organization, or if a leader lives by a totally different set of rules than the rest of the organization, it doesn't work," he affirms.

It takes an acutely-honed entrepreneurial sense to be able to identify the distinct issues plaguing each business and the specific management tools needed to address them, and Jonathan began accruing the experiences that lend expert nuance to his perspective from an early age. He grew up in an entrepreneurial family in Berkeley Heights, New Jersey, and from a young age, he knew he wanted to be an entrepreneur. His father, Dennis G. Smith, juggled the family's wholesale liquor distribution business—a venture his grandfather had single-handedly built—with more than a few other entrepreneurial efforts. Young Jonathan watched with fascination as his father leased cars, ran a temporary staffing company, acquired apartments, and flipped houses, all at the same time. He was an old school serial entrepreneur and encouraged thoughtful problem solving in his three sons, inventing brain teasers and demanding creative answers.

The value of hard work became readily apparent to Jonathan, and at the age of seven, he refused a $5 payday from his grandfather after spending the day "working" at his father's factory. Showing a sense of work ethic and integrity at a young age, Jonathan acknowledged that he had played more than he had worked and had not earned the $5, and this dedication to adding value—and to honesty—carries over to his work today. In fact, Jonathan offers a session guarantee that, if clients don't feel they get the value they expected, they don't have to pay.

Jonathan went on to attend college at Wesleyan University in Connecticut, where he completed an interdisciplinary major that emphasized history, economics, philosophy, and government. As he neared graduation, however, joining the family business began to look less and less likely, as profits had begun to decline. In fact, just a few years after Jonathan's graduation, his father declared bankruptcy—an event that, to a great degree, shaped his more cautious approach to business as an adult. "I like things structured so that there's very predictable revenue, and so that expenses are very predictable against those revenues," he says. "I don't believe in putting on an expense if you don't have some kind of recurring revenue." This philosophy has shaped Jonathan's hyper-analytical, almost scientific approach to the business world, setting him apart as a force for smart, organic growth.

After graduating from Wesleyan, Jonathan took a job with Arthur Andersen in Hartford, Connecticut, where he worked in accounting and attended an accounting graduate program part-time. After receiving his Master's Degree, he transitioned over to JP Morgan, where he realized his interest in the field was waning. He did, however, closely observe the structure of the giant firms, and absorbed everything he could of their efficiency. "It was amazing how eight people could run a business of 50,000 people as effectively as they could, with the controls they had in place," he remembers. Learning all he could, but lacking enthusiasm for the corporate world, Jonathan was cognizant that his caution in business might prove the perfect foil for his risk-taking father. Thus, the two men began to toss around the idea of a new venture, which would become Wave Dispersion Technologies in 1995.

Meanwhile, Jonathan left JP Morgan for Deutsche Bank, where his work was similar but his pay was increased by almost 50 percent. Unfortunately, he soon discovered that high dividends came at a high cost. Ever faithful to the values instilled by his father and grandfather, Jonathan was disappointed to find that his new employer placed little importance on these beliefs. "I learned what it was like to have a business that was a series of fiefdoms with few shared values," he says, "The fiefdom's only shared value was to make money at all costs."

During his tenure there in late 1990s, Jonathan was adamant that the mortgage-backed securities market, which Deutsche Bank played heavily in, was a terrible idea. "I didn't want to work in that environment," says Jonathan. "I didn't have enough power to change things, and they were making so much money doing those kinds of transactions. I knew their approach wasn't sustainable and that the process was totally illiquid." Time, of course, bore out these dire predictions with the Great Recession of 2008, and his experiences at the bank again reinforced his belief that strategy, planning, execution, and transparency are core tenets needed to create a strong and resilient business.

Jonathan's disillusionment with Deutsche Bank led him to leave for his first almost-fully entrepreneurial experience, which came in the form of a marketing position at a boutique investment firm. From there, he moved to Michigan to work with his brother's web development company, where he became interested in search engine optimization (SEO) and quickly excelled. "I basically taught myself SEO by practicing it, going to conferences, and reading about it," he says. "I was just voracious and wanted to learn how it worked." Jonathan's enthusiasm paid off, and in 2003, he was invited to speak at Google, where he was hosted by Sheryl Sandburg, the now-famous COO of Facebook. After his talk, Sheryl praised his work and invited him to join the team of Google, which was still a modestly-sized organization at the time. He turned her down, bound and determined to make his dream of true entrepreneurship a reality.

A year later, Wave Dispersion Technologies and its primary product, Whisprwave®, began experiencing success in earnest. Jonathan's friends at Morgan Stanley had agreed to serve as angel investors, and closed a deal with the United States Coast Guard. By this time, Jonathan had earned the nickname ChiefOptimizer. After the attacks of September 11, 2001, web development calls had morphed into search engine optimization requests, and he was just the man for the job. The skill came naturally, and he found it carried over into everyday life. "I can optimize search results, but today I optimize networks," he says. "I can see how people fit together. I am a connector at heart."

Jonathan's skills were critical as the fledgling business began to grow. "My role there is basically to run relationships," he says. "That entails either business development or government affairs. I run finance, as well as the legal piece, and I set up structure." In 2008, Wave Dispersion Technologies signed a $100 million dollar contract with the Critical National Infrastructure Authority in Abu Dhabi. "That was one of my proudest moments," Jonathan affirms.

In 2011, Jonathan founded ChiefOptimizer, a business he created in order to utilize the skill he'd long put to use in his professional and personal life. He calls his style of leadership "servant leadership," explaining, "I have great respect for the military and its commitment to lead by example. I'm not above doing whatever needs to be done to get the job done, and I can also motivate people to do amazing things because it's not about me—it's about the greater mission."

Jonathan has utilized this model to great effect, both in his businesses and in other settings. From 2007 to 2008, he served as the President of a faltering chapter of the Entrepreneur's Organization in Detroit. After accepting the volunteer position, he spoke personally at every forum under his purview, addressing issues and bringing ideas back to the board. Putting his belief in servant leadership to the test, he made sure members felt heard, and today, the chapter is flourishing as a perennial EO Rock Star Chapter.

Jonathan's contribution to the Entrepreneur's Organization is no anomaly. He's volunteered extensively and been involved with a number of charitable causes, none more dear to his heart than his work for an organization called Leader Dogs for the Blind. In support of this effort, he trained two Leader Dogs that went on to serve visually impaired persons, and he continues to provide leadership training with their Harness the Power of Leadership program. Jonathan has also been involved with the American Diabetes Foundation and The Leukemia and Lymphoma Society. In fact, in 2004, the Leukemia Society named him its "National Man of the Year" after he successfully raised over half a million dollars for their cause. And true to his reputation as the Optimizer, Jonathan prefers to contribute not only money, but also his time and expertise where he can. "I tend to donate my time to objective-oriented projects where I can make a difference by utilizing my entrepreneurial skills for social good," he explains. "I want to have that first-hand experience with the organization and its mission."

The importance of first-hand experience is a value he encourages in offering advice to young people entering the working world today. "I'm not the kind of guy who likes to sit on a soapbox and tell people what to do," he affirms. Instead, Jonathan leads by example, volunteering with the Global Student Entrepreneur Awards to work directly with college students to guide and encourage their ambitions. He also takes the initiative to mentor the young people he knows personally. In 2011, he traveled to Jakarta, Indonesia, as an Ambassador for Entrepreneurship for the U.S. Department of State, and he brought his 15-year-old godson, Matt, for the immersive cultural exposure.

The experience was so educational that Matt wrote his college admission essay about the trip, and, like Jonathan at his age, is now certain that entrepreneurship is the career path for him. "This type of experiential learning is the most effective and informative education possible," Jonathan says. "I believe in showing, not telling." It's this ambition, emphasis on connections, and unmatched ability to build a network that allow Jonathan to optimize not only his own life outcomes, but those of countless others, whether they're close family and friends, the employees and customers of the businesses he works to transform each day, or the young people he's inspired on the other side of the globe.

Edward L. Snyder

Communication is Key

Sitting on Edward Snyder's desk is a "Day-Timer" from 1932, the year his parents married. It belonged to his father, the founder of Snyder Cohn, PC, a CPA firm committed to helping businesses in the D.C. metropolitan area flourish. The "Day-Timer" is a symbol of the kind of hard-working, forward-thinking, and pragmatic approach to business that has become a hallmark of the Snyder family. Eddie's father, who married his mother on a Sunday in 1932 and was back in the office the next morning, recorded their wedding and every client meeting using initials rather than full names, protecting the privacy of those who trusted him long before HIPAA made it a requirement. He also meticulously recorded all expenditures and budgets, cognizant that how much money his company made was unimportant—what truly mattered was whether they were making more than they were spending.

"He was a natural-born leader who taught me tremendous organizational and business skills, and how to relate to people," Eddie remarks today. "He taught me to always be building toward something and moving forward. And, perhaps most importantly, he taught me that communication is key. To me, the "Day-Timer" represents the culture that my father created and we work hard to instill in others today."

While most young children think of school as the time where they learn the most, Eddie received his most valuable education not between the hours of nine in the morning and three in the afternoon, but instead in those early morning minutes on the drive to school. It was during those car rides that his father would impart the knowledge and wisdom that, later on, would prove more invaluable than anything Eddie learned in the classroom.

Beyond the simple joy of time together spent developing the bond between father and son, those early morning drives laid the core values of integrity, trust, and business acumen that form the backbone of Eddie's work today. "I learned common sense concepts and how things happen," Eddie remembers. "My father was one of seven children, and he was the leader, so I learned valuable leadership skills as well. By relaying his experiences to me and giving me the opportunity to relate to him, this wisdom and way of looking at the world was brought to life for me."

Eddie is now the chairman of the CPA firm originally established in 1927. David E. Snyder had formed the firm out of necessity at age 22, after graduating from Benjamin Franklin University into a harsh job market where he couldn't land a job. He wrote to friends and family declaring his intention to be a public accountant, and one by one, he picked up clients and referrals, slowly building the practice. Then, in the 1930s, he was struck with pleurisy, a lung disease that led him to the resolution that he would take on partners so his clients would never be left without service if he was incapacitated for some reason. He also formed the Society for Mutual Benefits for clients who couldn't get loans to get through hard times during the Great Depression. Everyone in the society had to agree to consider cosigning a loan or lending money to any member in need, as long as there were two guarantors on the loan. In this way, members would lend money to one another. "My father always did what he could to help his clients, and Snyder Cohn continues in that same tradition today," Eddie affirms.

The firm has stayed in the family for over 85 years, with Eddie working alongside his elder brother for at least fifty of them. Today, Snyder Cohn is comprised of seventy associates, a 40 percent increase since 1994, when Eddie became managing partner. With tax, outsource, and accounting and auditing divisions, the firm serves a wide range of industries that includes healthcare, food, hotel, retail, real estate, and the non-profit sectors. Snyder Cohn also works with individuals, either of high net-worth or private business owners. "Our primary focus is on entrepreneurs and non-profit organizations," Eddie relays. "We've been paperless since 2008, and we're extremely tech-savvy. Our tagline is, ' Supporting the life cycle of success.'"

Supporting the life cycle of success has become much more than a trademark of the company's culture over the past several decades— even more, it is the heart and soul of the business's day-to-day work and long-term vision. "We have experience and skill sets that fit a variety of businesses, and it's extremely gratifying to apply them to a given situation and watch businesses and contributions to society flourish," Eddie says. "I had a struggling client whom I helped by creating a simple financial plan. After coming up with a proactive strategy, they cut their staff by 40 percent, and a month later, they were profitable. We saved their business." Trust and reliability are basic company values that the Snyder Cohn team weaves together with listening and learning, creating a winning approach to achieve real success.

Eddie's natural affinity for accounting and proclivity toward entre-preneurship were cultivated consistently throughout his childhood, as his father was an accountant as well. It was perhaps his brother, however, who had the greatest impact on him. "When I was seven years old, he started hiring me to shine his shoes for a quarter," Eddie laughs. "We went on to work together for 53 years." His sister played quite a different role in his life, modeling a grace in how she carried herself. "She taught me how to play piano chords and was very beautiful," he remembers. "The lessons I learned from both my siblings were integrated into my character to create a good balance between my work and personal life today."

Eddie's mother, as well, had a strong impact on his desire to simply help others. "She was always looking out for everybody and was a natural caretaker," he remembers. "She was an impeccable homemaker and known as the best cook in town, infamous for her brownies and jello molds. She also got involved in cancer research." Eddie inherited the helping gene from her, and it now forms the *why* behind all that he does with Snyder Cohn. "It's so gratifying that people put their trust in us," he affirms. "When surveyed, our clients report that they know we have their best interest at heart. The opportunity to help people is so rewarding, and it's why I'm excited to come into work each day."

Beyond the skills Eddie assimilated on those early drives to school, he and his brother also followed in their father's footsteps by starting their own investment clubs at school. As did his brother, Eddie picked sixteen classmates, and the group began learning the ins and outs of finance and the investment world. They learned how to borrow money from a bank, invest, and pay it back. They learned about organizational structure and how to relate to others in a financial setting. They also had a president, vice president, treasurer, and secretary, which were rotated every six months so each member got the benefit of leadership experience.

With this unconventional immersion in accounting and finance, Eddie found himself fascinated with the concepts and began working at his father's CPA firm at the age of 13, earning $5 a week in the summers and sharpening his skills. Every night, his father would have him add together digits from the phone book just to get extra practice, and Eddie had such a natural affinity for the field that he knew he wanted to pursue a college degree to become a public accountant. "I had a lot of background at the start of college, to the point where all of freshman year accounting was a refresher," he says. A Washington native, Eddie attended Hebrew Academy grade school, Coolidge High School, and then the University of Pennsylvania's renowned Wharton School of Business for college. He then returned to the D.C. area and has lived in Silver Spring, Maryland, since 1969, building a life for himself as he's built his business skills and professional legacy at Snyder Cohn.

This life started with Maxine Snyder, the mother of his two children who was incredibly talented and a director of an agency that coordinated efforts of Hillels. "Becoming a parent was one of the most transformational and wonderful experiences of my life," he remarks. "It's been much less predictable than any other part of my life. The process of conveying values and being a good parent to your children is a role you take on indefinitely. My own mother is 99 now, and until recently she was making sure I wore a coat outside and that I was eating enough. It's just a tremendously fulfilling experience, and now that I'm a grandparent, there's just nothing like it."

Maxine was a nurturer, activist, and president of the PTA at the Hebrew Academy. "If she heard of any injustice anywhere at the school, she would get to the bottom of it at once," Eddie recalls. "To this day, people at the school revere her memory in awe." Maxine passed away ten years ago after a battle with lung cancer, and her friend, Ann Wimpfheimer, also lost her spouse tragically to lung cancer. "Ann was Maxine's friend in college who paid me a condolence call after Maxine passed away, and we got married three years later," Eddie says. "She and I are both very energetic, and for her, there is no such thing as idle time. We do lots of traveling, play tennis, and go hiking. She's given me new life. We both know what it means to come from tragedy and to move forward." Committed to lifelong learning, Ann has a Masters in Social Work and earned her PsyD after her husband passed. A very health-conscious and ecologically-minded woman, she was the catalyst for Snyder Cohn's decision to go green, and after blending their families together, Eddie and Ann are now proud grandparents.

In advising young people entering the working world today, Eddie emphasizes the importance of doing what you say you're going to do, being honest, and thinking about where the other person is coming from so you can best meet their needs. "A good place to start is to find shared values, from which you can forge a path forward," he recommends. Eddie likes to learn from his associates, and once a year in April, the firm holds a brainstorming session so that everyone has a seat at the table to discuss how Snyder Cohn can improve. "All seventy of us in the firm are assigned as a coach or mentor to one another to ensure the success of the group, and that includes listening with both ears," Eddie explains. "We try to keep our associates doing what they like the most." Thanks to this culture of communication, the firm operates at full capacity at all times, able to focus on the things that matter most to its clients and associates.

"When I see newer associates get frustrated because they don't understand why their client has made the choice they've made, I try to teach them to think innovatively and like a problem-solver," says Eddie, reminiscent of the lessons his father taught him on those early drives to school. "Think to yourself, what do they know that I don't know? And what do I know that they don't know?"

This simple and inquisitive effort to see eye-to-eye with people has been a major factor in Eddie's marked success. Thanks in part to this approach, Snyder Cohn recently gained acclaim as one of the top 100 best accounting firms to work for in the entire country—a testament to the attitude of care and respect that characterizes the firm's relationship with clients and associates alike. Indeed, to be heard and feel understood is an underestimated experience in today's fast-paced and often transient culture, but Snyder Cohn does it well.

"Without understanding where someone is coming from, communication is nearly impossible, and without clear and effective communication, growth of any kind—personal, professional, financial—is unlikely," Eddie affirms. "In order to communicate effectively with someone, you have to meet them where they are." By mastering the life skill of meeting others where they are, Eddie has been able to lead them forward to new success and new life satisfaction. "Listen with both ears and respond accordingly to meet others' needs," he says. "In this way, you come to find that, sometimes, the best communication involves very little talking."

BERNHARDT
WEALTH MANAGEMENT

Craig Strent

Embracing Change

Craig Strent pulled over on the side of the road, his stomach in such tight knots he thought he might be sick. For weeks, he had been plagued by anxiety over his decision to leave his job, with its promise of promotion to regional manager and accompanying handsome salary. It was the type of offer most twenty-five year olds only dream about, but it had felt wrong to Craig from the start.

The business, which Craig had helped build over the past three years, had been acquired by a Fortune 500 company, which planned to expand from nine branches to 54 virtually overnight. "The company had a broken foundation, and they were expanding too quickly for their own good. I just didn't trust what was happening," he explains. "My coworker, Eric Gates, and I had been talking about starting our own company for some time, and that seemed like our chance, even though it was a very risky career move."

Initially, his father thought he was crazy to even consider giving up such a promising package, urging him to save as much money as he could now and start his own company later if it didn't work out, but Craig felt that if it was ever going to happen, he needed to act now. "Also, Eric is the smartest guy I know in the mortgage business, and I didn't want to miss the opportunity to partner up and do business with him," Craig says.

Craig and Eric started operating their business out of a hallway in Greenbelt, and today, Craig is the CEO of Apex Home Loans, the largest independent mortgage banker headquartered in Montgomery County. Apex originates residential home loans throughout the District of Columbia, Virginia, Maryland, and Delaware, with Craig handling the marketing, customer relations, and business development along with his partner. Michael Parsons. Eric now focuses on the operations side of business with their fourth partner Stewart Zemil. "The key term that defines us as independent is that we are not affiliated with any national companies or owned by a bank. We lend our own money as a mortgage banker, as opposed to a broker who acts more like a middleman," he explains. "We control the loan and process in-house, fund it under our name, and then sell it individually or as a package to bigger banks."

In the early days, Apex utilized telemarketers and direct mail as their primary modes of customer recruitment. In the early 2000's however, they were hit by the liquidity crisis, forcing the company to completely change their model into an almost entirely new business. "Mortgage companies using the same model as us were going out of business every day, so we decided we had to try something new," he says. "In the past, we had relied on direct mail and telemarketing, so I loaded up my car with marketing materials and started attending networking events to seek out referral partners, which was a new method for us. I'd read that financial advisors could serve as an exceptional resource for mortgage referrals, so I sought them out and put together educational programs for them. After a lot of effort, follow-up, and repetition of the programs, word got around in the financial advisor community about our expertise in mortgages and financial planning. The referrals picked up significantly, and this became our primary driver of new business."

After its redesign into a completely referral-based business, Apex began to expand its network to include realt estate agents, accountants, estate planners, and attorneys, while continuing to market heavily to its existing database of customers and networking contacts. Thanks to this diversification, it was one of the only independent mortgage firms left still thriving in the wake of the housing crisis that started in 2008. Most other firms have become affiliated with a bank or a national company, or focus solely on brokering loans. "We were always an anomaly in our field," Craig remarks. "We contracted when others expanded, and vise versa. We always did the opposite of what the herd was doing, which served us well."

From 1999 to 2010, Apex operated as a mortgage broker, until they realized once again that their previous model was no longer relevant. "Just like in 1999, we realized in 2009 that our model was no longer effective," Craig explains. "Brokers were facing so many obstacles in the regulatory environment, so we decided to convert to being a mortgage banker." With that, Apex took on employees from Nationwide Home Mortgage in 2010, expanding from nine to 25 people, and have continued to grow to 60 employees in the past three years.

Craig was unusually successful for a man of his young age, but also unusually brave to face the risks that came with such a life-changing transformation. As it turned out, his gut instinct was correct: the previous company, who had promised him so much, was out of business within three years of Apex's conception. His finely honed intuition served him well, and Craig continues to draw upon this strength as he leads Apex today. "Since starting the company, I've operated on the theme of searching for the better and more efficient way to do our job, following the Japanese principle of *Kaizen*, or continuous improvement," he says. "As the environment changes, we change with it so that we are positioned to be the best possible offering in the market. I want our customers to look at us and our model and say, 'That's the best place to get my mortgage,' so we continue to change to make sure we're always the best and smartest option for our customers."

Craig learned from an early age to trust his instincts, and as a result, welcomed transition when the change felt needed. His parents divorced when he was nine years old, and after spending four turbulent years with his mother and older brother on Long Island, he moved in with his father. "The divorce had taken a heavy toll on both my mother and I, so we tended to clash as we worked through our readjustment," he explains. "Over time, things improved, and I soon realized that change can really be a positive thing. In fact, I've come to use it as a tool to accomplish goals."

His father was an accountant and the managing partner of a CPA firm, which later inspired Craig to study accounting for the last three years of high school. At the same time, his father encouraged him to explore other interests, first sending him on a summer bus tour of the United States and then helping him secure work as a golf caddy at the local club. He loved both experiences, but discovered a deep and unwavering passion for politics during a family trip to Washington, D.C. "I was especially moved by the Lincoln Memorial," he recalls. "It really sparked my interest in politics, and to this day I enjoy reading about Lincoln's life and legacy."

Craig has always found himself in natural leadership positions, gravitating to leadership roles in sports as the goalie in soccer and the catcher in baseball. He also involved himself in model congress and the world affairs club. "People always looked to me for an opinion because I was always up to date on public issues," he says. "If you had asked me what I wanted to be when I grew up at that age, I would have told you President."

Craig attended the American University, having felt the pull to D.C. since the family vacation in elementary school. He majored in accounting but decided to switch to International Business during his senior year, finding he enjoyed the material he was studying for the first time. He interned in the White House during the Clinton administration for the first semester of his senior year, and after realizing that it was not a field he wanted to make a career in, he applied for a three-year post-graduate program with MAERSK, a shipping company based in Denmark that would take him around the world.

His application, however, was not accepted, so for the first two months after graduating, he worked for US Assist, a customer service provider for American Express. He felt unsure about the future, until one of his fraternity brothers called that August, inviting him to work for his mortgage company. Without hesitation, Craig made the switch, and found that within sixty days he was flourishing in his new role.

In 1998, the company was sold to a larger firm, with hopes of taking the current mortgage platform and making it national. Craig, who was only 25 at the time, had done so well at the company that when they decided to expand, they promoted him to regional manager of the branch of his choice, prompting his decision to transform his future by breaking away to launch Apex. "The expansion was happening too quickly, and I felt I could do it better myself, so why not take a chance on start my own company?" he says. "I was young, and if I was going to fail, that was a good time to do it since I had no kids or large expenses yet. "

Luckily, Craig's wife, Amy, was fully supportive of his decision to try his hand at being a business owner. She had recently graduated from law school, so the couple had a small safety net beneath them to break his fall, should it happen. After carefully calculating the potential risks and benefits, he decided to turn down the company's offer and take the leap.

While Apex has changed its models several times since its inception, Craig is unrelenting in maintaining a consistent tone of honesty and integrity towards his customers. "People are terrified of mortgages," he says. "They hear horror stories, and all they want is a comfortable experience with someone they can trust. That's why we're different. We treat people fairly and are straightforward with them, so they come back again and again. If you do the right thing for your customers and your employees, your business will take care of itself." As a result, Apex has been recognized as one of SmartCEO's fastest growing companies in the region in their emerging growth category, as well as Small Business of the Year for Montgomery County and one of the top one hundred mortgage companies in America by Mortgage Executive Magazine. Most recently, it was named to the Inc. 5000 list as one of the fastest growing private companies in America. Apex even received a "Healthy Employer Award" from Community Health Charities for its voluntary payroll deduction program that allows employees to contribute to their favorite health organizations.

Throughout the many transformations the company has undergone, Craig has come to learn the value of networking and creating a presence in the local business community. "Small business owners frequently feel they are too small to make a difference in chambers or other business organizations, but it's important to expand your horizons and be a part of the conversation," he explains. "I've learned to get involved and stay involved. A lot of people abandon relationships if they don't get business out of it right away, but that's the wrong approach. I choose to go and help as many people as I can; I'll give before I'll receive. By connecting with people, I give myself a voice in the business community."

When Craig is not busy with Apex, he serves on the Board of Directors at Leadership Greater Washington and at the Greater Washington Board of Trade. In his personal life, he serves as his synagogue's golf chair for their annual outing and coaches his two sons' hockey teams. "I apply many of the valuable lessons I have learned in business to my role coaching the boys and their teams," he remarks. "Running a business and coaching sports teams are interchangeable roles, and I enjoy being able to apply lessons between them." Laying out his advice to young people entering the working world today, Craig says, "It's about hard work, staying accountable, and learning as much as you can. Whatever role you are in, be open minded and ready to adjust if the situation around you does. Make the most of your role and position yourself to be indispensable to the team." As Craig's story shows, embracing change in this manner is the only way to get from friction to dynamism, from wrong to right, and from a dream worth having to a reality worth living.

BERNHARDT
WEALTH MANAGEMENT

Nancy Tolbert

A Mind of Her Own

From the time she was a little girl, Nancy Tolbert was known for having a mind of her own, and she put it to understanding the world around her. If girls couldn't do all the things boys could do, she wanted to know why. If a teacher told her to do something that didn't make sense, she wanted to know the logic. With independent stubbornness, she demanded that the world around her adhere to laws of reason and justice. If a rule didn't resonate with her sense of how a fair society should be, it deserved to be challenged.

Growing up in an ethnic neighborhood in upstate New York where everyone knew everyone, it didn't take long for Nancy to notice that disabled individuals in her community were treated differently. "I can still remember one little girl who wasn't allowed to go to school, just because she was disabled," she recalls. "It was the same situation for another young man who lived down the street from us. He just roamed the streets all day—it was no way to teach him how to get on in the world. I wanted to know why these injustices were happening, but no one could tell me."

These unanswered questions never left her, and returned to the forefront of her thoughts when she defied the expectations of everyone around her by becoming the first of her family to graduate college. There, she met a particularly passionate professor who ignited her interest in disability justice. Now the Executive Director of CALMRA, Inc., Nancy continues to redefine what it means to have a disability in society today, providing the solace of support and the power of possibility to families as committed to change as she is.

CALMRA was first conceived of by Mary Solko, a Maryland resident who began to wonder what would happen to her developmentally disabled daughter when she could no longer care for her. Meeting the fear head-on, she built a coalition of people facing similar challenges. Over the course of several years, they met in the basement of the First United Methodist Church for brownies, coffee, and conversation. They envisioned lives for their loved ones that far surpassed the conditions of institutional living—lives where their disabled children, siblings, or other family members could live in a home-like setting and feel meaningful fulfillment.

At the time, Nancy was working for the state of Maryland, supervising a federally mandated program and providing case management to people living in the community with disabilities. She began working with Mary's daughter, getting to know Mary in the process. Though the coalition had originally wanted to bypass state funding, Nancy's input opened their minds to the stability it would lend, and after five years of deliberation, they resolved that they were ready to launch, and that Nancy should be their Executive Director.

At first, she resisted. "It's an extremely demanding role in an equally challenging industry," she remarks. "You're providing service everyday, all the time. When your budget gets cut, you can't cut back on staff or food. You have to figure something else out. At first, I wasn't sure I wanted to take on that responsibility."

It was Nancy's brother who ultimately changed her mind, pointing out that she could do her current job in her sleep. She had learned all she could in that capacity, and unless she pressed forward, she'd stagnate. "I realized he was right," she concedes. "I also realized I had seen the residential and support services available to the disabled in our community, and I knew I could do a better job." With that, Nancy accepted the position, and on July 27th, 1992, CALMRA opened for business.

In the beginning, the organization had no money and a shoestring budget, but it did have a goal: to help families who could no longer care for their children with cognitive disabilities in their home. It started as a program of the Arc of Prince George's County, and in her closet-sized office, equipped with only a folding table, chair, and phone, Nancy began building the organization. The Great Oaks Center, the institution serving the Southern region of Maryland, had recently closed down, so CALMRA began taking on its former clients. By October, it had opened two houses in residential communities, serving three people per house.

Today, CALMRA has around a hundred employees, including administrative staff and trained caregivers. Each of its sixteen homes across Prince George's and Montgomery County is staffed with a live-in employee, which makes them feel even more like home. "It can be very hard at first for families to transition their child into one of our houses," Nancy explains. "They know that person better than anyone, and they worry we won't take care of them as well. But we've seen some incredible and transformative success for our residents, and our philosophy is to incorporate the families as much as possible in their son or daughter's life, maintaining that contact. Our progressive, three-person setup provides an environment where individuals can create a life that's meaningful to them. It's not a place to get services; it's their home."

CALMRA has also opened a support service program to assist families who are able to keep their disabled children at home but need some extra help. Then, in 2010, they opened a senior center for individuals with disabilities, the Mary Solko Center. Inspired by CALMRA clients who were aging but not yet ready to retire, the center now serves thirty people, with plans to expand. Taken together, the various components of CALMRA operate on a budget of $6 million, with fundraisers modestly supplementing the state funding they rely on, and only seven percent of that spent on administrative costs. The organization completed a rigorous voluntary certification program to earn the Maryland Association of Nonprofit Organizations Seal of Excellence—a testament to its commitment to integrity, value, and impact.

This commitment has been a hallmark of Nancy's character from the time she was a little girl, chasing after her four older brothers because she wanted to go to school like them. When she finally got to Kindergarten, she couldn't understand why all the other children cried when their parents left. "I was so excited that we had finally made it to school, and I was shocked that the other kids weren't as thrilled as I was," she laughs.

Growing up in Syracuse, Nancy's mother worked as a cook in her uncle's restaurant after her father left, and then got a job cleaning safes. They lived in a flat above her grandparents' house, and when her older brothers went to school, Nancy would play checkers and do puzzles with her beloved great grandmother who lived with her grandparents. When her great grandmother passed away and she was told she had suddenly gone to Heaven, little Nancy wasn't satisfied. "I kept asking, what does that mean? How does that work?" she says. "In the wake of that experience, understanding the world became particularly important to me."

When Nancy was in seventh grade, her mother remarried, adding five stepsiblings to the mix. "It was hard to blend the families at first, and I was very headstrong, which didn't make it easier," she recalls. "But it got better with time."

Nancy attended Catholic school until, one day toward the end of her freshman year of high school, she showed up to a classroom to find there weren't enough seats. The school was run on a modular schedule, and she could easily have gone to another classroom for the period, but the nun told her she had to sit on the floor. When she protested, she was given detention, so the next year, she signed herself up for public school. "When my mom found out, she was furious, but I knew I needed a different environment," she says. "Not only was it more fair, but we got to wear regular clothes instead of uniforms. We had a winning football team, a golf course, a swimming pool, and an ice rink."

Nancy excelled at her new school and worked on the side, trading in her paper route and babysitting gigs for jobs at AMES, Olan Mills, and a local department store. She worked for the VA one summer, and at an ice cream factory the next. "I've never not worked," she says. She became editor of the yearbook her senior year—a leadership role that aligned with her understated, independent character. "I'm not really one for the limelight," she remarks today. "I like to get things done in my own way."

That meant one day getting out of Syracuse, and Nancy knew college was her best ticket, so she took charge of her life and made it happen. She put herself through the College at Brockport, a State University of New York. After exploring her options through her first couple years, she decided to major in social work. It fit well with her innate interests, which included volunteering on Thursday evenings with individuals with disabilities, learning sign language, and planning a Disability Awareness Week to highlight how inaccessible the campus was. Aside from the passion inspired by her professor for disability justice, she chose the profession because she knew she'd be readily employable when she finished her studies.

Upon graduating Suma Cum Laude, Nancy returned home for the first time since leaving. She spent a summer working her old job at the ice cream factory and was reminded how hard day-in, day-out, dead-end work is. Her brother was living in Maryland at the time and had a spare room in his townhouse, so she decided to move down and got a job as a counselor at a group home. She enrolled in graduate school at Catholic University, and for one intense year, she was working full time, taking classes full time, and participating in an internship for twenty hours each week. She was promoted to a supervisor role at work, and when the organization opened a group home down the street from the university, she pressed them to let her be a live-in supervisor. "I was there to help out the staff when they needed it, and it made for a much more stable home," she recalls. "It created a sense of ownership and accountability that was really meaningful, and that's what CALMRA is modeled after today."

When Nancy earned her masters degree, she became the social worker for the organization she was working for. The federal waiver program had just been launched, and they needed someone to do resource coordination. Before long, she was promoted to supervisor. Later, she was hired by the state to develop the deaf unit at their mental hospital, ensuring that the appropriate services were put in place. She then went on to work for Montgomery County doing child abuse investigations. During that time, she married Fred Tolbert, a friend of her brother's and the first native of the area she had met. "He's incredibly supportive," she remarks. "If I come home talking about an injustice, he gets angrier about it than I do."

Now, as a leader at CALMRA, Nancy tries to give her employees what she expects from others. People are free to do their jobs as they see fit, and nothing goes on in the organization without input from all levels. "I have an open door policy, and anyone can come talk to me about anything," she remarks. "We strive for transparency, and I try to make sure our mission is clear so that every staff member knows what we're about and how they fit into the overall mission." This leadership style has garnered incredible loyalty amongst staff, with some employees staying on for over two decades in an industry that generally sees high turnover. "Above all else, the people we serve come first," she affirms. "Their health and safety is our top priority at all times."

In advising young people entering the working world today, Nancy emphasizes the importance of ethics and focus. "Don't lose sight of what you're doing and why you're doing it, and always make ethical decisions," she says, echoing the Catholic upbringing that underpins her every action, word, and decision. Beyond that, her life path is a testament to the difference that hard work and a mission-driven mind can make. "There's no money to be made in this work, but that's not why I do it," she says. "It's about the meaning. That's why I would tell any young person that the key to success is having passion for whatever you do, whether it's for profit or not for profit. If you don't love it, why do it? I feel so lucky that I've found something I love to do." She may have a mind of her own, but Nancy's mission is expansive, and CALMRA is the perfect vehicle to bring it to life.

BERNHARDT
WEALTH MANAGEMENT

Valora Washington

Architect of Change

A s the fire roared before her eyes, filling the night air with smoke and a distinct sense of tragedy, eleven-year-old Valora Washington began asking questions. What was going on? Why did four young children live in an apartment above a bar? Where were their parents?

She had often noticed how the oldest child, a withdrawn boy who sat across the classroom from her and kept to himself, would collect his three younger siblings after school to walk them home. All four children died that night in the fire that had started in the bar below their apartment.

Later that week, as she joined her classmates on the sidewalk outside the school to watch the funeral procession pass, she looked at the four small coffins and decided something about life. Having watched a building burn down and grieved for the children who had been inside, she knew it wouldn't take just an architect to rebuild what had been lost—it would take an architect of change. "I remember thinking to myself right then and there that, when I grew up, no kid was going to be burning up on top of a bar," she says today. "Right at that moment, my whole vocation started."

Now the CEO of the Council for Professional Recognition, Valora has become an architect of change as a child advocate and is still doing her best to ensure that the innocent are given a fair start in life. "Working with young children and helping them get a strong footing is the best way to prevent problems down the road," she explains. Instead of fixing problems that already exist, her work has its sights set on keeping those problems from occurring in the first place.

"What we know from research is that family, teachers, and caregivers who work with a child influence that child the most," says Valora. "Historically in our country, people who work with young children under the age of five haven't had a lot of training because many people assume that anyone can teach young children. People think it's just kind of an extension of mothering. But actually, that's not true. Research shows that working with children in a particular way strengthens opportunities for learning and can have a lifetime impact on them in all kinds of ways. When children receive a high quality early education, they earn more money as adults, are more likely to be homeowners, less likely to drop out of school, and less likely to become teen parents. The impact of a good early childhood education benefits society as a whole."

The Council for Professional Recognition gives people working in early education a professional development framework for their work. The mission of the Council is to promote improved performance and recognition of professionals in the education of children from birth to five years old. Professionals who work in all types of early care and education programs like Head Start, pre-kindergarten, infant-toddler, family childcare, and home visitor programs are able to earn credentials through the Council. The Council is widely known for administering the Child Development Associate (CDA) National Credentialing Program™, which assesses and credentials early childhood education professionals.

The CDA credential has been awarded to over 325,000 people since it began in 1975, and approximately 18,000 new early childhood professionals are credentialed annually. The Council for Professional Recognition was created in 1985 as a means to oversee the professional assessment, which was a paper-based process until Valora came along. "We revolutionized the CDA," she explains. "I knew it needed to be upgraded or enhanced for the 21st century, so I joined the organization to do that specifically." Now, the exam can be administered electronically, and results can be obtained the day of testing, instead of the weeks it took with the paper process. In addition to updating the CDA to be administered electronically, Valora's team updated all of the competencies and materials to reflect the latest research.

Each candidate for the CDA assessment is observed by a professional development specialist, lending the credential new power and endurance. The national exam is offered in the language spoken by the candidate, and is currently being expanded internationally. "We recently awarded our first international credential in Dubai, and we're in negotiations to work with eight other countries right now," Valora says. "The exam is so crucial because our nation, unlike most of Western Europe, doesn't really have national childcare standards." The U.S. military also uses the credential extensively, requiring childcare workers employed at U.S. military bases all over the world to carry their credential.

The tremendous passion for social justice that Valora brings to her work each day was first honed by the example of her grandmother and by the emphasis her family placed on education and giving back to the less fortunate. "Many parents do not understand how important it is to talk to your children and to read to them," she says. "That's why there's a thirty-million-word vocabulary gap between poor children and middle class children before they get to kindergarten." Valora is grateful that her family always encouraged her to learn. "In my family, education has never been about personal development only," she points out. "It's also about how you can be of service. When you get your education, you're supposed to do something with it that is of service to other people."

Valora grew up in Columbus, Ohio and remembers her childhood fondly. Her father was a railroad worker and her mother a nurse. Her parents divorced and remarried other partners when she was young, but Valora never felt any chaos or tension in her family life. Her parents were still friendly after their divorce, and her extended family all lived in the same neighborhood. Everyone supported and looked out for each other.

Valora's stepfather was an elementary school principal, and her mother a lifelong student, underscoring the emphasis on education in her family. In fact, her grandmother received her high school diploma, her mother finished her Bachelor's degree, and Valora got her PhD all in the same year. Every day after school, Valora and her siblings would sit down at the kitchen table and do their lessons. "It was a daily routine," she remembers. "And in the summer, we would go to the library and read books—hundreds every summer." Even when she got her first job as a busgirl at a hotel in high school, it was to save money for college. In the environment she grew up in, college was the expected next step.

Valora considers her grandmother the most influential person in her life. Her grandmother volunteered with her church and with the Red Cross, always looking out for people in the neighborhood who needed help. "She worked, had eight children, volunteered, was a very active member of her church, cooked three meals a day, and was loved by all members of the neighborhood," says Valora. "We took real lunches to school. She cooked, baked, and sewed, making most of my clothes until I was a teenager. We grew vegetables in the garden, and we canned things for the winter. I was the eldest grandchild and I hung out with her a lot. I saw how people relied upon her and talked to her. All the things she did in her life were such an influence on me. My grandmother would not have called herself a social activist, but that's in fact what she was. She was always generous."

Valora was also profoundly influenced by the civil rights and women's movements in the U.S., hitting home for her the idea that anything is possible. "Not only is anything possible, but you can join with other people to make things happen," she says. "The social justice worldview of my generation focused on seeing education as a means for personal as well as community development."

After high school, Valora studied Anthropology at Michigan State University, as well as the many other subjects she found interesting but hadn't been exposed to before. She embraced the opportunity to study abroad in West Africa, where she became even more interested in childhood studies. "When I was over there, I noticed the children and how they were behaving," she recalls. "They had a lot of responsibility, with many of the older children taking care of the younger ones. Even a seemingly small task like collecting sticks was considered a contribution to the community. A lot of children these days have nothing to do except entertain themselves, but what they're doing isn't actually critical in any way, and they know that. The model of child behavior I saw in Africa definitely influenced my outlook on child development and my resolve to begin my career in the field."

With that resolve, Valora went straight from undergraduate to graduate school at Indiana University, receiving her PhD in Child Development at 24 years of age. Upon graduating, she accepted a position as an Assistant Professor at the University of North Carolina Chapel Hill and received tenure before age 30. She worked in academia for a while before entering the nonprofit world, finally deciding to leave teaching when she was offered the position of Associate Dean at Howard University. She then became Vice President at Antioch College in Ohio. While at Antioch, she was recruited by The Kellogg Foundation to work as a subject matter expert in early childhood education, where she remained for ten years and was the organization's first black Vice President.

After The Kellogg Foundation, Valora opened up her own nonprofit organization, the Community Advocates for Young Learners (CAYL) Institute. "CAYL focuses on leadership development for people in the field of early care and education," she explains. "We took mid-career people and tried to make them stronger leaders for young children and for the profession. To accomplish change, I knew we needed to come together to make things happen, both at the policy level and at the direct childcare level. CAYL teaches people the skills of how to impact the profession at the state level through state policy and so forth." Valora had been involved in the Council for Professional Recognition as a board member long before joining, and when the Founding Director retired, she took his place.

Although she has accomplished so much in the workplace, Valora is most proud of the work she has done for her family. Her most prized possession is a collection of old family photographs that she is working to digitize, giving family members priceless glimpses at moments in time that they could never have experienced otherwise. She has two adopted children, a son and a daughter. "What I'm most proud of is the time I've invested in my children," says Valora. "I made it to every sports event, musical performance, and play. I participated in the Girl Scouts and became the mother of an Eagle Scout." Valora made the decision to adopt a child when she was working as an evaluator in a foster care project. "I learned that the state can be a really poor parent," she remarks. "I told myself that I can't solve this whole huge problem, but I could at least help one child. So I got involved in some adoption advocacy, which led to my adopting my son. And then seven years later, I adopted my daughter."

In advising young people entering the working world today, Valora emphasizes the importance of staying true to your curiosity and giving back to the community by sharing what you know. "Instead of being only career-focused as a young adult, focus instead on what you're interested in and that will lead to a vocation," she encourages. "Think about what you do when you don't have to do anything. That's probably where your passion lies."

Beyond this, she reminds young people that they don't have to wait until they're older to give back. Just as her grandmother gave back to the community in abundance regardless of her circumstances, and just as the West African children she met were each given something important to do in the community, her leadership philosophy rests on the belief that each person has something important to give. "Young people these days are searching for meaning in their lives and want to contribute something meaningful to the community," says Valora. "There's always opportunity to share what you know. It's never too early to start. It's important to be an architect of change but also to try and help other people be architects of change. What I really believe is that you start with your everyday challenge—whatever is bothering you. That's the place where change first begins, and the structure of one's impact takes shape from there."

BERNHARDT
WEALTH MANAGEMENT

Benjamin Wilson

What's Possible

Benjamin Wilson grew up in the Deep South during the Civil Rights era, where the law was one thing but reality was quite another. Jackson, Mississippi was stringently segregated at the time, and at six years of age, he watched the integration of Arkansas schools on the news. He saw Freedom Riders brave violence to challenge the status quo, and he was twelve when Medgar Evers, a civil rights activist dedicated to integrating the University of Mississippi, was murdered.

In sixth grade, Ben watched James Meredith boldly gain admittance to the University of Mississippi as its first black student. Meredith's lawyer, Constance Baker Motley, was the first black woman to ever argue a case before the Supreme Court, winning not with physical power, but with something even more remarkable. "In that moment, I learned that powerful didn't mean big," Ben reflects today. "It means a different kind of strength—intelligence, courage in one's convictions, and bravery. I saw lawyers as having the ability to impact their communities and to make change for the better, and I wanted to do that."

Thanks to the visionary faith of his parents and his own ability to manifest that strength, Ben is now the Managing Principal of Beveridge & Diamond, P.C., the world's premier environmental law firm. With a hundred lawyers and offices in seven cities, its work spans the globe to address the expansive needs of its clients, and Ben oversees it all.

The firm was launched in 1974 during the Watergate Era, when President Nixon ordered Elliot Richardson, the Attorney General, to remove Archibald Cox, a Professor at Harvard Law School and the Watergate special prosecutor, from the case. When Richardson refused to do so, the order was passed on to Deputy Attorney General William Ruckelshaus, who also refused. After both men resigned in what became known as the Saturday Night Massacre, Ruckelshaus joined forces with several colleagues to launch Ruckelshaus, Beveridge, Fairbanks, and Diamond, an environmental law firm that would address issues of implementation related to the Clean Water Act, which had passed in the early 1970s.

The firm was a decade old by the time Ben came onboard in 1985 as a contract partner. He had three years to prove himself, and within the first, he had established himself as the busiest lawyer at his level. Ben and his team spent the subsequent decade establishing the firm as the best in environmental law, and now, companies readily identify it as such. "We wanted clients to see us as a firm that knew the substance of environmental law, but could also handle the work of major litigation matters," Ben explains. "Today, we've taken on these challenges for oil and gas companies, pharmaceutical companies, chemical companies, manufacturers, big box stores, and municipalities across the country."

The decision to name Ben the firm's Managing Principal in 2008 was the culmination of a lifetime of striving not for what is, but for what's possible—a dream set by his parents from the day he was born in Indiana. He was only several weeks old when they drove south to Jackson, where his father would earn his PhD and his mother would attain her master's degree. Both parents taught at Jackson State University, a historically black college where his father coached basketball and assisted with football. As a result, Ben and his three younger brothers grew up immersed in athletics and academia.

"What my parents saw, more than anything else, were opportunities for us that they, themselves, hadn't had," Ben remarks. "They knew integration would come, and that we'd have a chance to compete. So the question was, when you're put on the field, will you be able to play? Are you competitive? They didn't know where the opportunity would come, or when, or how, but they felt that it would. They had that sense of what was possible."

Ben's mother, in particular, was a woman of strong faith who believed that her son could do almost anything. She taught him that, as long as he worked hard and prepared himself for the future, he would have the freedom and capacity to define himself. "She saw the world not as it was, but as it could be," he affirms.

His mother wasn't the only one who saw such potential in Ben. As a boy, he attended junior high at an all-black school in his neighborhood, and one of his English teachers, Ms. Tatum, traveled to Connecticut one spring for a Shakespearean play festival. While there, she happened to sit next to the Dean of Admissions for a preparatory school that was looking for African American boys to integrate their institution. "I know just the boy," she said.

Ben did well on the standardized test required for admission, but the tuition costs were too much for the family's modest income. Thankfully, the school was able to award him a scholarship for half the tuition cost, and as long as Ben held paying jobs at the school, his parents could afford to cover the rest of the bill. "I'll never forget the day I left to start my ninth grade year. We had been at a football game, and we had to leave for the airport midway through, which was sacrilege," he laughs. "I took Southern Airways to Montgomery, Delta to Atlanta, Eastern

Airways to LaGuardia, and Allegheny Airlines to Bradley Field. A man picked me up, and I tried to memorize the winding route to the school in case I didn't like it and wanted to escape."

Ben arrived a few days early, when only the junior and senior boys were on campus, and thankfully, they were welcoming from the start. The academic terrain, however, was another story. Ben had been the best student at his school in Jackson, but the preparatory school demanded high caliber performance that introduced him to the challenges of critical thinking. "Teachers didn't just want the answer; they wanted the 'why' behind it," he says. "I remember studying all night for a test and only earning a 75. But I was extremely competitive and didn't like being second to anyone, so I resolved to fight my way up to the top. I'd size up other students like I'd size up the quarterback on an opposing team."

Ben's determined efforts paid off, and in tenth grade, he made the honor roll for the first time. "I couldn't wait to tell my mother—I knew she'd be so proud of me," he recalls. "But she died suddenly before I had the chance to give her the news. That's one of the biggest disappointments of my life." Despite the tragedy, Ben was committed to working hard—not just academically and athletically, but also in his various summer jobs. The family moved to Nashville soon there-after, and on his summer vacations home from school, he loaded ice onto boxcars, sold shoes at Sears, and put in hours of hard labor as a roofer. "Those jobs helped me understand why I was working so hard in school," he remarks.

Ben attended Dartmouth for college and then went on to Harvard Law School where, on the first day of class, he met a striking young woman named Merinda. "I liked her immediately and offered to give her a tour of Cambridge," he recalls. "It didn't take her long to realize I knew nothing about Cambridge!" Ben was particularly impressed by her unwavering commitment to her education. When they studied for exams together and he was ready to call it a night, she knew exactly how to motivate him to keep going. "I didn't know what kinds of challenges life would bring, but I had the sense that they'd be tough, so I wanted a partner that was tough too," he says. "We got married, and she has been that, and so much more. She's been supportive every step of the way, and I'm unendingly grateful to have her."

After law school, Ben took a position at a firm in Atlanta where he launched his career by writing a brief that was indisputably horrible. "It was sent back to me completely marked up in red, and as a result, I was sent to the equivalent of Siberia—the tax department!" he says. "It was the last thing I wanted to do, but since I knew at that point that my writing was poor, I decided to use that time to write articles about things I didn't know, developing both my skills and knowledge base."

From the tax-exempt status of private schools, to tax cases in the fifth circuit court, Ben built his proficiency day by day, making his time count for something. By the end of his tenure there, a number of his articles had been published, and his new excellence in writing served him well when the couple moved to Washington and he took a job in the Civil Division Commercial Branch of the Department of Justice, where he wrote prolifically. "Like that situation, most of my defining moments in life have not been as much about successes as they've been about failures," he remarks. "The key was to not accept that failure as a full definition my life or career, but to come back from it a better person with a stronger character."

While Merinda took a position at Sidley Austin LLP and embarked on an esteemed 25-year career in which she became a litigation partner at the firm, Ben pursued the position at the Department of Justice because he thought it would force him to swim—and he was right. "In my three years there, they taught me to dribble the ball with my head up, so that when I came out, I had court vision and could readily see the whole picture," he remembers. "I didn't have to worry about my writing or about trying cases because I had it all down. Instead, I could look at the witness's face and observe nonverbal communications, paying attention to internal dynamics and politics."

Next, Ben took a position at a firm and became a partner several years later. It wasn't long, however, before the firm lost its biggest client, and as there was little work left, he found himself investigating other options. He committed to pursuing innovative ways to bring in business, like finding work for the clients who owed the firm money so they had a means to make payments. He even began finding his own clients, but three weeks after he had secured his first one, his life took a character-defining turn when he fell from a man lift and broke his neck.

At George Washington Hospital, as his consciousness swam in and out, he fought for his life, only to emerge on the other side wondering whether it would be the kind of life he wanted to live. "I made my negotiation with God," he says. "I said I'd rather be dead than be paralyzed, where I couldn't be a father to my daughter or a husband to my wife. And to be honest, that realization brought a peace that I had never known before. I wasn't afraid to die anymore. I wasn't afraid to speak my mind or stand up to people of authority. In some profound way, I had gained that other kind of strength that had so inspired me as a kid."

Thirty-six hours later, the swelling had started to go down, and Ben found he could move his legs. Thankful for the ability to still feel pain, he refused morphine and relished the experience. Three weeks later, he was fired from his job at the law firm, but his newfound peace of mind helped as he asked himself the question his mother had taught him to ask with such optimism and faith: What's possible?

Looking for a job wasn't easy. He applied to several hundred law firms and wound up with two offers. The first was with a large firm where he wouldn't need to develop any clients for himself. The second, which paid a yearly salary of $25,000 less, required that he build a practice. "I never wanted to be in a position where I was beholden to someone else—where my destiny rested in the hands of another person," Ben avows. "Even though I had no idea how to do it, I wanted to have as much latitude as possible to create my own success, so I chose the second offer, which is what brought me to Beveridge & Diamond."

Despite his prowess in the field of law, Ben's success at the firm has rested, above all else, on his unparalleled ability to care about people. At the very beginning, he was put on a case with the Port of Oakland because he had met the client at his previous law firm, and it became the firm's single largest case that year. The next year, during the savings and loan crisis, Ben was put in charge of taking over the McLean Savings and Loan Association because he had also known the client through a connection, and the case again marked the largest that year. "Something like that seems to happen every year," he remarks. "By pursuing multiple lines of opportunity at once, focusing on who people are as people and taking a genuine interest in them, one out of four people we meet now results in an actual client relationship. Being nice to one person, no matter who that person is, can result in four clients for the firm. By being truly kind and genuine to people and being patient, the worst outcome is that you make a friend, and the best is that you make a friend who brings you work. It's a winning situation no matter what."

By developing his business sincerely, methodically, and personably, one step at a time, Ben has helped the firm build its practice profoundly over the years. He first became Managing Principal in 2008, just as the nation was entering the most difficult economic climate since the Great Depression, but his approach to leadership insulated the firm from the worst hardships. "Law firms were dumping people left and right, but we fired no lawyers, instead opting to freeze the salaries of staff and associates and asking partners to take a cut," he recalls. "There was a sense of collective sacrifice. We made a doomsday budget, and we stuck by it. We diversified our client base substantially. I encouraged a culture of open communication at every level, and I used unifying pronouns as I persuaded the team that we could win and then gave them the tools to do it. We made it through the crisis, and last year was our best year by far, but the best must get better. We're constantly asking ourselves what's possible, and how we can provide even greater value to our clients while keeping costs down—even if that means they're using us less."

As proud as he is of the team at Beveridge & Diamond, nothing can match the feeling he got when he saw this same determined attitude in his daughter, Rachel, as she played in a basketball game during her senior year at the University of Pennsylvania. Despite making a couple baskets and playing great defense, the team was playing poorly overall, yet when Rachel stood on the sidelines with her water bottle, she caught her father's eye, flashed him a big smile, and toasted in his direction. When the assistant coach asked her how she could be happy at a time like that, Rachel explained that her father measured players not when things were going well, but when things were difficult. It was her way of telling Ben that, even though things were going poorly, she was playing hard. "When she had every reason to give up, she didn't," he says. "If there's anything I'd impart to my daughter or anyone else, it's that you can't quit. You have to stick with it. That's the essence. That's how you truly push the limits to find out what's possible."

In offering further advice to young people entering the working world today, Ben stresses the importance of faith, especially through the difficult times when one's character is truly defined. "Whatever it is you believe in, hold it dear," he says. "It's not what happens in life, but how you choose to respond to it. Always treat others as you'd have them treat you. Be a real friend and make peace with all those you know. When all else fails, care about other people, because they'll always remember that."

For Ben, caring about people extends far beyond the bounds of the home or the workplace. Beyond serving on the board of Dartmouth College, speaking publically about the importance of diversity and inclusion in the legal profession, and doing pro bono work for the Washington Lawyers Committee on Civil Rights and Foreign Affairs, he chaired the board of the Healthy Babies Project, an organization dedicated to addressing D.C.'s dismally high infant mortality rate.

"D.C. has the highest infant mortality rate of any major American city, and too many high-risk pregnant mothers here struggle with alcohol, tobacco, and drugs," he explains. "We've supported the healthy births of over 7,000 high-risk babies—all children who now have the potential to grow up and make their own difference in the world."

In large and small ways, Ben's professional and personal efforts have always been about allowing himself and others to push the limits of what's possible. "I think that, in life, we're all trying to figure out our purpose and why we're here," he says. "I don't have all the answers, but it's important to work on something in life that's greater than yourself—that goes beyond the daily grind or the status quo and ensures that we leave things better than when we found them." It's this kind of vision that allows one to see things not as they are, but as they should be, and not as they could be, but as they will be.

About the Author

Having grown up on a farm in Nebraska, Gordon Bernhardt left the Midwest in the early 1980s for Washington D.C. to work as an assistant in the U.S. House of Representatives. He left behind the rural lifestyle but he carried with him the values of hard work, a focus on what you can control, and service to others—values that continue to influence his life, today.

After completing a bachelor's degree in Commerce at the University of Virginia, Bernhardt began a successful career in finance at a leading accounting firm and two different brokerage companies. In 1994, in order to make the kind of difference in people's lives that he hoped to make, he established Bernhardt Wealth Management, an independent registered investment advisory firm built on the principle of fiduciary care: providing investment and wealth management guidance, service, and advice that places clients' interests and needs ahead of everything else. By adhering to this higher standard, he removed the conflicts of interest that were prevalent elsewhere. Rather than be restricted by a large company's cookie cutter methodology, he and his team are able to create customized plans that are far more appropriate for individual clients. Today, Bernhardt Wealth Management is recognized as one of the top fee-only wealth management firms in the Washington D.C. region.

In addition to being an entrepreneur and wealth manager, Bernhardt is the author of *Buen Camino: What a Hike through Spain Taught Me about Investing and Life*, a memoir about the 35-day, 618-mile pilgrimage he completed in Spain and the lessons he learned along the way. He also writes a weekly finance blog. Bernhardt writes the *Profiles in Success: Inspiration from Executive Leaders* book series, and hosts a podcast with the same name, to expand the influence of outstanding leaders while inspiring the next generation of executives.

Find out more about Gordon Bernhardt at
www.BernhardtWealth.com and www.ProfilesInSuccess.com.

Pvt. Jonathan Lee Gifford was the first U.S. soldier killed in Iraq. He was killed just two days into the war on March 23, 2003. Spc. David Emanual Hickman was killed by a roadside bomb in Iraq on November 14, 2011. *The Washington Post* on December 17, 2011, said Hickman "may have been the last" U.S. soldier killed in Iraq. After reading an article about Gifford and Hickman my sister, Gloria, was inspired to write the following poem.

From Gifford to Hickman

by Gloria J. Bernhardt

From Gifford to Hickman…and all those in between,
You fought bravely amid chaos and dangers unforeseen.
Twenty-one guns have sounded, the riderless horse walks on.
Fond memories are remaining. A nation's child is gone.

Sons and daughters; fathers, mothers—broken hearts intertwined.
Hugs and kisses; their successes—major milestones left behind.
Your selfless gift—a life laid down; for fellow soldier, family, land.
Duty called—call was answered—no greater love hath man.

"I'm getting taller. I lost a tooth. I got 100 on my test!
Miss your pancakes and your tickles, goodnight kisses were the best.
Who will answer all my questions now? I've important stuff to learn!
You said you had a big surprise on the day that you'd return."

"I talk to you at bedtime—after lights go out at night.
I told Jesus that I miss you…sure wish you could hug me tight.
When Grandpa says I look like you, Grandma starts to cry.
I'm mad that you're not coming home…I need to say goodbye!"

From Gifford, to Hickman, through every soldier who has served,
Liberty's fruits are savored and freedom is preserved.
We live freely due to soldiers, willing to support and defend
Our Constitution, our country—against enemies 'til the end.

Sons and daughters; fathers, mothers—broken hearts intertwined.
Hugs and kisses; their successes—major milestones left behind.
Your selfless gift—a life laid down; for fellow soldier, family, land.
Duty called—call was answered—no greater love hath man.

"I had a dream the night before…you smiled and walked on by.
When I awoke, I thought it odd…it seemed like a 'good-bye'.
I couldn't put my finger on the dark cloud that remained,
When the phone began to ring…I knew my life had changed."

"I questioned God, 'Why MY child? Why do I have to lose?'
I imagined His response would be 'If not your child, then whose?'
Your bright life flashed too briefly… seems He only takes the best.
I'm thankful for the time I had. For that I'm truly blessed."

From Gifford to Hickman and every warrior who has passed,
The price you've paid bought freedom, but will we make it last?
Your last breath drawn for citizens in this country and abroad
Are we worthy of such gifts is known only but to God.

Sons and daughters; fathers, mothers—broken hearts intertwined.
Hugs and kisses; their successes—major milestones left behind.
Your selfless gift—a life laid down; for fellow soldier, family, land.
Duty called—call was answered—no greater love hath man.

"My world stopped spinning…I couldn't breathe! Lord, how can I go on?
My days are all one midnight…but they say it's darkest 'fore the dawn.
I can hear you say, 'I'm proud of you! I know that this is hard.'
What do I do without you here? What dreams do I discard?"

"I miss your laugh. I miss your smell. I even miss our fights.
No more messes. No embraces. It's more 'real' late at night.
I saw you in a crowd today; but you vanished in the throng.
Wishful thinking changes nothing! I know my "rock" is gone."

FOR Gifford, FOR Hickman…FOR all the fallen in between,
You've trudged through shadowed valley and joined heroes' ranks unseen.
Upon freedom's altar, we sacrificed our daughters and our sons.
Empty boots stand at attention. The flag is folded. Your mission's done.

© 2012 Gloria J. Bernhardt. All Rights Reserved.
Reprinted by permission.

BERNHARDT
WEALTH MANAGEMENT

Made in the USA
Middletown, DE
20 September 2022

73409472R00208